WISDOM
of the GODS FOR
YOU *and* ME

WISDOM
of the GODS FOR
YOU *and* ME

MY GITA *and*
MY HANUMAN CHALISA

DEVDUTT
PATTANAIK

Illustrations by the author

RUPA

Published by
Rupa Publications India Pvt. Ltd 2019
7/16, Ansari Road, Daryaganj
New Delhi 110002

Sales Centres:
Allahabad Bengaluru Chennai
Hyderabad Jaipur Kathmandu
Kolkata Mumbai

ISBN: 978-93-5333-511-3

Second impression 2020

10 9 8 7 6 5 4 3 2

Design and typeset in Garamond by Special Effects, Mumbai

'Arjuna, people worship limited deities,
limited as they are by their nature and
their yearnings. From me comes their faith.
From me comes fulfilment of their faith.
The restricted stay restrained. Those who shatter
the boundaries discover me: the limitless.'
—BHAGAVAD GITA
CHAPTER 7, VERSES 20 TO 23 (PARAPHRASED)

'Sankat kate
mite sab peera.
Jo sumirai
Hanumat Balbeera.

Problems cease
pain goes away.
When one remembers
Hanuman, the mighty hero.'
—CHAUPAI 36, HANUMAN CHALISA

Contents

MY GITA

MY HANUMAN CHALISA

My
GITA

In *My Gita*, acclaimed mythologist Devdutt Pattanaik demystifies the *Bhagavad Gita* for the contemporary reader. His unique approach—thematic rather than verse-by-verse—makes the ancient treatise eminently accessible, combined as it is with his trademark illustrations and simple diagrams.

In a world that seems spellbound by argument over dialogue, vi-vaad over sam-vaad, Devdutt highlights how Krishna nudges Arjuna to understand rather than judge his relationships. This becomes relevant today when we are increasingly indulging and isolating the self (self-improvement, self-actualization, self-realization—even selfies!). We forget that we live in an ecosystem of others, where we can nourish each other with food, love and meaning, even when we fight.

So let My Gita *inform* your *Gita.*

Why *My Gita*

T he Bhagavad Gita, or The Gita as it is popularly known, is
part of the epic Mahabharata.

The Bhagavad Gita

The epic describes the war between the Pandavas and the Kauravas on the battlefield of Kuru-kshetra. The Gita is the discourse given by Krishna to Arjuna just before the war is about to begin. Krishna is identified as God (bhagavan). His words contain the essence of Vedic wisdom, the keystone of Hinduism.

Ramkrishna Paramhansa, the nineteenth-century Bengali mystic, said that the essence of The Gita can be deciphered simply by reversing the syllables that constitute Gita. So Gita, or gi-ta, becomes ta-gi, or tyagi, which means 'one who lets go of possessions.'

Gi-ta to Ta-gi

Given that, it is ironical that I call this book 'My Gita'.
I use the possessive pronoun for three reasons.

Reason 1: *My Gita* is thematic

The Gita demonstrates many modern techniques of communication. First, Arjuna's problem is presented (Chapter 1), and then Krishna's solution (chapters 2 to 18) is offered. Krishna begins by telling Arjuna what he will reveal (Chapter 2); he then elaborates on what he promised to tell (chapters 3 to 17); and finally, he repeats what he has told (Chapter 18). Krishna's solution involves analysis (sankhya) and synthesis (yoga)—slicing the whole into parts and then binding the parts into a whole.

The solution itself is comprehensive, involving the behavioural (karma yoga), the emotional (bhakti yoga) and the intellectual (gyana yoga). However, no one reads The Gita as a book, or hears every verse in a single sitting.

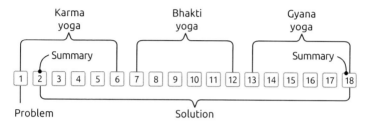

Chapter Architecture in The Gita

Traditionally, a guru would only elaborate on a particular verse or a set of verses or a chapter of The Gita at a time. It is only in modern times, with a printed book in hand, that we want to read The Gita cover to cover, chapter by chapter, verse to verse, and hope to work our way through to a climax of resolutions in one go. When we attempt to do so, we are disappointed. For, unlike modern writing, The Gita is not linear: some ideas are scattered over several chapters, many ideas are constantly repeated, and still others presuppose knowledge of concepts found elsewhere, in earlier Vedic and Upanishadic texts. In fact, The Gita specifically refers to the Brahma sutras (Chapter 13, Verse 5), also known as Vedanta sutras, said to have been composed by one Badarayana, sometimes identified with Vyasa. Further, at places, the same words are used in different verses to convey different meanings, and at other instances, different words are used to convey the same idea. For example, sometimes the word 'atma' means mind and sometimes soul; at other times other words like dehi, brahmana and purusha are used for soul instead of atma. This can be rather disorienting to a casual reader, and open to multiple interpretations.

So *My Gita* departs from the traditional presentation of The Gita—sequential verse-by-verse translations followed by commentary. Instead, *My Gita* is arranged thematically. The sequence of themes broadly follows the sequence in The Gita. Each theme is explained using several verses across multiple chapters. The verses are paraphrased, not translated or transliterated. These paraphrased verses make better sense when juxtaposed with Vedic, Upanishadic and Buddhist lore that preceded The Gita and stories from the Mahabharata, the Ramayana and the Puranas that followed it. Understanding deepens further when the Hindu worldview is contrasted with other worldviews and placed in a historical context.

For those seeking the standard literal and linear approach, there is a recommended reading list at the end of the book.

Reason 2: *My Gita* is subjective

We never actually hear what Krishna told Arjuna. We simply overhear what Sanjaya transmitted faithfully to the blind king Dhritarashtra in the comforts of the palace, having witnessed all that occurred on the distant battlefield, thanks to his telepathic sight. The Gita we overhear is essentially that which is narrated by a man with no authority but infinite sight (Sanjaya) to a man with no sight but full authority (Dhritarashtra). This peculiar structure of the narrative draws attention to the vast gap between what is told (gyana) and what is heard (vi-gyana).

Krishna and Sanjaya may speak exactly the same words, but while Krishna knows what he is talking about, Sanjaya does not. Krishna is the source, while Sanjaya is merely a transmitter. Likewise, what Sanjaya hears is different from what Arjuna hears and what Dhritarashtra hears. Sanjaya hears the words, but does not bother with the meaning. Arjuna is a seeker and so he decodes what he hears to find a solution to his problem. Dhritarashtra is not interested in what Krishna has to say. While Arjuna asks many questions and clarifications, ensuring the 'discourse' is a 'conversation', Dhritarashtra remains silent throughout. In fact, Dhritarashtra is fearful of Krishna who is fighting against his children, the Kauravas. So he judges Krishna's words, accepting what serves him, dismissing what does not.

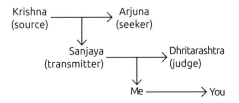

Overhearing The Gita

I am not the source of The Gita. But I do not want to be merely its transmitter, like Sanjaya. I want to understand, like Arjuna, though I have no problem I want to solve, neither do I stand on the brink of any battle. But it has been said that the Vedic wisdom presented by Krishna is applicable to all contexts, not just Arjuna's. So I have spent months hearing The Gita in the original Sanskrit to appreciate its musicality; reading multiple commentaries, retellings and translations; mapping the patterns that emerge from it with patterns found in Hindu mythology;

and comparing and contrasting these patterns with those found in Buddhist, Greek and Abrahamic mythologies. This book contains my understanding of The Gita, my subjective truth: my Gita. You can approach this book as Arjuna, with curiosity, or as Dhritarashtra, with suspicion and judgement. What you take away will be your subjective truth: your Gita.

The quest for objective truth (what did Krishna actually say?) invariably results in vi-vaad, argument, where you try to prove that your truth is the truth and I try to prove that my truth is the truth. The quest for subjective truth (how does The Gita make sense to me?) results in sam-vaad, where you and I seek to appreciate each other's viewpoints and expand our respective truths. It allows everyone to discover The Gita at his or her own pace, on his or her own terms, by listening to the various Gitas around them.

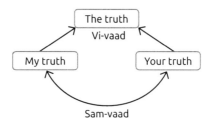

Argument and Discussion

Objectivity is obsessed with exactness and tends to be rather intolerant of deviation, almost like the jealous God of monotheistic mythologies. But meanings change over time, with the personality of the reader, and with context. Subjectivity challenges the assumption that ideas are fixed and can be controlled; it celebrates the fluid. Modern global discourse tends

My Gita

to look at truth qualitatively: it is either true or false. That which is objective is scientific and true. That which is subjective is mythic and false. Hindu thought, however, looks at truth quantitatively: everyone has access to a slice (bhaga); the one who sees all slices of truth is bhaga-van. Limited truth is mithya. Limitless truth is satya. Satya is about including everything and being whole (purnam). The journey towards limitless truth expands our mind (brahmana).

The Gita itself values subjectivity: after concluding his counsel, Krishna tells Arjuna to reflect on what has been said, and then do as he feels (yatha-ichasi-tatha-kuru). Even Sanjaya, after giving his view on what Krishna's discourse potentially offers, concludes The Gita with the phrase 'in my opinion' (mati-mama).

Reason 3: *My Gita* is not obsessed with the self

Traditionally, The Gita has been presented as a text that focusses on self-realization (atma-gyana). This suits the hermit who isolates himself from society. This is not surprising, since most early commentators and retellers of The Gita, such as Shankara, Ramanuja, Madhwa and Dyaneshwara, chose not to be householders. The original Buddhist monastic order may not have survived in India, but it did play a key role in the rise and dominance of the Hindu monastic order. The monastic approach willy-nilly appeals to the modern individualist, who also seeks self-exploration, self-examination, self-actualization and, of course, selfies.

Shankara

But the Mahabharata is about the household, about relationships, about others. It is essentially about a property dispute. Arjuna's dilemma begins when he realizes that the enemy is family and he fears the impact of killing family on society as a whole. Krishna's discourse continuously speaks of yagna, a Vedic ritual that binds the individual to the community. He elaborates on the relationship of the individual, whom he identifies as jiva-atma, with divinity, whom he identifies as param-atma, which is etymologically related to 'the other' (para). The Buddha spoke

My Gita

of nirvana, which means oblivion of individual identity, but Krishna speaks of brahma-nirvana as an expansion of the mind (brahmana) that leads to liberation (moksha) while ironically also enabling union (yoga), indicating a shift away from monastic isolationism. That is why, in Hindu temples, God is always visualized with the Goddess as a householder, one half of a pair. The devotee looks at the deity (darshan) and the deity, with large unblinking eyes, looks back; the relationship is 'two-way' not 'one-way'.

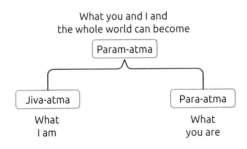

Relationships

In Chapter 5, Verse 13, of The Gita, Krishna describes the human body as a city with nine gates (nava-dvara-pura): two eyes, two ears, two nostrils, one mouth, one anus and one genital. A relationship involves two bodies, two people, the self and the other, you and me, two cities—eighteen gates in all. That The Gita has eighteen sections, that it seeks to make sense of the eighteen books of the Mahabharata—which tells the story of a war between family and friends fought over eighteen days involving eighteen armies—indicates that the core teaching of The Gita has much to do with relationships. It serves the needs of the householder rather than the hermit.

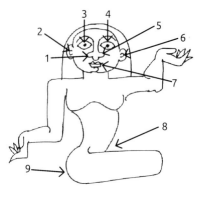

Nine Gates

Before starting on these eighteen chapters we shall briefly explore the history of The Gita. After these eighteen chapters, we shall discuss the impact of The Gita on Arjuna.

Writing *My Gita* helped me expand my mind. I discovered more frameworks through which I could make better sense of reality. I hope reading this book informs your Gita and helps you expand your mind. Should the urge to find a fixed single objective truth grip you, remind yourself:

> *Within infinite myths lies an eternal truth*
> *Who sees it all?*
> *Varuna has but a thousand eyes*
> *Indra, a hundred*
> *You and I, only two.*

Before *My Gita*:
A Brief History of The Gita

Before the Bhagavad Gita, or God's song, there was the Vyadha Gita, or the butcher's song.

Vyadha Gita

The Vyadha Gita is found earlier in the Vana Parva, Book 3 of the Mahabharata, when the Pandavas are still in exile in the forest, having lost their kingdom to the Kauravas in a gambling match. The Bhagavad Gita is found in Bhisma Parva, Book 6 of the Mahabharata, just before the war between the Pandavas and the Kauravas.

In the forest, the Pandavas encounter the sage Markandeya, who tells them the story of a hermit who would burn birds alive with a fiery glance of his eye, if they accidentally dropped excrement on him while he was meditating. When the hermit threatened to curse a housewife because she kept him waiting for alms while attending to her household chores, she admonished him for his impatience, and advised him to go to learn the secret of the Vedas from a butcher in Mithila. The butcher's long discourse—the Vyadha Gita—on dharma, karma and atma so moved the hermit that he returned to his home to serve his old parents, whom he had abandoned long ago.

In both the Vyadha Gita and the Bhagavad Gita, the discourse takes place in a violent space: a butcher's shop and a battlefield, respectively. In both, there is a separation of the physical (prakriti) and the psychological (purusha), which is the hallmark of Vedic wisdom. In both, the householder's way of engagement is valued over the hermit's way of withdrawal.

What distinguishes the Bhagavad Gita is that it talks explicitly about God (bhagavan) and devotion (bhakti). It marks the transition of the old ritual-based Vedic Hinduism into the new narrative-based Puranic Hinduism.

Approaches to Hindu History

The history of Hinduism spreads over 5,000 years and can be seen in eight phases that telescope into each other. The first is the Indus phase, then come the Vedic phase, the Upanishadic phase, the Buddhist phase, the Puranic phase, the Bhakti phase, the Orientalist phase and finally the modern phase. Relics from the Indus–Saraswati civilization reveal ancient iconography that is considered sacred in Hinduism even today. But much of the knowledge of that period remains speculative. The subsequent three phases constitute Vedic Hinduism, when there were no temples and the idea of God was rather abstract. The final four phases constitute Puranic Hinduism, characterized by the rise of temples and belief in a personal god, either Shiva, or one of his sons; Vishnu, or one of his avatars; or the Goddess, in her many local forms. We can go so far as to call Vedic Hinduism pre-Gita Hinduism and Puranic Hinduism post-Gita, to indicate the pivotal role of The Gita in Hindu history.

The Vedic phase began 4,000 years ago, the Upanishadic phase 3,000 years ago, the Buddhist phase 2,500 years ago, the Puranic phase 2,000 years ago, the Bhakti phase 1,000 years ago and the Orientalist phase only 200 years ago. The modern phase is just emerging, with Indians questioning the understanding of Hinduism that has so far been based on Western frameworks.

Dating of Hindu history is always approximate and speculative, and often a range, as orally transmitted scriptures precede the written works by several centuries, and parts of the written work were composed by various scribes over several generations, in different geographies. Everything is complicated by the fact that writing became popular in India only 2,300 years ago, after Mauryan Emperor Ashoka popularized the Brahmi script through his edicts.

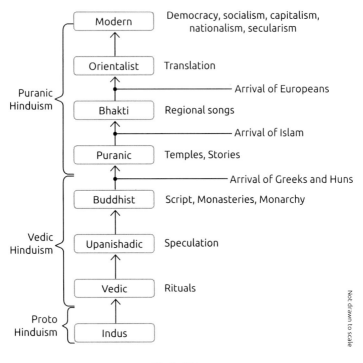

Hindu History

Before we proceed, we must keep in mind that the historical approach to Hinduism is not acceptable to all Hindus. The ahistorical school of thought sees all Hindu ideas as timeless. The rather chauvinistic proto-historical school sees all Hindu rituals, stories and symbols, Vedic or Puranic, as having been created simultaneously over 5,000 years ago. These have become political issues, which influence scholarship.

History seeks to be everyone's truth, but is limited by available facts. More often than not, what is passed off as history is mythology, someone's understanding of truth shaped by memory, feelings and desire, available facts notwithstanding. However, it is never fantasy, or no one's truth.

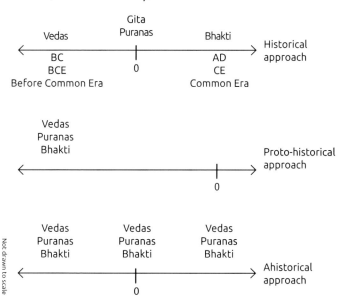

Historical, Proto-historical and Ahistorical Schools

We must also guard against a masculine view of history based on conflict and triumph alone: natives versus colonizers, polytheism versus monotheism, Hindus versus Buddhists, Christians versus Muslims, Shias versus Sunnis, Shaivites versus Vaishnavites, Protestants versus Catholics, Mughals versus Marathas, democracy versus monarchy, theists versus atheists, capitalists versus socialists, liberals versus conservatives. This has been popularized by Western academics and their love for the Hegelian dialectic, where thesis creates antithesis until there is resolution and a new thesis. This approach assumes that history has a natural direction and purpose.

An alternate, feminine view of history looks at every event as the fruit of the past (karma-phala) as well as the seed of future tendencies (karma-bija), without the need to play judge. Thus, we can see the writing of the Gitas as a response to, not an attack on, Buddhist monasticism, and the feminization of Buddhism as a response to, not an appropriation of, the idea of the Goddess found in Hindu Puranas. No idea emerges from a vacuum. Different ideas amplify from time to time. Old ideas coexist with new ones. Contradictory ideas influence each other. Here the world has no beginning, no end, no value, no purpose. All meaning is created by humans, individually and collectively: the boundaries we establish and fight over.

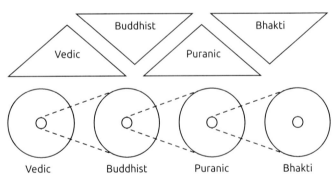

Masculine and Feminine Approaches to History

In most parts of the world, a new idea suppresses and wipes out the old idea, but in India, thanks to the abstract nature of

My Gita

Vedic ideas, new worldviews—be they native ones like Buddhism or Bhakti or foreign ones like Islam and Christianity—simply helped reaffirm the Vedic way in different ways. The same idea manifests as 4,000-year-old Vedic rituals, 2,000-year-old stories, 1,000-year-old temple art and architecture and 500-year-old devotional poetry.

This resilience of the Vedic way led to the Vedas being described in later texts, such as the Brahma-sutras, as being of non-human origin (a-paurusheya). This means Vedic ideas are not artificial: they are a reflection of nature (prakriti) as it is. It is common, however, to glamorize the Vedas by claiming them to be superhuman or supernatural.

Veda essentially refers to a set of hymns, melodies and rituals put together nearly 4,000 years ago that symbolically and metaphorically communicate knowledge (vidya)—observations of seers (rishis), people who saw what others did not, would not, could not see. The Upanishads speculated on these ideas while Buddhism and other monastic orders challenged the rituals inspired by these ideas. These inform The Gita. The ideas in The Gita were illustrated and often elaborated in the Puranas, including the great epics, the Ramayana and the Mahabharata. These were simplified during the Bhakti period and communicated in regional languages. They were expressed in English from the eighteenth century onwards. That is why any study of The Gita has to take into consideration Vedic, Upanishadic, Buddhist, Puranic, Bhakti and Orientalist ideas.

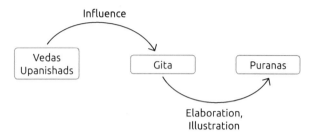

Influence, Illustration and Elaboration

Gitas and the Reframing of Hinduism

Two thousand years ago, South Asia was torn between two extremes. On one side were kings who established great empires, such as those of the Nandas, Mauryas, Sungas, Kanvas, Satavahanas, Kushanas and Guptas, which heralded great prosperity but also involved great violence. On the other side were hermits (shramanas) such as the Jains, the Ajivikas and the Buddhists, who spoke of the household as the place of suffering and sought solace in the solitude offered by monasteries (viharas). More and more people, including kings, were choosing the hermit's way of life over marriage, family vocation and family responsibilities, causing great alarm. Chandragupta Maurya embraced Jainism. His grandson, Ashoka, embraced Buddhism.

For 2,000 years before this, society was dominated by Vedic lore. At the heart of the Veda was the ritual called yagna, which involved exchange, giving in order to get, thus establishing a relationship between the yajamana, who initiated the ritual and the other—family, friends, strangers, ancestors, gods, nature and cosmos. It was all about the household.

My Gita

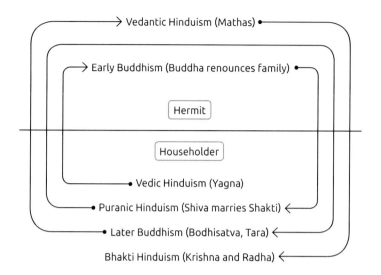

Tension Between Hermit and Householder

There were hermits in these Vedic times too: the rishis, who were married but chose philosophical exploration over material ambitions; the sanyasis, who had chosen to renounce the household after completing all household duties; and the tapasvis, who chose to be celibate in the pursuit of occult powers (siddhi). The Vedas presented a world where there was no conflict between the householder's way and hermit's way, as in the legendary kingdom of Mithila ruled by Janaka.

Vedic ideas were transmitted via the hymns of the Rig Veda, melodies of the Sama Veda, rituals of the Yajur Veda and even the spells of the Atharva Veda. The idea of including the Atharva Veda in the list of Vedas is a much later phenomenon. Still later, the epic Mahabharata and even the Natya Shastra—that discusses art and aesthetics—came to be seen as the fifth Veda.

Vedic transmission is highly symbolic, with the onus of transmitting the ideas resting on priests (brahmanas, or Brahmins) and the onus of decoding them resting on the patron (yajamana). As the centuries passed, as society grew in size and complexity, as economic and political realities shifted, as tribes and clans gave way to villages with multiple communities, which gave rise to kingdoms and later empires, the transmission began to fail. The transmitters of Vedic lore, the Brahmins, assumed the role of decoders. In other words, the librarian became the professor! Consequently, hymns and rituals stopped being seen as symbolic puzzles that when deciphered unravelled the mysteries of the world. Instead, they became magical tools to attract fortune and ward off misfortune.

This trend towards materialism over self-enquiry may have contributed to the rise of the shramanas, who were known for their disdain of Brahmins and Brahmanic rituals. The need for reframing Vedic ideas was felt even within the Vedic fold.

The reframing of Hinduism happened rather organically over a period of another 1,000 years. No authority spearheaded it. Sages began communicating Vedic ideas choosing stories as their vehicle, instead of rituals and hymns. The stories were based on traditional accounts of events, both experienced and imagined. These were 'open source' narratives, with plots and counter-plots gradually turning into pieces of a complex jigsaw. Everyone worked anonymously and attributed their work to one Vyasa, who was the son of a fisherwoman. He was also credited with reorganizing the lost Vedas. The word 'vyasa' means compiler: compiler of Vedic knowledge, as well as compiler of Puranic stories.

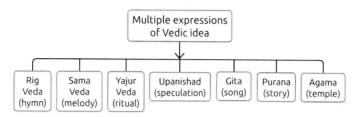

Transmission of the Veda

The narratives by 'Vyasa' were called the Puranas, or chronicles, which included the epics Ramayana and Mahabharata that spoke of family quarrels over property. They were also called Itihasa. Itihasa, taken literally, means stories from the past. Itihasa, taken symbolically, means stories that will always be true: past, present or future. They reiterated the concept of 'iti', which means 'as things are'—accepting the reality of sex and violence, desires and conflicts in relationships, household and life.

Those who affirmed iti were the astikas. Those who denied iti were the nastikas. Later, as Hinduism turned more theistic, iti denoted faith in God, and so astikas and nastikas would come to mean believers and non-believers.

Unlike monastic orders of Buddhism, which spoke of withdrawal and renunciation, these narratives spoke of liberation despite engaging with society and upholding responsibilities. Household quarrels and property disputes were always resolved using Vedic wisdom presented in the form of conversations. Often, the conversations were turned into Gitas, made lyrical using the anushtup metre, where each verse has four sentences and each sentence has eight syllables.

The Mahabharata itself has many Gitas, besides the butcher's song and God's song. In the Shanti Parva, Book 12 of the

Mahabharata, Bhisma reveals nine Gitas to the Pandavas: the prostitute's song (Pingala Gita), the priest's song (Sampaka Gita), the farmer's song (Manki Gita), the ascetic's song (Bodhya Gita), the king's song (Vichaknu Gita), the retired man's song (Harita Gita), the demon's song (Vritra Gita), the philosopher's song (Parasara Gita) and the swan's song (Hansa Gita). Outside the Mahabharata, there are the Ashtavakra Gita, Vasishtha Gita, Ram Gita, Shiva Gita, Devi Gita, Ganesha Gita and many more.

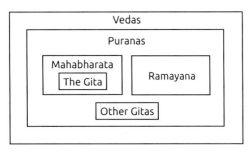

Locating The Gita in a Sea of Scriptures

The Bhagavad Gita, of course, remains the most widely read of the Gitas. It is the counsel of a chariot-driver called Krishna to the chariot-rider and archer, Arjuna, just before the start of a war at Kuru-kshetra between the five Pandava brothers and their hundred Kaurava cousins. It is so popular that today, when we say Gita, we mean the Bhagavad Gita.

In its final form, the Bhagavad Gita had 700 verses, split into 18 chapters, of which 574 are spoken by Krishna, 84 by Arjuna, 41 by Sanjaya and 1 by Dhritarashtra. There are suggestions that the Bhagavad Gita originally had 745 verses. It is a conversation, though it does seem like a discourse, which takes place over ninety minutes while fully armed soldiers on either side wait

My Gita

impatiently to do battle. Whether this event is a time-bound physical objective truth (history) or a timeless psychological subjective truth (mythology) remains a matter of opinion.

Commentaries, Retellings, Translations

Interpretations of The Gita started appearing nearly five centuries after its final composition. The reason for this gap remains a mystery. The Vedic idea was widely prevalent, but no special attention was given to this particular conversation in the Mahabharata between Krishna and Arjuna.

Commentaries on The Gita start appearing from approximately the time Islam entered India. One of the world's oldest mosques was built on the Malabar coast in the seventh century, and Adi Shankara, who wrote the first elaborate commentary on The Gita and made it an important scripture for Vedanta, was also born in the Malabar coast region in the eighth century. A relationship cannot be denied. Whether this was pure coincidence or the cause for the resurgence of The Gita remains a matter of speculation, mired in contemporary politics.

With Islam, India was exposed to Abrahamic mythology: the idea of one formless God, one holy book, one set of rules and one way of thinking that included a violent rejection of hierarchy as well as idolatry. Christian and Jewish traders had introduced many of these ideas before, but nothing on the Islamic scale. As many Muslims settled in India, as many kingdoms came to be ruled by Muslims, as many Indian communities converted to Islam, they were bound to influence Hindu thought. However, the extent of Islamic influence provokes fierce debate.

The Gita readings took place in five waves spread over 1,200 years.

The first wave involved Sanskrit 'commentaries' (bhasyas) by Vedanta scholars, the most celebrated of whom were Adi Shankara from Kerala in the eighth century followed by Ramanuja from Tamil Nadu in the eleventh century and Madhva Acharya from Karnataka in the thirteenth century. They were concerned about the nature of God, and the relationship of divinity and humanity. Was God within or without? Was God embodied (sa-guna) or formless (nir-guna)? Their language was highly intellectual. What is significant is that all three commentators were celibate monks, who either did not marry or gave up marriage and established Hindu monastic orders (mathas), suggesting very clearly that Hinduism, once champion of the householder's way, had ended up mimicking the hermit's way of Buddhism it had previously always mocked. It contributed to the gradual separation of the more intellectual Vedanta from the more sensory Tantra, with the former becoming more mainstream and the latter being seen more as the occult.

The second wave involved 'retellings' in regional languages, the earliest of which was in Marathi by Gyaneshwara (thirteenth century), followed by the works of Niranam Madhava Panikkar in Malayalam (fourteenth century), Peda Tirumalacharya in Telugu (fifteenth century), Balarama Das in Odiya (fifteenth century), Govind Mishra in Assamese (sixteenth century), Dasopant Digambara and Tukaram in Marathi (seventeenth century) and many more. The tone in these regional works was extremely emotional, with the poets speaking of God in extremely personal and affectionate terms. Gyaneshwara even refers to Krishna as 'mother', and visualizes him as a cow that comforts the frightened calf, Arjuna, with the milk that is The Gita. It is through works such as these, usually presented as songs, that the wisdom of The Gita reached the masses. It is in this phase that the Bhagavad Purana, or simply Bhagavata, which describes the earlier life of Krishna as a cowherd, became the dominant text of Hinduism. It is also during this phase that The Gita started being personified as a goddess, and hymns were composed to meditate on her (Gita Dhyana) and celebrate her glory (Gita Mahatmya). Gita Jayanti, the eleventh day of the waxing moon in the month of Margashisha (December), was identified as the day when Krishna revealed this wisdom to Arjuna, and the world.

Gyaneshwara

The third wave involved 'translations' by Europeans— eighteenth-century European Orientalists such as Charles Wilkins, who was sponsored by the East India Company, and nineteenth-century poets such as Edwin Arnold, who also introduced the Buddha and many things Eastern to Europe. They sought an objective, hence correct, reading of The Gita, implicitly introducing the suggestion that commentaries and retellings and poetic renditions were mere interpretations—subjective, contaminated by artistic liberty, hence inferior. The translators were Christian and, like Muslims, immersed in Abrahamic monotheistic mythology, who saw God as the primary source of knowledge and humans as sinners who needed to follow the way of God. Naturally, they saw The Gita's God as judge, even though such a concept was alien to Hinduism. The Gita naturally became a directive from God, a Hindu Bible! These translations, and the meanings given by Orientalists to Sanskrit words, with assumptions rooted in Abrahamic mythology, continue to be subscribed to and have a profound impact on the understanding of The Gita in modern times.

The fourth wave involved 're-translations' by Indian nationalists. The Indian National Movement gained momentum in the early part of the twentieth century, and there was an increased urgency to bind the diverse peoples of the Indian subcontinent into a single narrative. The Gita seemed like a good book to do so. But different leaders saw it differently. Sri Aurobindo found in The Gita mystical ideas of an ancient civilization, while B.R. Ambedkar pointed out that The Gita seemed to justify the draconian caste system. Bal Gangadhar Tilak found the rationale for righteous violence in it, while Mahatma Gandhi found inspiration for the path of non-violence. This was the period that the world was introduced to the words of the Buddha that were compared with the words of Krishna. Eventually, Arjuna's dilemma was radically re-articulated: it became less about 'how can I kill family?' and more about 'how can I kill?'

The fifth wave involved 're-framing' following the end of the two World Wars that replaced colonial empires with republics and democratic nation states. The world, traumatized by violence, was confused as to how to interpret The Gita. J. Robert Oppenheimer infamously equated the nuclear bomb with

Krishna's cosmic form. Aldous Huxley saw The Gita as part of the perennial philosophy that bound all humanity. It became the definitive holy book of the Hindus that spoke of peace. Spiritual gurus started projecting The Gita as a directive from God with a well-defined goal of liberation (moksha) and turned Hinduism into a 'religion'. Management gurus used The Gita to explain leadership, ethics, governance and the art of winning. By the 1980s, before the Internet explosion, there were an estimated 3,000 translations of The Gita in almost fifty languages, and nearly a thousand in English.

Some American academicians, in recent times, have challenged the notion that The Gita has anything to do with peace. They tend to project Hinduism as the outcome of an oppressive violent force called Brahminism that sought to wipe out Buddhist pacifism and propagate a hierarchical system that promoted patriarchy and untouchability. The Gita then becomes a complex justification of violence. Any attempt to challenge this view is dismissed as religious fundamentalism or Hindu nationalism. Such a naïve, or perhaps deliberate, force-fitting of Hinduism into the conflict-based masculine historical template, long favoured in the West, is increasingly being condemned as Hindu-phobia, especially by the Hindu diaspora. Increasingly, historians are drawing attention to the deep prejudice and cultural context of many South Asian scholars, as well as nationalists, that influence the way they make sense of facts.

To eyes that can see, each of these waves is a response to a historical context, be it the amplification of Hindu theism in the Buddhist and Islamic periods or the transformation of India into a British colony or the rise of the national movement or the end of empires, the rise of secular democracies with atheistic ideologies or an increasingly digitized global village having an identity crisis, where everyone seems to be tired of violence but no one seems to be able to give it up.

You and I live in unique times. We have access to the history of The Gita, its creation and its transformation over time. We have a better understanding of geography, of history, of different mythologies and philosophies from around the world, with which we can compare and contrast ideas of The Gita. We have access to research on animal, human and developmental psychology. We are also aware that any study of The Gita eventually becomes a study of how humans see the world, how Indians saw the world, how the West wants to see India, how India wants to see India and how we want to see The Gita.

Rather than seeking a singular authentic message, you and I must appreciate the plurality of ideas that have emerged over the centuries and seek out what binds them, and what separates them. In the various translations, commentaries and retellings, we do find a common tendency to appreciate the relationship between the self (Arjuna) and the other; those who stand on our side (Pandavas); those who stand on the other (Kauravas); the one who stands on everybody's side (Krishna); and of course, property (Kuru-kshetra). Our relationship with the other, be it a thing or an organism, and the other's relationship with us, is what determines our humanity. And this is a timeless (sanatana) truth (satya), a discovery of our ancestors, which we will explore in *My Gita*.

My Gita

My Gita

Vishwa-rupa

In the following chapters, you and I will explore eighteen themes of The Gita. We will continuously journey between the outer world of relationships and the inner world of thoughts and emotions. We will begin by appreciating how we look at the world and ourselves (darshan). Then we will understand the architecture of the world we inhabit, composed of the tangible and the intangible, both within and around us (atma, deha, dehi, karma). After that, we will see how humans can socially connect (dharma, yagna, yoga). Then we will appreciate the idea of God (deva, bhagavan, brahmana, avatara), located in all of us, that helps us cope with our fears that disconnect us from society. Lack of faith in the divine within makes us seek solace outside, in property (kshetra, maya). Because of this, a tug-of-war ensues between the inside and the outside. As long as we cling (moha), we are trapped. As soon as we let go, we are liberated (moksha). We become independent and content in our own company (atma-rati) yet generous and dependable for the other (brahma-nirvana).

The sequence of themes in *My Gita* is slightly different from the sequence of themes in The Gita as some concepts have been elaborated to facilitate understanding.

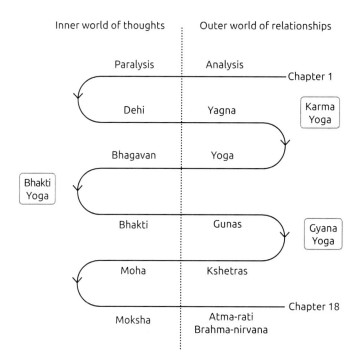

Inner world of thoughts | Outer world of relationships

Paralysis | Analysis — Chapter 1

Dehi | Yagna — Karma Yoga

Bhagavan | Yoga

Bhakti Yoga — Bhakti | Gunas — Gyana Yoga

Moha | Kshetras

Moksha | Atma-rati Brahma-nirvana — Chapter 18

The Architecture of My Gita

Themes in The Gita	Chapter	Themes in *My Gita*
Arjuna's despair	1	Observation (darshan)
Summary of analysis (sankhya)	2	Rebirth (atma)
Informed action (karma)	3	Mortal Body (deha)
Appreciating exchange (gyana)	4	Body's immortal resident (dehi)
Detached action (sanyasa)	5	Cause and consequence (karma)
Inner journey (dhyana)	6	Appropriate conduct (dharma)
Inner potential (vi-gyana)	7	Exchange (yagna)
Rebirth or liberation (askhara)	8	Introspection (yoga)
Special secret (raja-guhya)	9	Trust (deva–asura)
Description of divinity (vibhuti)	10	Potential (bhagavan)
Sight of divinity (vishwa-rupa)	11	Expanding the mind (brahmana)
Form or formless (bhakti)	12	Contracting the mind (avatar)
Proprietorship (kshetra)	13	Tendencies of matter (guna)
Tendencies of matter (guna)	14	Proprietorship (kshetra)
Potential (purushottam)	15	Measurement (maya)
Believers (deva-asura)	16	Attachment (moha)
Diversity of devotion (shraddha)	17	Liberation (moksha)
Summary of solution (moksha)	18	Union (brahma-nirvana)

1.

You and I do not have to judge

Hindu mythology does not have the concept of Judgement Day (or qayamat in Arabic). The God of Hinduism is no judge. Hence, Krishna gives no commandments in The Gita. He simply explains the architecture of the world. As long as we judge, we cannot see the world for what it is; we are simply spellbound by the boundaries that we build separating those whom we consider family from those whom we consider enemy, as we realize in Chapter 1 of The Gita. This chapter introduces the concept of **darshan**, or observing, that is implicit in the Vedas and The Gita and the Mahabharata, but becomes an explicit ritual in temples of Puranic Hinduism where devotees are invited to gaze upon the enshrined deity, and the deity looks back at them, without a blink.

The Gita begins with how Dhritarashtra, Duryodhana and Arjuna view the same battlefield. Below is what Dhritarashtra says in the very first verse of The Gita. It is the only verse he speaks:

> Sanjaya, tell me what is going on between my sons and Pandu's sons, as they gather in Kuru-kshetra, where they have to do what they are supposed to do?—*Bhagavad Gita: Chapter 1, Verse 1 (paraphrased)*.

Dhritarashtra is the head of the Kuru family, whose two branches are about to clash on the battlefield. Naturally, he is curious about what is going on there. He is also concerned whether the right thing is being done there, for he refers to Kuru-kshetra as dharma-kshetra. However, he refers only to his sons, the Kauravas, as mine (mama) and his nephews simply as the Pandavas, the sons of Pandu, not as 'my brother's sons'. Thus, he expresses his exclusion of the Pandavas from his heart: he sees them not as family but as outsiders, intruders, even enemies. He does not realize that this exclusion is the root of the adharma that is the undoing of the Kuru clan. Dhritarashtra's blindness is not so much the absence of sight as the absence of empathy.

Dhritarashtra's blindness extends to his eldest son, Duryodhana, whose conduct on the battlefield is then described by the royal charioteer Sanjaya.

> King, your son is not surprised that the enemy is well-prepared; after all, their commander, Dhristadhyumna, is also the student of his tutor, Drona. He declares that the Pandavas may have the mighty Bhima leading a

limited army, but he has the veteran and the invincible Bhisma on his side leading his limitless army. Having said so, he orders his soldiers to guard Bhisma at all costs.—*Bhagavad Gita: Chapter 1, verses 2 to 11 (paraphrased)*.

Duryodhana's words as described by Sanjaya reveal irritation, insecurity and agitation, despite the fact that he has eleven armies, and the Pandavas only seven.

Sanjaya

Sanjaya then proceeds to describe Arjuna's entry into the battlefield. Arjuna looks confident, bow in hand, on his chariot drawn by four white horses, with the image of Hanuman, the mighty monkey god, on the flag fluttering above. He asks his charioteer, Krishna, to take him to the centre of the battleground in the space between the two armies. There, in no man's land, the enormity of the unfolding tragedy dawns upon him: on either side are family and friends. Elders, teachers, uncles, nephews, sons-in-law, fathers-in-law. Before him are those he should be protecting, and those who should be protecting him. Instead, they are planning to kill him, and he them. Why? For a piece of land! How can that be right, or good? What impact would it have on civilization?

> Krishna, Dhritarashtra's sons are family. How can we slaughter them, they whose greed blinds them to the horror of the situation? If we kill family over property, why will women bother with fidelity, why will communities respect boundaries? All rituals will be abandoned and all ancestors will be forgotten. Those who unravel the fabric of family will surely sink into hell.—*Bhagavad Gita: Chapter 1, verses 37 to 45 (paraphrased).*

This response, full of fear and confusion, is very different from the views of Dhritrashtra and Duryodhana. The Kaurava father and son have clearly drawn boundaries dividing those they consider their own and those they consider as outsiders, intruders, even enemies. Arjuna's boundaries, however, wobble: how can family be enemy?

The Mahabharata describes Arjuna as a highly focussed archer, who could shoot his arrow into the eye of a flying bird without being distracted by the clouds above, or the trees below. Yet, at Kuru-kshetra, Arjuna looks beyond the target and 'sees' family and friends. He questions the morality of his wanting to kill them, and the consequences of such violence on society as a whole. It is not the violence that bothers him; he has killed before. What bothers him is violence against family, those he is meant to protect.

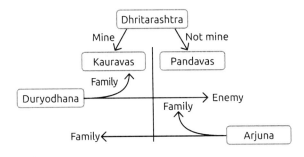

Observing Kuru-kshetra

Here is the very reverse of the psychological blindness displayed by Dhritarashtra and Duryodhana: Arjuna's vision is expanding, focus is giving way to perspective, attention (dhayana) to awareness (dharana) as his gaze finally rejects the boundary separating the self from the other, and action from responsibility. This is darshan!

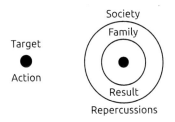

Focus and Perspective

In darshan, there is no judgement because there are no boundaries, no rules, no separation of right and wrong, mine and not mine.

Dhritarashtra is unable to do darshan because of memories (smriti); he bears a deep grudge. He was born blind, yet it was he who was never seen. Not by his uncle, Bhisma, who decided that Dhritarashtra's younger brother, Pandu, should be made king instead of him. Not by his wife, Gandhari, who decided to share his blindness by wearing a blindfold, rather than compensate for it. Not by his beloved son, Duryodhana, who preferred the advice of his maternal uncle, Shakuni, to his own. Not by his advisor, Vidura, who always praised Pandu's five sons, but never his hundred. Unseen by all, he is simply paying the blindness forward.

Arjuna also has many reasons not to do darshan: the Kauravas tried their best to kill him and his brothers when they were children; they humiliated him and his brothers repeatedly in a gambling hall; they dragged the Pandavas' common wife, Draupadi, by the hair and attempted to disrobe her in public; they refused to return Indra-prastha, the Pandava lands, even though the Pandavas had kept their side of their agreement and spent thirteen years in exile; the Kauravas even refused offers of compromise for the sake of peace. Yet, Arjuna finds it hard to respond to the Kauravas' blindness with blindness.

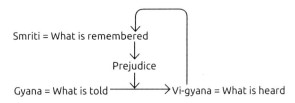

Memories Distort Observation

In an attempt to goad Arjuna into action, Krishna reminds him of the sufferings of his brothers and his wife and of his duties as a warrior, a brother and a husband. Krishna even questions

Arjuna's manliness (Chapter 2, Verse 3) when he mocks his action as those of a non-man (kliba). He speaks of the glory of paradise that awaits him if he dies, and the satisfaction of victory that awaits him if he lives. But none of these have any impact on Arjuna. He refuses to let memories strip him of empathy. He does darshan and that makes him a worthy recipient of The Gita.

Long before the war, when negotiations for peace had broken down, Krishna had revealed his cosmic form (virat-swarup)—the same form he shows Arjuna during the course of his discourse—to both Dhritarashtra and Duryodhana, perhaps to impress upon father and son that his words needed to be taken seriously. But Dhritarashtra, granted momentary sight, had simply declared his helplessness before such awesomeness and shrunk back into blindness, while Duryodhana had seen it as a magician's trick. Both father and son refused to see what was shown. They clung to the view that they were the victims. Thus, showing does not guarantee seeing. Telling does not guarantee hearing. Gyana is not vi-gyana.

In judgement, the world is divided: good and bad, innocent and guilty, polluted and pure, oppressor and oppressed, privileged and unprivileged, powerful and powerless. In darshan, one sees a fluid world of cause and consequence, where there are no divisions, boundaries, hierarchies or rules.

Judgement	Darshan
↓	↓
Right / Wrong	Fears
Mine / Not mine	Hungers
↓	↓
Rana-bhoomi	Ranga-bhoomi

Rana-bhoomi and Ranga-bhoomi

A world created based on judgement evokes rage. Life becomes a battleground (rana-bhoomi) like Kuru-kshetra, where both sides feel like victims, where everyone wants to win at all costs, where someone will always lose. A world created by observation evokes insight, hence affection, for we see the hunger and fear of all beings. Life becomes a performance on a stage (ranga-bhoomi) aimed to nourish and comfort the other, while deriving nourishment and comfort from their delight. Krishna's performance (leela) leads to him being worshipped as Ranga-natha, lord of the stage. He never judges, so he sees no one as a victim. This is how he begins The Gita:

> Arjuna, you grieve for those whom you should not feel sorry for, and you argue as if you are a man of wisdom. But the wise grieve for no one: neither the living, nor the dead.—*Bhagavad Gita: Chapter 2, Verse 11 (paraphrased).*

Do you see me as hero, villain or victim? If yes, then you are not doing darshan. If you can empathize with the fears that make people heroes, villains and victims, then you are doing darshan. For then you look beyond the boundaries that separate you from the rest.

2.

You and I have been here before

Our body is mortal and so it seeks security and creates boundaries. But within this body is the immortal **atma** that does not seek security and so, does not care for boundaries. Wrapped in mortal flesh, it experiences life and death, again and again. By introducing the idea of immortality and rebirth in Chapter 2 of The Gita, Krishna changes the scope of the discussion, for without death serving as a boundary, there is no fear, no yearning for food or meaning, nowhere to come from, or go to, for the end is no longer the end and the beginning is no longer the beginning. Rather than change the world that defies control, rather than seek validation from things temporary, we engage, observe, discover and enjoy.

Arjuna, the wise know that you and I and the rest existed before this event, and will continue to exist after this event. The resident of this body experiences its childhood, youth and old age before moving on to the next. This body gets attached to the world around it, and so fears death. But the wise, aware of the inner resident's immortality, aware that the flesh goes through cycles of birth and death, do not fear change, or death. They know that what matters is the immortal, not the mortal.—*Bhagavad Gita: Chapter 2, verses 12 to 16 (paraphrased).*

With these words Krishna simply renders death irrelevant. He transforms the battlefield into one of the infinite experiences of the immortal resident (dehi) of the mortal body (deha). Later, he identifies dehi as atma, purusha, brahmana and kshetragna. It inhabits various bodies, again and again, lifetime after lifetime. This means that this is not the first time we have experienced the world, and it will not be the last. We have been here before and will return again. Our birth is a re-birth. Our death is a re-death.

Arjuna, you wear fresh clothes at the time of birth and discard them at the time of death. You are not these clothes.—*Bhagavad Gita: Chapter 2, Verse 22 (paraphrased).*

In Chapter 4, Krishna declares he has transmitted this knowledge before, to the sun or Vivasvat (the first celestial being), then to Manu (the first man), and then to Ikshvaku (the first king), and that this knowledge is often forgotten.

Krishna, Vivasvat lived long ago. You live now. How could you have taught him?—*Bhagavad Gita: Chapter 4, Verse 4 (paraphrased).*

Arjuna is naturally startled. Krishna responds by revealing that he has lived before, as has Arjuna; he remembers it, but Arjuna does not, for Arjuna is trapped in the outer world of tangible objects and has no insight into the inner world of intangible thoughts.

Arjuna, at the dawn of Brahma's day, all forms burst forth. At dusk, they withdraw into formlessness. The children of Brahma stay entrapped in the wheel of rebirths as their mind is drawn by their senses. But those who fix their minds on me break free from this wheel of rebirths, of fluctuating between form and formlessness.—*Bhagavad Gita: Chapter 8, verses 16 to 26 (paraphrased).*

The idea of rebirth forms the cornerstone of Hindu thought. It is also the mainstay of Buddhist and Jain philosophies. But there are differences. Buddhists do not believe in the existence of the immortal resident (atma), and Jains do not believe in the concept of God (param-atma), but they both agree on the concept of rebirth (punar-janma). In Jainism and Buddhism, the world of rebirths is called samsara, propelled by action (karma) and memories of past actions (samskara). These are sometimes referred to as dharma mythologies, distinguishing them from Abrahamic or non-dharma mythologies such as Judaism, Christianity and Islam that believe in only one life, and an afterlife in heaven or hell. Science endorses only one life, as the afterlife or rebirth defies scientific measurement.

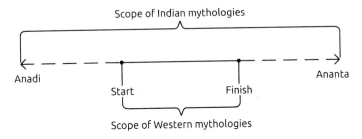

Dharma and Non-dharma Mythologies

The idea of rebirth can be seen at metaphysical, social and psychological levels. Together they change our view of life.

At a metaphysical level, rebirth helps us explain the inexplicable, and replace conflict with acceptance and peace. Why are some people born into rich families and some into poor families, some to loving parents and some to cruel parents, some with talent and some without? Who is to be blamed?

In Abrahamic mythology, the explanation of everything is God's will. Our sufferings are the result of disobeying God's will and law, having fallen under the spell of the Devil. All will be well if we repent of our sins, accept God's love and demonstrate it by following His law. This assumption fuels guilt.

In Greek mythology, wealth and power are seen as having been cornered by the privileged few, and heroes have to fight these oppressors, bring justice and offer equal opportunities to all. This assumption fuels rage.

Science offers no explanation, as science is not about 'why', but about 'how'. For the why, the social sciences invariably turn to

My Gita

Greek mythology with its oppressor-oppression framework that resurrected after the European Renaissance, 600 years ago. Or it creates a new god: the people.

In Hindu mythology, there is no one but ourselves to blame for our problems: neither God nor any oppressors. The idea of rebirth aims to evoke acceptance of the present, and responsibility for the future. Our immortal soul is tossed from one life to another as long as our mind refuses to do darshan. This is made most explicit in the story of Karna in the Mahabharata.

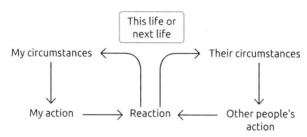

My Action, My Circumstance

Karna is a foundling brought up by a charioteer, who rises to be a king through sheer talent and effort, and discovers much later in life that he is of royal blood, abandoned at birth by his mother Kunti, who went on to marry King Pandu. Kunti's children are none other than the Pandavas, who constantly mock his lowly status and who are the enemies of his benefactor and best friend, Duryodhana. Before the war, Karna has the option to switch to the opposite side, where as the eldest of the Pandavas, he would become the rightful heir to Pandu and the first of Draupadi's husbands. But Karna chooses to stay loyal to the Kauravas. During the war at Kuru-kshetra, everyone and everything turns against him. First, Bhisma does not let him fight as long as he is alive. Then Drona makes him use his best weapons prematurely. Arjuna's celestial father, the rain god Indra, tricks him into giving up his invulnerable armour, taking advantage of his charitable nature. To mock the Pandavas, Duryodhana gets their uncle, Shalya, to serve as Karna's charioteer, but that turns out to be a terrible decision as Shalya spends all his time praising Arjuna and demotivating Karna. When the wheel of Karna's chariot gets stuck in the ground, Shalya refuses to pull it out, claiming he is a king, not a charioteer. The mantra taught by Parashurama to release wheels stuck in the ground does not work. So Karna throws down his bow and tries to pull the wheel out himself, and in that unarmed, helpless moment, goaded by Krishna, Arjuna strikes him dead. Karna, who sought all his life to be an archer and a king, thus dies as a charioteer, the profession of his foster father that he shunned.

Karna's story is a tragic one. Though technically an insider, circumstances make him an outsider, who is never ever allowed into the family. He is used and exploited by all, not just the Kauravas, but also his birth mother, Kunti, who comes to him only at the brink of war and tries to take advantage of his charitable nature. Even Krishna tries to tempt him away from his friend and benefactor, Duryodhana. Despite his charity, his integrity and his loyalty, he suffers all his life. We see him as a victim, but Krishna does not. For Krishna knows his previous lives.

In one story, Karna was an asura blessed with a thousand armours called Sahasrakavacha. To destroy each armour, a warrior had to acquire special powers by meditating for a thousand years. Even with these powers, destroying the armour would need a thousand years. So Nara and Narayana, twin sages, avatars of Vishnu, attacked this asura simultaneously—while one meditated, the other fought, taking turns to acquire the power and to destroy the armour. By the time they had destroyed all but one of the thousand armours, the world came to an end. But the world was reborn; the asura was reborn as Karna, Nara as Arjuna and Narayana as Krishna. We are told that only Krishna knows the full story and so, while Karna is a victim if we know only his present story, he becomes a villain if we know another backstory.

In another story, when Vishnu descended on earth as Ram, he killed Vali, the son of Indra, and sided with Sugriva, the son of Surya. So when Vishnu descended as Krishna, he was obliged to restore the balance in the cosmos by killing Karna, son of Surya, and siding with Arjuna, son of Indra. Here, one story is one half of another story, and Karna's misfortune neutralizes his fortune in another life. Free of any obligations or expectations, he would thus be liberated from the wheel of rebirths. So his killing, which we feel is a sad incident, becomes a wonderful event.

In a third story, when Vishnu descended as Parashurama, he trained Bhisma, Drona and Karna, who ended up siding with the Kauravas and upholding adharma. Since he could not kill his own students, Vishnu again descended as Krishna, and supported the Pandavas, who fought and killed the Kauravas and their commanders. Here Krishna is reborn to correct the errors of a previous life, one of them being Karna.

In the Puranas, stories of past lives are continuously used to counter assumptions of another story. It reminds us that our story is part of a grand jigsaw puzzle. We are part of a larger narrative. Stories of the past impact stories of the present that impact stories of the future. We may not know these stories, but we have played roles in them. We must not assume that the story we encounter, experience or remember is the only story in the world. Our lives are the outcomes of roles performed in other stories. Even if we don't remember those stories or those roles, we cannot escape their consequences.

> 'Arjuna, when I take form, particles of myself form the various beings in this world and I draw the mind and the senses to me. It is I who experience the world through the senses. When I lose form, I carry memories of these experiences to the next form, just as the breeze carries fragrances. The wise see me enjoying and transporting myself so. The unwise don't.'—*Bhagavad Gita: Chapter 15, verses 7 to 10 (paraphrased).*

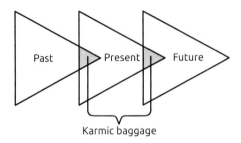

Impact of Past on Present and Present on Future

At a social level, the idea of rebirth expands the canvas of our lives and brings perspective. It reminds us that the world existed before us and the world will exist after us. Like us, many people have sought to change the world and make it better, even perfect, but while changes do take place technologically, no real change takes place psychologically—people are still jealous and

My Gita

angry and ambitious and greedy and heartbroken. While the West valorizes social transformation, The Gita is focussed on individual psychological expansion.

The world into which we are born is imagined as a stage full of actors but with no script, or director. Everyone assumes they are the hero, but discover they are not the protagonists of the ongoing play. We are forced to play certain roles and speak certain dialogues. But we revolt. We want our own script to be performed and our own dialogues to be heard. So we negotiate with fellow actors. Some succeed in getting heard with some people, others fail with most people, no one succeeds with everybody. We cling to our scripts, submit to other people's scripts, speak dialogues we do not want to, only to stay relevant and connected to the larger narrative, or at least to a subplot. Heroes emerge. Villains emerge. Heroes of one plot turn out to be villains of other plots. Eventually, all leave the stage but the play continues. Who knows what is actually going on? Vishnu, the ranga-natha? All we can decipher are the patterns, as does he.

In the Puranas, Vishnu sees the devas and asuras in eternal combat: the devas feel they are entitled, and the asuras feel they have been tricked; the devas do not share, and the asuras always scare. The force of the devas and the counterforce of the asuras, their alternating victories and defeats, keep the world moving. Vishnu sleeps and awakens, and smiles, turning the unproductive fight into a productive churn whenever he can, as Brahma and his sons struggle continuously to control life, rather than accept and enjoy it, despite Vishnu's numerous interventions.

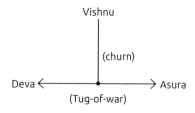

Deva, Asura and Vishnu

In the Ramayana, Vishnu encounters Ravana, who refuses to give up Sita, even if it means the death of his son and his brother, and the burning of his kingdom. In the Mahabharata, Vishnu encounters Yudhishtira, who gambles away his kingdom, his brothers, his wife, even his own identity, rather than simply accept defeat. He encounters Duryodhana, who would rather plunge his family into a war that will kill millions than give up a 'needlepoint of land'. There is pride, jealousy, rage and the rationalization of all desires. These patterns are neverending, and can be experienced in every society, at all times.

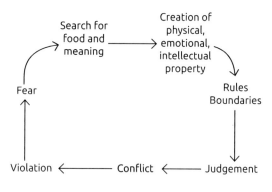

Darshan Breaks the Cycle

The idea that life has no beginning (anadi) and no end (ananta), that our existence has no borders, no starting or finishing line, stands in direct contrast to modern ideas based on Greek mythology, where life is like an Olympic race where we have to 'win'. The winners of Greek mythology found a place for themselves in the afterlife, called Elysium. In Abrahamic mythology, those who align to the will and word of God reach heaven, the rest go to hell. Rebirth takes away the sense of urgency and the quest for perfection that are the hallmarks of Western thought. The Gita does not speak of changing the world. It speaks of appreciating the world that is always changing. Belief in one life makes us want to change the world, control it or resign to the way things are. Belief in rebirth enables us to appreciate all three possibilities, without clinging to any.

Taken psychologically, the idea of rebirth is about having multiple opportunities to break the cycle of fear and find meaning, without 'consuming' anyone.

When you live only once, the value of your life becomes the sum total of your achievements. Hence the need to align or achieve, which are the driving forces of Western thought. In Christianity and Islam it involves conversion to the right way of living. In Greek mythology (or secularism), it is about being a hero by either winning a race, or overthrowing oppressors. In either case, we end up controlling, hence consuming, the other. This is entrapment.

But when you live many lives, alignments and achievements are rendered meaningless. What matters is wisdom: an understanding of why this world exists, why we exist, and why we live, again and again, in a merry-go-round. When we understand, we do not seek control of the other, hence are liberated. We engage with the world, but are not entrapped. We are no longer dependent, but we stay dependable.

Arjuna draws attention to the fact that it is tough to stay aligned to a single course, howsoever noble.

> Krishna, what happens to he who strays from the path of insight? Does he lose out on both: happiness promised by wisdom and pleasures promised by indulgence? Does he perish like a torn cloud?—*Bhagavad Gita: Chapter 6, verses 37 and 38 (paraphrased).*

Krishna replies that nothing is wasted or destroyed in the cosmos. All efforts are recorded and they impact future lives. Knowledge acquired in the past plays a role in the wisdom of future lives.

> Those unsuccessful in realization in this life will be reborn. Their efforts will not go in waste. They will ensure they are born in a wise family, where they can strive again. They will be driven to wisdom on account of memories and impressions of previous lives. By striving through many lives, they untangle themselves to unite with divinity.—*Bhagavad Gita: Chapter 6, verses 41 to 45 (paraphrased).*

In a way Krishna is alluding to Yama, the god of death in the Puranas, who has an accountant called Chitargupta, who keeps a record of all deeds. This record determines the circumstances of our future lives: the parents we shall have, the gender we shall acquire, the fortunes and misfortunes we shall experience. How we respond to what we carry forward from our previous lives will determine what we carry forward to our future lives. Escape is possible if there is nothing to carry forward.

> Arjuna, there are two paths, one of return and the other of no return. The wise, the connected, know the difference and choose the one of no return.—*Bhagavad Gita: Chapter 8, verses 26 and 27 (paraphrased).*

Thus, rebirth offers a second chance. In the Ramayana, Ram's ancestors, the sons of Sagara, are burned to death by the fiery glance of the sage called Kapila because they wrongly accuse him of stealing their horse. Their grandson begs Indra, who had stolen the horse in the first place, to let the celestial river Mandakini flow down on earth as the Ganga. Washed by its waters, the sons of Sagara get the chance of a second life. Another life is another chance: either to stay entrapped in the cycle of fear, or break free by discovering the architecture of the world and observing it without judgement. This is why, in Hindu funerals, the corpse is first burned and then the ashes and bones are cast in the river. Fire and running water represent the two paths mentioned in Chapter 8 of The Gita, one offering liberation and the other offering entrapment.

> Arjuna, the two paths are twins: like fire and smoke, the waxing and waning moons, the course of the rising sun towards the north before rains and towards the south after.—*Bhagavad Gita: Chapter 8, verses 24 and 25 (paraphrased).*

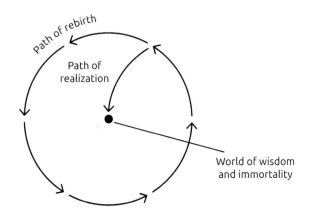

Path of rebirth

Path of
realization

World of wisdom
and immortality

The Two Paths of Rebirth and Liberation

This life is not the first time you and I have experienced each other. We have been here before, but we have not learned, from past experiences, that much of life defies explanation and control, that life always offers a second chance and that the world existed before us and will continue to exist after us. As long as we resist reality, we will not discover the immortal, and go from lifetime to lifetime, hungry for meaning and validation.

3.

You and I experience life differently

Is the idea of immortality and rebirth real or conceptual? What is real? Can the conceptual be real? Our understanding of reality is a function of the capabilities of our body or **deha**, home of the atma. What is real for a plant is not real for an animal, what is real for one human is not real for another. Nature is all about diversity. This understanding of the body, the instrument through which we experience and express reality, is not explicitly a part of The Gita, but certainly a part of Vedic knowledge elaborated in the Upanishads, that Krishna assumes Arjuna to be familiar with.

The body of a rock is different from the body of a plant, which is different from the body of an animal, which is different from the body of a human. And so, what a rock experiences is different from what a plant, animal or human experiences. Human experiences are further complicated by different modes of expression: some humans express accurately, others imaginatively; some speak literally and others use metaphors. Further, what is reality for humans cannot be the reality of God. Hindu mythology constantly refers to this four-fold division of the world—the world of elements, plants, animals and humans. Symbolically, it is represented by the swastika.

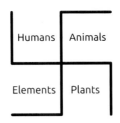

Four-fold Division of the World

The elements (bhutas)—sky, earth, wind, water and fire—constitute the world. However, they do not experience the world, as they do not possess organs (indriyas) to sense or respond to what is around them. Stars, rocks and rivers are not sentient. They move, but do not act. They do not seek opportunities or avoid threats. They do not feel or think. If they do, we do not know, as they cannot express themselves, or at least we cannot fathom their responses. They do not seem to experience death, as they do not demonstrate any struggle for life. Even fire, that needs fuel to survive, does not seek out fuel. It simply dies out when the fuel is exhausted. Elements are therefore considered lifeless (a-jiva).

Plants, animals and humans constitute the living (sa-jiva). They depend on air (prana) and so are called breathers (prani). To stay alive, and keep breathing, living organisms seek food. To find food, plants grow and animals run. Both experience hunger and fear. They want to eat, not be eaten. They want to live, not die. They fight to survive.

Plants have sense organs (gyana-indriyas) to sense the external world and respond to water, sunlight and change of seasons. But they are immobile (a-chara), unable to run from danger, unlike animals (chara) which clearly have more response organs (karma-indriyas). The five sense organs are eyes, ears, nose, tongue and skin. The five response organs are hands, legs, mouth, anus and genitals.

Animals, especially ones with larger brains, display a greater degree of emotions (chitta) and some degree of intelligence (buddhi). They remember things. They make choices. They solve simple problems. They form packs to find food, hives to store food and herds to protect themselves. They establish pecking orders to get a greater share of food and mates. They take care of their young. Some even display personality.

Humans are dramatically different. In us, senses, emotions and intelligence are highly developed. But what really makes us unique is our imagination (manas). While plants and animals experience hunger, fear and death, humans can imagine infinite hunger and infinite fear and infinite death. Humans can also imagine a world without hunger, fear or death. Hence, the idea of immortality! The ability to conjure up a conceptual reality (how the world should be) different from emotional experience (how the world feels) or sensory experiences (what is actually sensed) is unique to human beings and unique for every human being. Your reality is different from my reality, because your body is different, your filters are different, your experiences are different, your knowledge is different.

Krishna experiences every slice (bhaga) of reality, that of elements, plants, animals as well as humans. That is why he is called God (bhaga-van) in The Gita.

> Arjuna, know that I am the sun, the moon, the fire. I am the sap that makes plants blossom. I am the digestive fire and breath of animals. I eat. I think, remember, understand and forget as humans do. I am the transmitter, the teacher, the scholar and the wise. I am the perishable and the imperishable. And that which supports both.—*Bhagavad Gita: Chapter 15, verses 12 to 18 (paraphrased).*

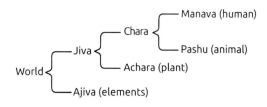

Many Bodies in Nature

In Vedanta, the body is visualized as a series of containers. The flesh is the outermost container and is made up of the senses. It is composed of food and serves as food, and so it is called the container of food (anna-kosha). It is animated by the container of breath (prana-kosha). Within are the container of thoughts (mana-kosha), the container of beliefs (vi-gyana-kosha or buddhi-kosha) and finally the container of emotions (chitta-kosha). In plants, there are only the containers of the flesh and the breath. In animals, there are the containers of the flesh, breath and emotions. In some animals there is also the container of thoughts, influencing emotions. Only in humans is found the container of beliefs, ideas that humans use to make sense of the world around. Our thoughts and beliefs shape our emotions; our emotions also determine our thoughts and beliefs.

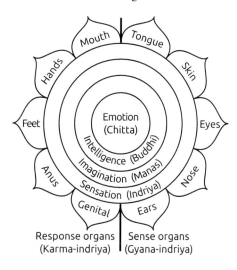

Five Containers of the Body

These five containers create three realities: sensory reality that depends on the flesh (indriyas), emotional reality that depends on the heart (chitta) and conceptual reality that depends on imagination (manas) and intelligence (buddhi). Elements (bhutas) inhabit none of these realities. Plants (a-chara) inhabit the sensory reality. Higher animals (chara) inhabit the emotional reality as well. But only humans (manavas) inhabit all three.

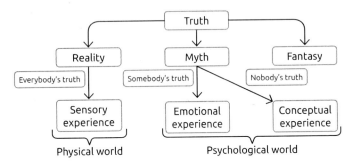

Three Realities

What distinguishes humans from the rest of nature is our ability to imagine reality. We can conjure up the opposite of what we experience. While the senses experience pain, our mind can imagine happiness. While the senses experience pleasure, our mind can imagine sorrow. While the senses experience form, our mind can imagine formlessness. While the senses experience finiteness, our mind can imagine infiniteness. While the senses experience mortality, our mind can imagine immortality.

Imagination helps us create concepts, which filter our sensory inputs and ultimately impact our emotional experience. Thus, we can imagine a rock or river to be a deity and so condition ourselves to feel joyful whenever we encounter that rock or river. Our emotional experiences can also inform and shape our concepts. So, when a rock or river gives us joy in some way, we declare it must be a deity. Concepts therefore help us rationalize emotions; emotions help us rationalize concepts—it is a two-way process.

My Gita

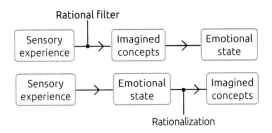

Mental Processes

When presented with the same stimuli, all plants and animals of the same species usually respond in a similar way. Variations are few, and mostly in higher animals. However, the same set of stimuli is read differently by different humans who harbour different concepts. This is why Dhritarashtra, Duryodhana and Arjuna respond to the battleground of Kuru-kshetra very differently. The journey from human to divine is to achieve conceptual clarity and appreciate the world as it is, while empathizing with how others perceive it.

But are concepts real? Are they not products of the imagination? How can we value imagination?

This distinguishing of the imaginary from the real overlooks the fact that humans are humans because of the ability to imagine. All the things that we value—justice, equality, free speech, human rights—are actually concepts churned out of imagination, just like ideas such as God, heaven, hell, rebirth and immortality. We may classify these ideas as secular or religious, rational or supernatural, value one over the other, but they are essentially creations of humans, by humans, for humans. They are artificial constructions, not natural phenomena. They have no independent existence outside humans.

Even our identity (aham) is essentially how we imagine ourselves, a concept. Nature does not care for our tribal roots, our social structures or our cultural hierarchies. It does not care for how we qualify our actions or judge each other. Yet our identity matters to us, as do our concepts, because we are human. Our concepts establish our humanity and help us cope with the terror of nature and biology.

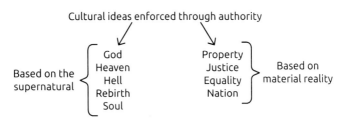

Imagined Concepts

That Arjuna grants himself an identity (Pandava, Kaunteya, Kuru), gives meaning to people around him (friends and family), ascribes value to his action (good or bad) and predicts its reactions (collapse of society) stems from his ability to imagine, construct or inherit boundaries and inhabit conceptual spaces. It is an indicator of his humanity.

> Arjuna, the senses exist beyond the physical; mind beyond the senses; intelligence beyond the mind. Beyond intelligence is your sense of self. By knowing who you really are you will conquer all yearning.—*Bhagavad Gita: Chapter 3, verses 42 and 43 (paraphrased).*

The conceptual reality of Krishna—where immortality is a fact—makes him function without fear, and gain insight about life without imposing the filter of conflict. The conceptual reality of Dhritarashtra and Duryodhana—where victimhood is a fact—makes them function in rage, imagine persecution and harbour an intense desire to change the world. Which imagination is the appropriate one?

Science does not share The Gita's enthusiasm about imagination. Science values the finite, the measurable entity, while The Gita values the infinite (ananta) and the immortal (nitya), which are unmeasurable concepts.

The reality constructed by science is dependent on measuring instruments. However, it is easier to measure things than feelings. This is why physics, chemistry and biology are considered 'pure' sciences, while psychology is considered a 'pseudo' or 'imperfect' science. We can at best use bodily responses to emotions to understand the functioning of the mind, as neuropsychology and behavioural science tend to do.

The humanities, subjects such as sociology, history, economics, management and politics, which involve humans, are no longer called 'social sciences' because while the data may be computed scientifically, the analysis is invariably influenced by the prejudice of the analyst, the philosophy he subscribes to and the concepts he believes to be true.

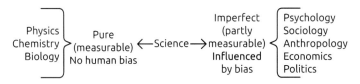

Classification of Sciences

That being said, concepts do play a key role in science, especially mathematics. Zero (shunya) and infinity (ananta) are called imagined numbers, because their existence cannot be proven in material reality. I can show you one tree, two trees, three trees, but I cannot show you 'zero trees' or 'infinite trees'. These have to be imagined.

Civilizations existed and thrived without the knowledge of these concepts for centuries. Buddhist, Jain and Hindu philosophers of India conceived both infinity and zero over two thousand years ago in their attempt to understand both the psychological and the physical world. The hermits preferred the concept of withdrawal into oblivion, hence zero, while the householders preferred the concept of embracing everything, hence infinity. Today, zero and infinity play a key role in calculus and help scientists around the world solve technological problems of the real world.

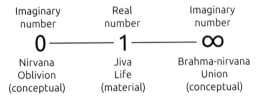

Concepts in Philosophy and Math

Like infinity and zero, immortality is also a concept. By introducing it, Krishna increases the canvas of Arjuna's experience and expands the denominator of his existence. It makes him look at life differently—this life is not the only life we live; it is but one of many lives; our actions have infinite consequences; we have limitless choices, if we open our mind to them. Thus, a shift in

My Gita

imagination brings about a dramatic shift in identity, meaning, value, assumptions and aspirations.

> Arjuna, people worship limited deities, limited as they are by their nature and their yearnings. From me comes their faith. From me comes fulfilment of their faith. The restricted stay restrained. Those who shatter the boundaries discover me: the limitless.—*Bhagavad Gita: Chapter 7, verses 20 to 23 (paraphrased).*

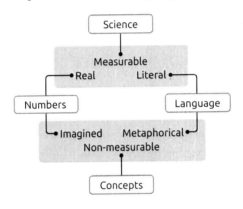

Literal and Metaphorical

Those who are comfortable with imagination appreciate metaphors and symbols. Those who are not prefer the literal. Only through metaphors and symbols can one convey the conceptual. Without poetry, you cannot communicate ideas that are not material and measurable, like love, or justice or remarkability. But The Gita recognizes that the world is made up of different people, those who can only deal with the tangibility of mortality and those who can deal with the intangibility of immortality and rebirth. Krishna does not expect people to experience the world the same way as he does, or respond to the world exactly as he does. This is why Krishna has a 'menu-card' approach to solutions, suiting different capabilities and capacities.

> Arjuna, immerse your mind in me and I will uplift you from the ocean of recurring death. If you cannot do that, then practise yoga and work on your mind. If you cannot do that, then do your work as if it is my work. If you cannot do that, then make yourself my instrument and do as I say. If you cannot do that, then simply do your job and leave the results to me.—*Bhagavad Gita: Chapter 12, verses 6 to 11 (paraphrased).*

My deha is different from yours. My hungers are different from yours. My assumptions are different from yours. My capabilities are different from yours. My experiences are different from yours. My expressions are different from yours.

4.

You and I seek meaning

The immortal resident of the body, the **dehi**, watches how the body experiences the world around it. But what is dehi exactly? Is it the senses that make the body responsive to external stimuli? Is it the mind within the body, or thoughts and ideas and imaginations within the mind, or concepts that filter all sensation and influence emotions? It is something unmeasurable, mystifying and debatable, like consciousness? Or is it conceptual clarity that bestows tranquillity? Does that conceptual clarity involve appreciating the unique human ability to give meaning to ourselves and the world around? We shall explore these ideas in this chapter.

Right at the start of The Gita, Krishna refers to dehi, the immortal that dwells in the body.

> Arjuna, weapons cannot pierce it, fire cannot burn it, water cannot wet it, wind cannot dry it. It is everywhere, at all times, fixed, immovable.—*Bhagavad Gita: Chapter 2, verses 23 and 24 (paraphrased).*

Later, he refers to dehi as atma, the immortal located in the body, but beyond the reach of the senses and the mind.

> Arjuna, detached, tranquil, assured, the observer resides in the city of nine gates.—*Bhagavad Gita: Chapter 5, Verse 13 (paraphrased).*

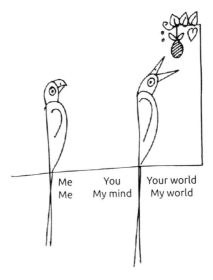

Bird Watching the Bird Eating Fruit

The Rig Veda speaks of a bird that watches another bird eating fruit. This is a metaphor of the world (fruit), the body (bird eating fruit) and the dehi (bird watching bird eating fruit). We can watch others, and ourselves, seeking 'fruit'.

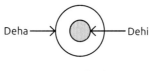

Deha and Dehi

Krishna describes dehi, located inside the body, very much the same way as he describes purusha, located inside all of nature that surrounds the body. If dehi is within the self, purusha is within the other.

> Arjuna, prakriti is responsible for all events around you. Purusha, resident of nature, experiences these events as painful and pleasurable circumstances.—*Bhagavad Gita: Chapter 13, verses 20 and 21 (paraphrased).*

The body we inhabit, and nature that is all around our body, is tangible (sa-guna). What resides in our body, and in nature, is not (nir-guna). Deha and prakriti are within the reach of the senses; they are bound by the rules of space and time, which means that they can be measured and are impermanent. Dehi and purusha, however, are outside the reach of the senses, and are not bound by rules of space and time, which means that they cannot be measured and are permanent.

Deha is part of prakriti. But is dehi a part of purusha? Since both are immortal and infinite, neither can be confined by space, nor can they be separated. In other words, dehi is the same as purusha.

> Arjuna, it is both in and out, inside the animate and the inanimate, far as well as near, difficult to gauge as it is subtle. It is not divisible yet appears divided in separate beings. It is what brings together and creates anew.—*Bhagavad Gita: Chapter 13, verses 15 and 16 (paraphrased)*.

Deha is that which separates us from other entities. Dehi is that which unites us to others. Deha establishes individuality. Dehi establishes universality. We discover deha through analysis (sankhya), by figuring out what isolates us from the world. We discover dehi through synthesis (yoga), by figuring out what connects us with the world. Arjuna's deha is not the same as Duryodhana's, Arjuna's deha is not the same as that of the horses that pull his chariot, but the dehi in Arjuna enables him to feel the fear and hunger in every living creature, and its absence in non-living creatures.

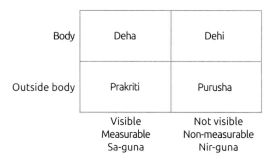

	Visible Measurable Sa-guna	Not visible Non-measurable Nir-guna
Body	Deha	Dehi
Outside body	Prakriti	Purusha

Deha and Prakriti

Dehi and purusha are the same, yet they are also differentiated. Dehi is called jiva-atma and purusha is called param-atma, as dehi's experience is limited by the deha it resides in, while purusha's experience is unlimited, as it resides in limitless prakriti. Dehi or jiva-atma experiences a slice (bhaga) of reality. Bhagavan, who experiences every slice of reality, is then param-atma. The jiva-atma, who seeks fulfilment and fullness, is the bhagat or bhakta. Every living creature is a jiva-atma. For every jiva-atma, other living creatures are para-atma (the individual other). The collective of all living creatures makes up the param-atma (the collective other).

This relationship of the deha, prakriti and atma is best visualized in art as a spoked wheel, where the hub represents my body (deha) and the rim presents the body of the world around me (prakriti). The atma within us (jiva-atma) radiates like the spokes of a wheel and connects with the atma (para-atma) within everyone around us. All of this together constitutes param-atma, the potential that everyone, including us, can realize. Such a spoked wheel whirls around Krishna's finger, indicating that param-atma is more than the sum total of all individual jiva-atmas. The jiva-atma depends on the param-atma but the param-atma is not dependent on the jiva-atma.

Arjuna, he is the perceiver of all sense objects without the senses. He is unattached, yet sustainer of all. He is devoid of all tendencies, yet the enjoyer of all material tendencies.—*Bhagavad Gita: Chapter 13, Verse 14 (paraphrased).*

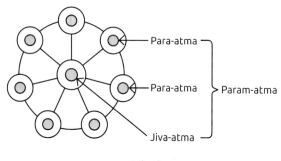

Wheel

Exploration of the relationship between jiva-atma and param-atma, between dehi and deha, purusha and prakriti, bhagavan and bhakta, has led to the many schools of Vedanta, schools that seek the essence of the Vedas. Advaita saw no difference between divinity and humanity; dvaita saw a complete separation; bheda-abheda saw humanity as part of the divine.

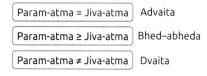

Different Schools of Vedanta

Many see dehi as the seed of the purusha-tree. Each seed is separate from the tree, dependent on the tree, yet containing the tree. This idea is expressed in a beautiful hymn on completeness (poornamadah poornamidam) found in the Isha Upanishad: 'This is complete, that is complete, from completeness comes completeness, when completeness is added or subtracted, it still remains complete.' This hymn refers to the concept of infinity and the capability of human imagination. You are complete in yourself; I am complete in myself; yet we are part of a wider human narrative. Like the seed of the tree, we are part of completeness, as well as our complete selves.

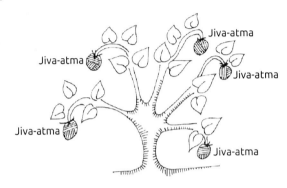

Fruits of the Param-atma Tree

So what exactly is dehi/atma/purusha? Various metaphors are used to describe it in The Gita: the ocean that is fed by rivers but never overflows (Chapter 2, Verse 70); the sky that is ever-present but always detached (Chapter 13, Verse 33); the sun that illuminates everything (Chapter 13, Verse 34). From Chapter 7 onwards, Krishna personifies the idea and starts equating himself with dehi and purusha, using the first person. Though Krishna sports a male form, he refers to his 'wombs', indicating the metaphorical nature of the language used.

> Arjuna, forms and formless are my two wombs. I am the start and the end, the thread on which the world is strung like jewels. Nothing else but me.—*Bhagavad Gita: Chapter 7, verses 6 and 7 (paraphrased).*

Some identify dehi/purusha/atma with the soul. But soul is a Christian concept and in Christian mythology, especially, there is talk of souls that can get corrupted and bodies without souls. Dehi/purusha/atma of The Gita is eternally pure and permeates everywhere, even beings deemed most sinful and foul.

Some say dehi is not material, hence it must be something spiritual. We must be careful of this term, spiritual. It is an eighteenth-century European term that once referred to everything from the psychological to the paranormal and the occult, a meaning that is still popular in New Age religious orders. The West formally separated the psychological from the paranormal only in the twentieth century after the works of Sigmund Freud and Carl Jung, though religious folk continue to insist that the paranormal is real.

If not material, then dehi/purusha/atma can be mental. But it is also distinguished from all things that constitute the mind: senses (indriyas), emotions (chitta), imagination (manas) and intelligence (buddhi). Some, therefore, identify it with consciousness, the ability to be self-aware. But scientists and gurus disagree on what consciousness exactly is. Scientists restrict consciousness to living organisms, especially higher ones, while gurus attribute consciousness to all of nature, even the inanimate.

Some identify the soul/spirit/consciousness as conscience (viveka). But conscience is an outcome of imagination and judgement: how we imagine ourselves and how we want others to judge us. Animals do not have a conscience, but for Hindus, atma is present in everything.

Ultimately, the exact identity of dehi/purusha/atma will always be elusive, not just because it defies objective measurement, but also because you and I experience reality very differently, and use different words to describe our experiences. What is dehi to you may not be dehi to me. Also, what I thought dehi was today may not be what I realize dehi is tomorrow. Initially, dehi may be the mind, then it becomes intelligence, then consciousness, then imagination, concept, meaning, then something else which defies language. But it exists. And that is the point.

> Arjuna, it exists in the heart of all beings that which is worth knowing, the knowledge itself, and that which is reached through knowledge. It is the light that illuminates life, and all of darkness too.—*Bhagavad Gita: Chapter 13, Verse 17 (paraphrased).*

What we can be sure of is that dehi cannot be an entity, as by definition it cannot be measured. It has to be a concept. It can at best be experienced, hence it is a subjective truth, indifferent to the rules of science.

> Arjuna, it has no beginning and has no qualities, and so does not change. It is located in the body, but it does nothing and covets nothing.—*Bhagavad Gita: Chapter 13, verses 31 and 32 (paraphrased).*

According to the five-container architecture of the body described in the Upanishads, our breath resides within our flesh, our mind resides within our breath, our concepts reside within our mind and our emotions reside within our concepts. We can only see the flesh and breath. We can sense the emotions by the way they are expressed through the body and the breath. Sensations received by the mind are filtered by concepts to create emotions. Emotions affect our mind and shape our concepts. When there is conceptual clarity, we experience tranquillity (ananda), no matter what the sensory experience is. Atma then becomes an idea that offers conceptual clarity, that establishes connection (yoga) with the world as it really is, not what we imagine it to be.

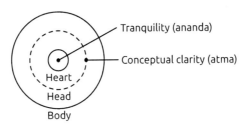

Atma as Conceptual Clarity

In the absence of conceptual clarity, the dominant emotion is fear, fear of losing opportunities, fear of threats, fear of achievement, fear of abandonment, fear of invalidation. The emotion of fear impacts the way we think and what we believe. It contaminates the filtering of sensations and choice of responses. It creates a vicious cycle where atma is eclipsed by aham, our judgemental self.

Conceptual clarity draws attention to language, a key theme of the Vedas. Many animals use language to communicate. Their language is descriptive. Human language is used to analyse, construct and convey complex meaning. Through sound, image or gesture meaning is conveyed. That which is expressed (shabda) contains layers of meaning (shabda-brahmana), some literal, some metaphorical. These evoke multiple emotions (rasa) and experiences (bhava). Shabda is tangible (sa-guna), shabda-brahmana is intangible (nir-guna). Only through shabda, can shabda-brahmana be expressed and experienced. If we imagine our body as a shabda, then we are containers of meaning. Only through our bodies can that meaning be expressed and experienced. When Hindus say that everything around us has atma, and bow to rocks and rivers, plants, animals, and humans, it is an acknowledgement that everyone and everything is meaningful and valid.

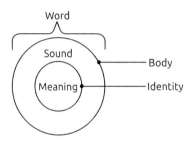

Atma as Meaning

Like animals that seek food for their survival, humans yearn for meaning for their sanity: what is our value, our purpose and our identity in this world? As long as we seek validation from the world around us, we are entrapped by aham. As soon as we realize that all meaning comes from within, that it is we who make the world meaningful, we are liberated by atma.

Arjuna, this fabulous all-encompassing being who resides within you, who is me really, and you really, is that which observes, approves, enables and enjoys ultimately.—*Bhagavad Gita: Chapter 13, Verse 22 (paraphrased).*

When we say that everything around us has atma, and we bow to rocks and rivers, plants and animals, to people around us, living and dead, we essentially mean that everything around is meaningful and valid. Who decides this? The dehi within, as well as the purusha without. We give meaning to others. We get meaning from others. We give meaning to each other. We may die but things continue to be meaningful, for atma never dies. There is always someone to give meaning.

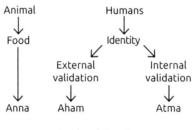

Food and Meaning

Plants and animals, including humans, seek food. Additionally, humans also seek meaning: the dehi within the deha, the meaning within the word, the soul within the body, the metaphorical within the literal.

5.

You and I have to face consequences

The quest for food, security and meaning propels the living into action. Every action has reactions. Reactions create circumstances that we constantly experience. Can we control our circumstances, create fortune and avoid misfortune, by regulating our actions and the actions of others? Or can we simply withdraw from activity, turn away from all sensory seductions, save ourselves from disappointment and heartbreak, and thus find peace? Is there such a thing as good action and bad action? Can good actions have bad reactions and bad actions, good? Answers to these questions constitute the doctrine of **karma** that means both action as well as reaction, which Krishna elaborates in Chapter 3 of The Gita.

In nature, gravity forces movement in all things inanimate. Plants defy gravity and grow towards the sky, propelled by the fear of death to seek sunlight and consume it as food, along with minerals and water pulled up by their roots. Animals graze and hunt and migrate for food. The act of eating is violent, as elements and plants and animals are devoured by the hungry. Where there is life, there is hunger. Where there is hunger, there is food. Where there is food, there is violence. Where there is violence, there are consequences. Nature is violent, as the hungry seek food. This is the fundamental truth of life.

In human society, violence is regulated. Forests are destroyed to make way for fields. Riverbanks are destroyed to create dams and canals. Natural ecosystems are wiped out to make way for human settlements. In the Mahabharata, the Pandavas burn the forest of Khandava-prastha to build their city of Indra-prastha. The price is high: the resident snake people, the nagas, never forgive them or their descendants.

In human society, violence transforms: it is not just physical. It is also psychological, as people are stripped of their freedom, bound by rules, located in hierarchies and restricted by boundaries. Culture is created by domestication: the violent control of the earth and the violent control of the human mind.

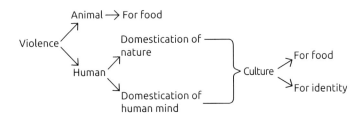

Forms of Violence

My Gita

So when Arjuna wonders if it is better to withdraw from the battle, Krishna does not endorse this apparently noble choice. For non-violence is only possible when one gives up hunger, and no one, not even a hermit, can give up all hunger. His body needs nourishment and for that he needs food. The act of cultivation of food is violent, as is the act of keeping away those who wish to steal our food. Only the non-living (a-jiva) are non-violent as they are not hungry. The living (sa-jiva) eat; eating involves violence.

> Arjuna, even when you do nothing, you still act. By simply withdrawing from society, you do not get freedom. Everyone who is born, who is alive, who is dependent, acts, compelled to do so by nature itself. He who controls the senses but has a mind full of cravings is a pretender who fools himself. Do what you have to do, rather than not doing anything at all. You need to act if you want your body to function.—*Bhagavad Gita: Chapter 3, verses 4 to 8 (paraphrased).*

The atma, resident of the body, is never hungry, and so does not crave food, and so is not violent. It witnesses this hunger-propelled violence, without judgement.

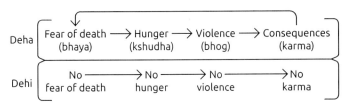

Hunger and No Hunger

From fear of death comes hunger, hence the quest for food, hence violence. Fear of death by violence makes animals sexual, so that they reproduce and ensure that at least some part of their being outlives death. And that which is reproduced carries with it the fear of death, hence hunger, hence violence and sex. Thus, cause is an action (karma) and the consequence is also an action (karma). Karma is both action and reaction. Each moment is a fruit (karma-phala) of the past and a seed (karma-bija) of the future. And just as every seed need not germinate, just as the quality of the fruit depends on various external factors like sunlight and quality of soil and availability of water, the reaction of every action is unpredictable. With unpredictability comes uncertainty, which amplifies fear.

> Arjuna, fair or unfair, the results of any action depend on five things: the body, the mind, the instruments, the method and divine grace (luck? fate?). Only the ignorant think they alone are responsible for any outcome.—*Bhagavad Gita: Chapter 18, verses 13 to 16 (paraphrased).*

This acceptance of uncertainty is the hallmark of mythologies that believe in rebirth. Here, the world is always changing and so the point is to observe it, rather than judge or control it. Western mythologies, in contrast, speak of a world that is either imperfect (Abrahamic mythology) or chaotic and unfair (Greek mythology). There is a yearning to change, to convert, to revolt, to make the world a better place. There is always a goal. Actions are classified as good or bad, right or wrong, moral or amoral, ethical or unethical, depending on the goal.

My Gita

Arjuna, as I do not bind myself to the fruit of my action, my actions do not entrap me.—*Bhagavad Gita: Chapter 4, Verse 14 (paraphrased).*

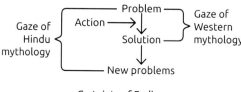

Certainty of Endings

This criticality of a climax or goalpost is alien to Vedic thought.

Arjuna, those who yearn for pleasure, power and paradise, constantly have their eye on the fruits of their birth, their actions, their rites and rituals. They focus on the Vedas cosmetically. They don't see the meaning within. They never attain wisdom.—*Bhagavad Gita: Chapter 2, verses 42 to 44 (paraphrased).*

Hindu mythology sees destinations as artificial milestones. What is natural, however, is action. Every action has a reaction, immediate results and long-term repercussions. Karma refers to both action and reaction. It is cause as well as consequence. It is stimulus as well as response.

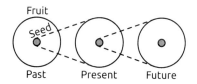

Karma-bija and Karma-phala

In nature, there is continuous transformation: spring gives way to summer that brings in the rain, then autumn and finally winter. All animals go through four phases of life: childhood, youth, maturity and old age. Cultures (sanskriti), too, go through multiple phases (yuga): Krita, Treta, Dvapara, Kali. The presence of Ram or Krishna does not impact the flow of events. Pralaya or dissolution of culture is as certain as the death of a living being. And just as nature renews itself every year with the rains, just as cultures go through many lifetimes (kalpa), renewing themselves after every collapse (pralaya), so are humans reborn after death.

> Arjuna, that which is born will die and that which will
> die will be born. So it is pointless to cling and mourn.
> —*Bhagavad Gita: Chapter 2, Verse 27 (paraphrased).*

This idea is made explicit through stories. The Ramayana does not begin with the birth of Ram or end with his death. Before he was Ram, he was Parashurama at the end of the Krita yuga. After he was Ram, he will be Krishna at the end of the Dvapara yuga. These are various lifetimes of Vishnu, who otherwise reclines in Vaikuntha, located on the shoreless ocean of milk, observing worlds rise and fall like waves of the sea.

But humans can imagine: we can imagine a world that is stable and controlled, all evidence in nature and culture notwithstanding. We can imagine attracting fortune and keeping misfortune at bay. And so we can classify actions as good and bad. Actions that help others and us are good. Actions that do not help others or us are bad.

For example, Arjuna imagines the horror that can follow if he kills his family, people he is expected to protect. It will result in a world where no one is trustworthy, a world where no boundaries are valid, where no commitment is sacred, and where integrity has no value. So he concludes his action is paap: karma that will result in misfortune. He considers not fighting family as punya: karma that will result in fortune. But Krishna points out that it is difficult to distinguish between action that is meritorious and action that is not.

> Arjuna, there is appropriate action, incorrect action and inaction, difficult to distinguish. The wise can spot action in inaction and inaction in action. The wise act without clinging to the results of action, are content with whatever is the outcome, and so are unburdened by merit or demerit.—*Bhagavad Gita: Chapter 4, verses 17 to 22 (paraphrased).*

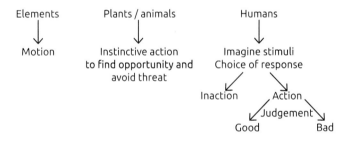

Action of Various Entities

In the Ramayana, for example, Dashratha keeps his word to Kaikeyi and agrees to give her the two boons she is entitled to. Integrity is good. But the result is the exile of Ram. That is bad. A reaction may be good in the short term but not in the long term. In the Bhagvata Purana, Krishna kills Kansa, the dictator of Mathura. This is good. But Kansa's enraged father-in-law, Jarasandha, burns Mathura to the ground. This is not good. An apparently good action can have a bad reaction. In the Ramayana, Sita goes out of her way to feed a hermit and ends up getting kidnapped. Likewise, an apparently bad action can also have good results. In the Mahabharata, the burning of the Khandava-prastha forest, which kills many forest creatures, enables the building of the Pandava kingdom of Indra-prastha.

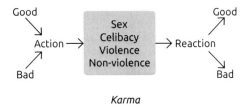

Karma

The complexity of karma is demonstrated in the following Telugu folk tale based on the Mahabharata: a little girl was drinking milk from a pot when Karna's chariot rolled past. Startled, she dropped the pot. The pot broke and the earth soaked up the milk. The girl began to cry. Karna saw this, stopped the chariot and decided to get the milk back for the little girl. He took the moist earth in his hand and squeezed out the milk in the pot, much to the girl's astonishment and delight. Everyone praised the great warrior. Thus, Karna's action yielded an expected output. But the outcome was unpredictable. The earth was furious that Karna had squeezed milk out of her. She swore that one day she would take her revenge. So on the battlefield of Kuru-kshetra, she grabbed hold of Karna's chariot wheel, squeezing it as hard as he had squeezed her, forcing him to alight and pull the wheel free. And while he was thus distracted, with his back to the enemy, he was shot dead. His blood fell on the ground and the earth soaked it all up. Karna's action thus had two reactions, an immediate one and a subsequent one. The immediate one was perceivable. The subsequent one was not. The latter reaction created the circumstances of Karna's death.

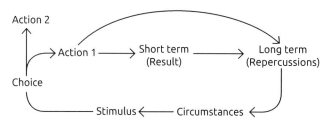

Sequence of Cause and Consequence

In the Hindu scheme of things, circumstances are not created accidentally, or by others, but by our own actions of the past. We can appreciate this by analysing the Ramayana. Who is responsible for Sita's abduction by Ravana? Should we blame her for taking a risk and feeding a hermit? Should we blame Lakshmana who cruelly cut the nose of Ravana's sister Surpanakha? Or should we blame Surpanakha who tried to kill Sita so that her husband, Ram, would be free to love other women? Should we blame Ram who refused to indulge Surpanakha's desires because he wanted to be faithful to his wife? Or should we blame Sita for accompanying Ram into the forest where rules of marriage have no meaning? Should we blame Ram's stepmother, Kaikeyi, for demanding his forest exile? Or should we blame Ram's father, Dashratha, for giving boons to Kaikeyi that the royal family was bound to uphold? Even if we identify the cause, can we control the action and determine future consequences? Maybe we can imagine control over our actions, but we have no control over other people's actions, hence the results.

> Arjuna, you have control over your action alone, not the fruits of your action. So do not be drawn to expectation, or inaction.—*Bhagavad Gita: Chapter 2, Verse 47 (paraphrased).*

Those who believe in karma do not blame. They do not judge. They accept that humans live in a sea of consequences, over which there is limited control. So they accept every moment as it is supposed to be. They act without expectation. This is nishkama karma.

> Arjuna, you can choose actions, not reactions. Do not choose action because of the reactions. Do not choose inaction either.—*Bhagavad Gita: Chapter 2, Verse 27 (paraphrased).*

I want to control your actions and reactions. You want to control my actions and reactions. We want to control the world around us, make it predictable. To act is karma. Karma yoga is when we act without seeking control over the outcome.

My Gita

6.

You and I can empathize

If karma yoga is action without expectation, then what should the motivation of our action be? Plants and animals act in order to find food and security only for themselves and their young ones. Humans can also act to find food and security for others, even strangers. Can this be human motivation? To realize this potential is **dharma**. Dharma is the first word uttered in The Gita. It is often confused as righteousness. The conflict between dharma and adharma is a point raised by Arjuna in Chapter 1. Empathy is not about controlling others through rules. This is why Krishna continuously distinguishes between sva-dharma and para-dharma, appropriate conduct of the self and the other.

Dharma is popularly translated as 'righteousness', which involves following punya and shunning paap. It has also come to mean religion, which is essentially about rules that come from a supernatural or superhuman source. So much so that today verses from The Gita are often translated using the tone of a judge and saviour, similar to that in Western mythologies. It appeals to our yearning for a hero. So, verses 7 and 8 of Chapter 4 are typically translated as, 'Arjuna, in age after age, whenever humanity forgets the righteous way, and functions in unrighteous ways, I manifest to save the good and punish the bad, to restore order in the world.' Such a translation, full of moral outrage, makes no sense to one with a perspective of infinity, who subscribes to the idea of karma, and so acts without an eye on any particular outcome. So we need to revisit the traditional meanings of dharma.

Hero, Saviour and Avatar

In Jainism, dharma refers to natural movement that stabilizes nature; adharma is artificial stillness that destabilizes nature. In Buddhism, dharma is the path that helps us accept the transitory nature of all things, including the self. In Hinduism, dharma means realizing our potential: changing ourselves into the best we theoretically can be. What is that?

Humans are the only living creatures who can expand their mind and see the world from another's point of view. This ability

My Gita

enables humans to empathize, to care for the other. To empathize is dharma. Failure to empathize is adharma. With this definition in mind, the above verse can be translated very differently:

> 'Arjuna, in age after age, whenever humanity forgets its potential and functions as it should not, I manifest to inspire those with faith and shake up those without faith, so that humanity never ever forgets what it is capable of.'—*Bhagavad Gita: Chapter 4, verses 7 and 8 (paraphrased).*

In any situation, plants and animals think only of themselves, their hunger and fear. At best they may think of the hunger and fear of their young ones, or that of their herd and pack. Dogs do think of their masters, but only their masters, no one else. They are driven by the instinct of self-preservation and self-propagation. They do not have the wherewithal to function in any other way. Humans, however, can sense other people's, even strangers', hunger and fear, and create resources to provide for and protect others. It is the one thing that makes humans special.

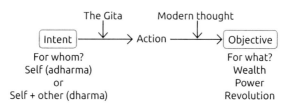

Role of Empathy in Action

Plants and animals do not help others consciously. They cannot help, because they simply do not have the neurological wherewithal to do so: the enlarged neo-cortex that only humans have (we can imagine otherwise though, as we often do in fables or on anecdotal evidence). They do not expect help either. Humans can help and expect to be helped, which comes from the ability to imagine and respond to other people's suffering. Animals have no choice but to follow their instinct. Humans do have a choice. When we do exercise our choice, when we value other people's needs alongside our own, we are following dharma. When we stay focussed on our own needs at the cost of others', we are doing adharma.

Animal	Human
↓	↓
Instinctively focussed on self-preservation or self-propagation	Imaginatively comes up with resources to also support others

Empathy

In nature, plants and animals use their strength and size and cunning to survive. This is called 'matsya nyaya', literally 'fish justice', which means the same thing as 'jungle law' in English— might is right, survival of the fittest. But words like justice and law are human concepts that we impose on nature to make sense of it. Justice and law presuppose the existence of a judicial system of judges and lawyers; in nature, there is no such system. Forces and counter-forces within nature ensure self-regulation. Dominating the weak, consuming the weak, in order to survive, is the way of animals. For them, it is instinct, not aspiration. When humans display animal behaviour, such as domination and territoriality, it is adharma, as they are indulging the self.

In the Ramayana, when Hanuman is crossing the sea, Surasa,

a sea monster, blocks his path. Hanuman begs her to let him go as he is on a mission. The sea monster does not understand. Realizing that the creature is unable to appreciate his situation and is blinded by hunger, Hanuman increases his size, forcing Surasa to open her mouth really wide. Hanuman then quickly reduces himself to the size of a fly, darts into Surasa's mouth and slips out before she can snap her wide jaws shut. In this story, Surasa is no villain for blocking Hanuman's path and Hanuman is no hero for outsmarting Surasa. In nature, there are only hungry predators and their food, the prey; villains and heroes are human perceptions.

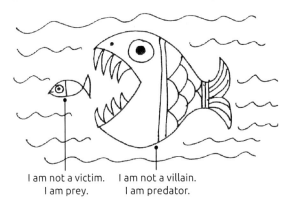

I am not a victim.   I am not a villain.
I am prey.   I am predator.

Big Fish and Small Fish

In nature, every creature has to fend for itself. There are no rules in the jungle. Rules exist only in human culture to restrain the strong and enable the weak. Ram submits to these cultural rules; Ravana does not. However, in the Mahabharata, despite rules, the way of the jungle thrives. In fact, rules are exploited to further domination and territoriality. At Kuru-kshetra, a hundred Kaurava brothers use the might of their eleven armies to twist rules and deny the five Pandava brothers, who have only seven armies, access to Indra-prastha, which is Pandava land and their livelihood. The Pandavas cannot afford to burn another Khandava-prastha, destroy more forests and ecosystems, to create another city simply to accommodate the Kauravas' greed. Besides, there are no guarantees that the Kauravas will not crave that new city too. Withdrawal would mean starvation for the Pandavas, and legitimization of the Kauravas' bullying. The Pandavas act according to dharma—they have no choice but to fight for their survival, as no one empathizes with them, no one even accepts their offer of compromise. The Kauravas, though, practise adharma as they could have empathized, shared, compromised and prevented the war, but they choose not to.

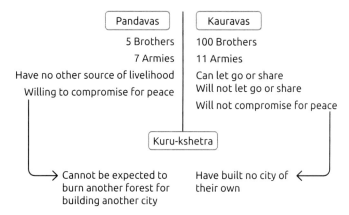

Matysa-nyaya in Kuru-kshetra

The Gita acknowledges the diversity and dynamism of the world. Everyone is born with a different capability (varna): some advise society (Brahmins), some protect society (Kshatriyas), some feed society (Vaishyas) and some serve society (Shudras). Everyone has to go through different stages of life (ashrama): a student (brahmacharya), a householder (grihastha), a retired person (vanaprastha) and a hermit (sanyasa). The Puranas tell us that society is constantly changing; every culture goes through four phases (yuga) moving from innocence (Krita) to maturity (Treta) to struggle (Dvapara) to decay (Kali). How does one uphold dharma in different contexts?

Typically people come up with rules—traditions (riti) and laws (niti), and equate them with dharma. Compliance then becomes dharma and non-compliance adharma. But things are not so simple. What matters more than action is intent, which is not tangible, hence rather invisible.

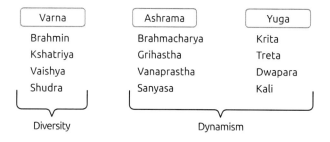

Diversity and Dynamism

Rules vary with context. In the Ramayana, which takes place in Treta yuga, Vishnu is Ram, eldest son of a royal family. In the Mahabharata, which takes place in Dvapara yuga, Vishnu is Krishna, youngest son of a noble family, who is raised by cowherds but who performs as a charioteer. They are expected to behave differently. Ram is obligated to follow the rules of the family, clan and kingdom, and uphold family honour. Krishna is under no such obligation. This is why Krishna tells Arjuna to focus on dharma in his context (sva-dharma) rather than dharma in another's context (para-dharma).

> Arjuna, better to do what you have been asked to do imperfectly than try to do perfectly what others have been asked to. All work has inadequacies; even fire is enveloped by smoke.—*Bhagavad Gita: Chapter 18, verses 47 and 48 (paraphrased).*

In the Ramayana Ram upholds rules, while Ravana breaks them. In the Mahabharata Duryodhana upholds rules, while Krishna breaks them. As eldest sons of their respective clans, Ram and Duryodhana are obliged to uphold rules. Ravana, son of a Brahmin, and Krishna, raised by cowherds, are under no such obligations. Dharma, however, is upheld only by Ram and Krishna, not Ravana and Duryodhana. Ram is constantly concerned about his city Ayodhya's welfare, while Ravana does not care if his Lanka burns. Krishna cares for the Pandavas, who happen to be the children of his aunt, but the Kauravas do not care for the Pandavas, who happen to be the children of their uncle. Dharma thus has nothing to with rules or obligations. It has to do with intent and caring for the other, be it your kingdom or your family.

Ravana argues his case passionately, as do those who fight on the Kaurava side, from Bhisma to Drona, Karna and Shalya. They justify their actions on grounds of justice, fairness, legitimacy, duty, loyalty, fidelity and commitment. None of them sees the other (para); they are too blinded by the self (aham). Logic

My Gita

serves as a lawyer to defend their stance.

But while Ravana and Duryodhana judge, Ram and Krishna never do so. They never complain or justify. Ram does not justify the mutilation of Surpankha (karma-bija) and silently accepts the end of his happiness that follows (karma-phala), for after that event Sita is kidnapped, and even after her rescue, the two are separated thanks to gossip. Krishna does not resist when the killing of the Kauravas (karma-bija) causes their mother Gandhari to blame and curse Krishna and his family (karma-phala).

Dharma Versus Riti and Niti

Vishnu is not angry with Ravana or Duryodhana or Duryodhana's commanders, for he can see the roots of their self-obsession and psychological blindness. These come from a sense of isolation and abandonment. They feel they have to fend for themselves and there is no one who can help them; and so, rather than realize their human potential, they regress to their animal nature, focussing on outrunning imagined predators, fending off imagined rivals and consuming imagined prey. When humans behave as animals do, despite the human ability to outgrow animal nature, it is adharma. It evokes compassion in Vishnu. For him, the villainy of Ravana and Duryodhana is viparit-bhakti, reverse love, born of hunger, fear and a yearning for love.

Arjuna, no one is hurt when you walk this path of humanity; no one is killed; even a little effort helps you fear less.—*Bhagavad Gita: Chapter 2, Verse 40 (paraphrased).*

Dharma is more about empathy than ethics, about intent rather than outcome. I follow dharma when I am concerned about your material, emotional or intellectual hunger. I follow adharma when I focus on my hunger at the cost of yours.

7.

You and I can exchange

Empathy enables exchange. I can satisfy a hunger of yours and you can satisfy a hunger of mine. This refers not just to physical hunger, but psychological hunger as well. This act of mutual feeding informs the **yagna**, the ancient Vedic ritual, which establishes the human ecosystem of mutuality, reciprocity, obligations and expectations that we shall explore in this chapter. Yagna is a key theme in chapters 3 and 4 of The Gita. In Vedic tradition, technically, the word 'karma' refers to yagna. Karma yoga begins when we acknowledge that we are always part of an exchange.

Krishna declares that the only action worth doing is yagna. Yagna refers to the Vedic fire ritual, 4,000 years old, nowadays abbreviated to the havan.

> Arjuna, all actions other than yagna entrap us. Yagna alone liberates us.—*Bhagavad Gita: Chapter 3, Verse 9 (paraphrased).*

The association of yagna with a battle seems strange. However, in The Gita Krishna looks upon it as a metaphor, indicative of relationships. To appreciate this, we have to look at the basics of a yagna.

He who initiates the yagna is called the yajamana. He invokes a deity (devata) and offers him food (bhog) exclaiming, 'Svaha!', meaning, 'This of mine I give you'. He hopes that the invoked deity will give him what he desires (prasad), exclaiming, 'Tathastu!' or 'So be it'. This indicates an exchange.

Yagna

Yagna is a very special form of exchange, where we can give and hope to receive. It is give and get, not give and take. When

My Gita

we take without giving, we become the oppressors. When we give and don't get, we become the oppressed. Feeding the other is dharma. Not expecting reciprocation is nishkama karma.

> Arjuna, the wise define renunciation as giving up action and detachment as giving up expectation.—*Bhagavad Gita: Chapter 18, Verse 2 (paraphrased).*

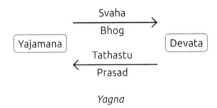

Yagna

The yagna is mentioned in the first verse (rig) of the first hymn (sukta) of the first book (mandala) of the collection (samhita) known as Rig Veda because it is a reminder of our humanity. No animal feeds another except its own offspring; at best, its pack or herd. Humans can feed everyone around them. Humans can also return the favour. To trade is a very unique human phenomenon. Trading behaviour has been documented in chimpanzees and vampire bats, but nothing on the human scale.

Exchange creates a network of expectations and obligations. Yagna thus is the cornerstone of sanskriti (culture). This idea echoes the sentiment of modern economists who see the market as the foundation of society.

When humans began exchanging, we stepped out of the animal world. From exchange came ideas of mutuality, reciprocity, expectation, obligation, debt and balancing accounts that shaped culture. Yagna is a ritual reminder of this very human ability.

Arjuna, way back, Brahma created humans through yagna and declared that yagna will satisfy all human needs. Use yagna to satisfy the other and the other will satisfy you. If you take without giving, you are a thief. Those who feed others and eat leftovers are free of all misery. Those who cook for themselves are always unhappy. Humans need food. Food needs rain. Rain needs exchange. Exchange needs action. Exchange began with divinity, that primal spark of humanity. Those who indulge themselves, those who do not repay it backwards, as well as pay it forward, break the chain, are miserable and spread misery.—*Bhagavad Gita: Chapter 3, verses 10 to 16 (paraphrased).*

In the Kalpa-sutras, which elaborate Vedic household rituals, the yajamana is advised to perform five yagnas (pancha-yagna) to feed everyone around: the self, the other, family, birds and animals and ancestors. When we do that, the boundary between family and stranger is removed. As the Upanishads say: the whole world becomes family (vasudaivah kutumbakam).

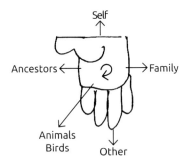

Yagna for Relationships

In most writings, yagna is translated as 'sacrifice'. This translation came from the European Orientalists of the eighteenth century who never really conducted the ritual or witnessed it. They probably equated the yagna with the blood sacrifices seen in tribal communities around the world to appease fearsome spirits, or even with the sacrifice of Abraham's son demanded by Abraham's God as a mark of love and obedience.

Later, scholars realized that there was another word for sacrifice in the Vedic texts, bali, and that yagna was clearly a larger concept. Historians drew attention to the practice of honouring deities (puja) with food, flowers, incense and lamps, that became popular in Puranic times. This had its roots in the Vedic practice of pouring ghee into fire. Both are acts of invocation and libation. Yagna came to be seen as an earlier form of puja. So yagna was then translated as 'worship'.

But the Puranas show yagna in a very different light. In the Ramayana and the Mahabharata, kings perform yagna to get children. Mantras chanted yield instant results: a god is obliged to give a woman a child, or turn an ordinary arrow into a deadly missile. Yagna thus assumes expectation and obligation, giving in order to get. Yagna is clearly an exchange.

The word 'exchange' is rarely used to explain yagna. It is problematic. It lacks nobility. We have learned to valorize sacrifice, where there is giving without getting. We even celebrate worship, where getting is a surprise, a bonus, not the outcome of any expectation. This, despite the fact that the last hymn of every yagna and puja is always the chant of expected outcomes (phala-stuti). Perhaps we have been conditioned to be ashamed of human yearnings, maybe by mendicants of the Buddhist, Jain and Hindu orders who chose to renounce the world. Perhaps our preference for socialism in the post-Independence era made us frown upon the idea of exchange, as it reeks of a trader mentality. How can we trade with the divine?

By calling the battle at Kuru-kshetra a yagna, Krishna indicates that Arjuna is part of an exchange. Either he is the yajamana who will please his brothers, or he is the devata who has to repay the debt he owes his brothers. The Pandavas depend on him, and he is indebted to the Pandavas. To deny these dependencies, these expectations and obligations, is to deny humanity.

The monastic order rejected the yagna. In essence, they rejected the other. For yagna is all about paying cognizance to the hunger of the other. The other is both an individual (para) as well as the collective (param). Yagna is about the relationship between the individual (aham) and the other (para/param) through exchange.

In the Shiva Purana, when the hermit Shiva beheads Daksha and destroys his yagna, all the gods beg him to give life back to the yajamana and restore the yagna, for without it they will starve. Thus, the devatas depend on the yajamana as much as the yajamana depends on the devatas. There is interdependence at play here.

> Arjuna, those who offer food to the gods and survive on the leftovers find brahmana. Not those who offer nothing. Different yagnas are thus laid at the mouth of the brahmana. It all begins with choosing an action. Rather than choose to give up the world, choose to understand the brahmana, which demands action, hence yagna. Thus, informed by the wise, you will see all beings in yourself, and all beings as part of me.

My Gita

There will be no confusion.—*Bhagavad Gita: Chapter 4, verses 26 to 35 (paraphrased).*

In Puranic lore, he who gives upon getting is a deva; he who seeks retrieval of what he thinks has been stolen is an asura; he who grabs, takes without giving, is a rakshasa; he who hoards is a yaksha! He who does not participate in the yagna, does not give or want to get, is a shramana or tapasvi, the hermit, much feared in the Puranas as the cause of drought, hence starvation. Within us is the yajamana, the devata, the asura, the rakshasa, the yaksha and the shramana. They manifest in different interactions.

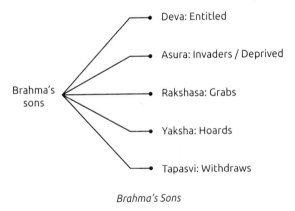

Brahma's Sons

Once, as Shiva was passing by a yagna-shala, where a yagna was being conducted, the wives of the yajamanas, the yagna-patnis, ran after him, begging him to satisfy them. The yajamanas got upset and created, out of the yagna, a whole bunch of monsters. Shiva destroyed all the monsters and then began to dance. He used various gestures of his hands and feet to convey the wisdom of the yagna that escaped the yajamanas, that the yagna existed to satisfy the yearnings of those around them, not to create monsters to defend themselves.

A similar story is found in the Bhagavat Purana, where Krishna, while tending to his cows, comes upon a few yajamanas performing yagna and asks them for food. They ignore him. So he goes to their wives and the yagna-patnis feed him all the offerings they had prepared for the yagna. The yajamanas are furious but then realize that their wives look content, while they feel angry and frustrated. The yagna had yielded results for their wives, not them, for the yagna-patnis had fed the hungry and discovered the true meaning of the yagna.

> Arjuna, like a well surrounded by water, hymns and rituals are of no value to the one who has understood the meaning.—*Bhagavad Gita: Chapter 2, Verse 46 (paraphrased)*.

Human hunger is not just about food. We seek emotional and intellectual nourishment too. We seek meaning, validation, significance, value, purpose, power and understanding. We seek ideas about wealth, power, relationships and existence. We seek entertainment. We seek food to liberate us from the fear of the predator, security to liberate us from the fear of the prey and meaning to liberate us from the fear of invalidation. This transforms every meeting into an exchange. Lovemaking is yagna. Child-bearing is yagna. Child-rearing is yagna. Feeding is yagna. Teaching is yagna. Service is yagna. War is also yagna. Exchange can be used to satisfy our desires, or repay our debts. It can entrap us, or liberate us. It depends not on the action, but on the thought underlying the action.

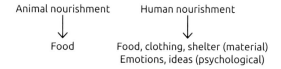

Animal nourishment	Human nourishment
↓	↓
Food	Food, clothing, shelter (material)
	Emotions, ideas (psychological)

Different Types of Yagna Food

A wish (sankalpa) always precedes a yagna. It is about asking
for whom are we performing the action: for the benefit of the self
(aham) or the benefit of the other (para)? Who is the beneficiary
(aradhya)? And who is merely the instrument (nimitta)? In
nishkama karma, the devata is the aradhya and the yajamana is
the nimitta.

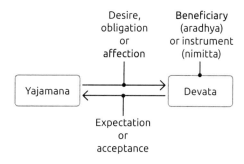

Approach to Exchange

In the Ramayana, disruption happens because characters
act for their own pleasure at the cost of others and resolution
follows when Vishnu acts for the pleasure of others, not his
own. It is Dasharatha's desire for sons, Kaikeyi's desire for the
kingdom, Surpanakha's desire for pleasure and Ravana's desire for
domination that cause disruption. Ram works not for his personal
happiness, but the happiness of Ayodhya. In the Mahabharata, it

is Shantanu's desire for a young wife, Dhritarashtra's desire for the throne and Yudhishtira's desire not to lose a gamble that causes disruption. Krishna works not for his personal happiness, but for the happiness of the Kurus.

Krishna asks Arjuna to fight the war not for his own sake but for the sake of others. He has to consider himself merely the instrument, for the karma-bija of the war has already been sown and the karma-phala of carnage is inevitable.

> Arjuna, I am time that destroys worlds. Even without you, these warriors are doomed to die. So arise and fight; destroy your opponents and claim your success. It is I who has already killed them. Make yourself merely my instrument.—*Bhagavad Gita: Chapter 11, verses 32 and 33 (paraphrased).*

To do yagna is to recognize that we live in a sea of assumed expectations and obligations. You and I can hoard, grab, give in order to get, get before giving or simply withdraw from the exchange. We can act out of desire, duty or care. We can choose to expect or control outcome, or not.

My Gita

8.

You and I withdraw in fear

What stops us from empathizing and exchanging? What makes us want to control the other, or simply withdraw, find peace in the isolation of the cave? The process of discovering the source of disconnection is called **yoga**, though the word yoga itself means 'to connect'. It involves moving through the many containers that constitute deha in order to discover dehi. Krishna starts speaking of yoga in Chapter 5 of The Gita, elaborating it further in Chapter 6. Yoga is what we will explore in this chapter. With this, we move from the outer social world to the inner psychological world, from karma yoga to bhakti yoga.

Each of the eighteen chapters of The Gita is titled 'yoga'. These are then bunched together to give us three types of yoga: behavioural (karma), emotional (bhakti) and intellectual or cognitive (gyana). So what does the word 'yoga' exactly mean?

Colloquially, Indians use the word 'jog' for yoga. In astrology, jog means alignment of the stars that results in favourable conditions for an activity. From jog comes the word 'jogadu', the resourceful individual, a word typically used in the eastern parts of India for one who is able to create alignment and connections in a world full of misalignment and disconnections. The word 'jogadu' has given rise to the words 'jugad' and 'jugadu' in the northern parts of India, where it means improvisation and even by-passing the system. Sadly, today, jugad is used in a negative sense, for it is practised for the self at the cost of the other, in the spirit of adharma, not dharma.

The word 'yoga' has its roots in the sound 'yuj' which means to yoke, like a horse to a chariot. The word 'vi-yoga' refers to disconnection or separation. Thus, 'yoga' has something to with binding things together, or connecting things.

Traditionally, yoga has been used as a complement to sankhya. Sankhya means enumeration and refers to analysis, the tendency to break things down into their constituent parts. Yoga is its complement and refers to synthesis, the tendency to bind parts to establish a composite whole. In art, sankhya is visualized as an axe (parashu), used to slice things into parts, while yoga is visualized as a string (pasha), used to tie things together. Ganesha, the scribe of the Mahabharata—and hence The Gita—holds these symbols in his hands to remind all of these two techniques of enquiry. Krishna uses both sankhya and yoga to solve Arjuna's problem. He establishes boundaries using sankhya and then dissolves them all using yoga.

> Arjuna, practise yoga with conviction and without dismay, for it will connect you with that from which you are disconnected, and unhook you from your sorrow.
> —*Bhagavad Gita: Chapter 6, Verse 23 (paraphrased).*

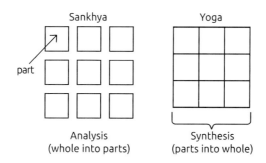

Analysis and Synthesis

Nature is full of discrete units: planets, stars, rocks, rivers, plants, animals and humans. These units are naturally drawn together or pulled apart by certain forces of attraction or repulsion. In the physical world, these forces have been observed at inter-planetary as well as sub-atomic levels. In the biological world, they manifest as animals seeking opportunity, such as food and mates, and shunning threats, such as rivals and predators. This attraction (raga) and repulsion (dvesha) is part of life.

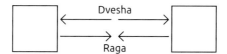

Raga–Dvesha

Yoga enables us to be aware of these natural forces of attraction and repulsion, and not be swept away by them. Krishna equates the senses to cows (indriya-go-chara) that graze on the pasture made of various kinds of stimuli. Yoga turns our mind into the cowherd who determines what the senses should or should not graze upon. Thus, yoga has much to do with the mind, and it complements yagna that has much to do with society. Yagna is the outer journey, while yoga is the inner journey that Arjuna has to undertake.

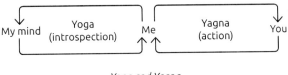

Yoga and Yagna

Arjuna feels that if he withdraws from the battle, all problems will be resolved and there will be peace. However, not fighting a war does not tackle the underlying hunger and fear. It simply denies and suppresses the hunger and fear and the consequent rage, which then ends up festering secretly as people 'pretend', awaiting to explode more intensely at a later date. Outer peace does not guarantee inner peace. Further, it does not take into consideration the other's thoughts and feelings. Arjuna's desire for peace, howsoever noble, may not be shared by Bhima or Duryodhana, who are ready for war. Forcing his noble view on them would be judgement, devoid of empathy, hence adharma. Arjuna may not want to do yagna, but he cannot stop others from doing so. Our decision to act or not act cannot be insensitive to the feelings of those around us. Hence, any discussion on yagna is complemented with discussions on yoga. While yagna focusses on tangible giving and getting, yoga focusses on discovering intangible thoughts and emotions of the yajamana as well as the devata, the boundaries that we create and use to include some as family and exclude others as enemy.

> Arjuna, your mind is your friend and your enemy. If you control the mind, it is your friend. If your mind controls you, it is your enemy.—*Bhagavad Gita: Chapter 6, verses 5 and 6 (paraphrased).*

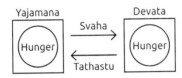

Mind of the Yajamana and the Devata

The value of the mind slowly amplifies as The Gita progresses. In Chapter 3 of The Gita, Arjuna asks whether Krishna values knowledge over action. Krishna replies that he values *informed* action. In Chapter 5 of The Gita, Arjuna asks if Krishna values action over renunciation. Krishna replies that he values *detached* action. Informing the mind about the exchange and detaching action from the expectation of results demand that Arjuna take an inner journey.

> Arjuna, the exchange of knowledge is greater than the exchange of things for ultimately all exchange culminates in the mind.—*Bhagavad Gita: Chapter 4, Verse 33 (paraphrased).*

Krishna introduces yoga as an inner yagna, where we are our own yajamana and devata, our own beneficiary and instrument. We choose our stimulus. We choose our response. Here, the fire is not in the altar outside, but can be our body, our senses, our mind, even our breath and our digestive fire.

> Arjuna, there is yagna everywhere, where offerings are made to various fires. Worldly stimuli can be offered to the sensory fires. The sensory experience can be offered to the mental fire. The mental understanding can be offered to the wisdom fire. Breath is offered to the fire of life, as is food. Fasting is offered to the fire of restraint.—*Bhagavad Gita: Chapter 4, verses 26 to 28 (paraphrased).*

Patanjali, in his Yoga-sutra, written around the time of The Gita, defines yoga as stopping the rippling and twisting of the mind (chitta-vritti-nirodha) caused by various experiences and memories that result in disconnection. He gives an eight-step process to stop the ripples and untwist the mind, so as to restore connection. With each step we move inwards through the containers that constitute the body.

With yama, we limit social engagements by not indulging in sex, violence, falsehood, theft and greed. Then, with niyama, we discipline ourselves by practising cleanliness, contentment, austerity, reflection and having faith in divinity. Third comes asana, where we activate the body using various postures. Fourth is pranayama, through which we regulate the breath. With pratyahara, we withdraw from sensory inputs. With dharana, we become aware of the big picture and gain perspective. With dhyana, we become attentive and focussed. With samadhi, we go further within, experience our emotions and discover fear!

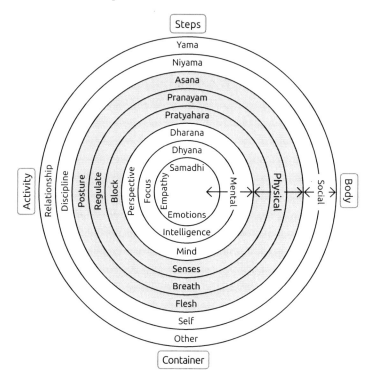

Patanjali's Yoga

Fear (bhaya) is a neuro-biological fact. It is the first emotion that manifests with the arrival of life. It is a critical emotion, essential in the struggle for life. For it evokes hunger (kshudha) and makes the organism seek food (bhog) to nourish itself.

Fear of death by starvation makes trees grow, seek out and grab sunlight as well as water and nutrients from the soil, so that they can nourish themselves. This same fear makes animals wander endlessly in search of pasture and prey, and form packs that collaborate to increase the chances of finding food. Fear of being killed makes the prey shun the predator, and form herds to increase the chances of survival. Then there is the fear of losing food to a rival that makes animals compete. Fear of dying also creates the restless urge to undertake extra efforts to find a mate, reproduce and risk death to raise an offspring, so at least a part of the creature outlives death.

In humans, the fear is amplified by imagination. We can imagine hunger, our hunger and the hunger of those around us, current and future hunger, and so our quest for food is insatiable. We can imagine predators and so feel insecure all the time. This amplified fear goads human imagination to invent various physical and social instruments to create excess food, distribute and secure it; and themselves.

The greatest human fear is validation. We seek meaning (artha): who are we? What is our role in the world? Surely we are not just animals—predator, prey, rival or mate? This fear gives rise to the notion of property and to hierarchies in society. Out of fear, we do not share. Due to fear, we fight over property.

Fear crumples our mind (chitta), knots it, twists it, creates ripples and waves and eventually wrinkles our mind. These wrinkles in the mind are called impressions (samskaras). They appeared with the first experience of fear in the first living organisms. The experience of all feeders and food, every plant and animal, has been stacked up over millions of years. The crumpling has been intensified by imagination (manas). It causes disconnection. The frightened, hence crumpled, hence disconnected, mind is referred to as aham. The mind that is not crumpled, hence connected, is referred to as atma. Yoga is about un-crumpling and reconnecting, moving from aham to atma.

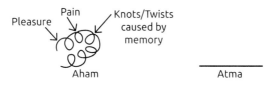

Aham to Atma

The Gita reveals a familiarity with all the practices referred to in the Yoga-sutra. Krishna speaks of using the breath to make the journey from the outside to the inside.

> Arjuna, ignore the onslaught of external stimuli and focus between your eyebrows, regulating inhalation and exhalation at the nostrils, to liberate yourself from fear, desire and anger, and discover me within you, I who receive and consume every offering of your yagnas.—*Bhagavad Gita: Chapter 5, verses 27 to 29 (paraphrased).*

There is reference to meditation in The Gita: sitting still and calming the mind until one's breath is natural and rhythmic.

> Arjuna, sit still on a mat that is neither too high nor too low. Your head, neck and back aligned, still your senses, focus your mind, gazing at the nose-tip.—*Bhagavad Gita: Chapter 6, verses 11 to 13 (paraphrased).*

The point is to make one's way through the turbulence of the mind and discover the tranquillity beyond.

> Arjuna, use your mind to ignore sensory stimuli, outgrow that desire, disconnect from intelligent arguments and ideas, rein in the restless fickle wandering emotions, expand your mind and discover the tranquillity within. —*Bhagavad Gita: Chapter 6, verses 24 to 27 (paraphrased)*.

And having once realized the fear within, the yogi is able to see the fear without, in others around, in individuals as well as in the collective, for he is connected.

> Arjuna, those connected see everything equally, for they discover me everywhere, in everyone and everything. They always see me, and I see them. They always establish me everywhere. I am always established in them.—*Bhagavad Gita: Chapter 6, verses 29 to 31 (paraphrased)*.

This is where The Gita departs from the Yoga-sutra. While the Yoga-sutra speaks of samadhi as complete withdrawal from the material world, Krishna's Gita speaks of samadhi very differently, as the ability to see the world with perfect equanimity, without judgement.

> Arjuna, one who has attained samadhi is not disturbed by unhappiness, nor does he crave happiness. He is not consumed by craving, fear or anger. He is at peace in pleasant and unpleasant circumstances. He is content

in wisdom.—*Bhagavad Gita: Chapter 2, verses 55 to 56 (paraphrased).*

This divergence from the Yoga-sutra is not surprising, as mythological tales inform us that Patanjali was a serpent who overheard Shiva revealing the secret of yoga to Shakti. Shiva is a hermit. His path is suitable for the tapasvi who does not wish to engage with the world. Krishna speaks to the yajamana, the householder, and the whole point of yoga is to facilitate engagement with the world. If the tapasvi is focussed on the inner journey, and if the yajamana is focussed on the outer journey, then the yogi takes the inner journey in order to be better at the outer journey.

Arjuna, the yogi is far superior to a hermit who withdraws from the world, to a scholar who understands everything but does nothing, or a householder who does everything without understanding.—*Bhagavad Gita: Chapter 6, Verse 46 (paraphrased).*

Patanjali

Yoga brings awareness and attention to fear. By recognizing the reality of his own fears, the yogi is able to appreciate the fears of those around him. He observes why he withdraws and why those around him withdraw. He does not seek to amplify fear by trying to control people. He works towards comforting them, enabling them to outgrow their fear. Thus is born empathy and the ability to let go. The yajamana performs nishkama karma.

A yogi looks within to appreciate the mind that occupies the body, the thoughts that occupy the mind, the fears that occupy the thoughts, the opportunities and threats that occupy the fears, and the fears of others that occupy those opportunities and those threats.

9.

You and I hesitate to trust

Connecting with the other is not easy, especially when we look upon each other as predator or prey, rival or mate. In such a situation we trust no one but ourselves, as animals tend to do. Or we trust the other only in situations of extreme helplessness, as only humans can. Thus, we become **asuras** and **devas**. Krishna discusses the difference between the two in Chapter 16 of The Gita, but we discuss it much earlier in *My Gita* as we need to understand 'gods' before we plunge into conversations about 'God'. These beings are not 'out there' in the world, but very much 'in here' in our minds.

The words 'deva' and 'asura' refer to divinities in the Veda, and are roughly translated as gods and demons, but Krishna uses them differently. A deva is one who accepts the reality of atma; an asura does not. Thus, Krishna sees devas and asuras not in supernatural terms or as inherently good or evil, but as people who value the dehi and those who don't, respectively. The asuras are trapped by the literal and the measurable, while the devas appreciate the metaphorical and the non-measurable. Those who do not look beyond the body and material reality, says Krishna, have no hope of freedom, despite any material accomplishments.

> Arjuna, those who think as devas do are eventually liberated and those who think as asuras do are forever trapped. Fear not, you think like a deva.—*Bhagavad Gita: Chapter 16, Verse 5 (paraphrased)*.

While asuras are equated with non-believers (nastikas) and devas with believers (astika), the split is not so simple. Devas may believe, but do they experience?

Non belief ⟶ Belief ⟶ Experience
(asura)   (deva)   (bhagavan)

Non-Belief, Belief, Experience

The Gita presents atma as a fact, hence in Chapter 17, Verse 23, the phrase 'om tat sat' is used, which roughly translates as 'that which is forever true'. It is the closest we get to the definitive article 'the' in Sanskrit. This fact, however, can never be measured, therefore from a scientific point of view it can never be proven. It can, however, be experienced (anu-bhava). Believing is a cognitive process, an acceptance of a conceptual truth. Experience is an emotional process, the journey from the head to the heart. To enable anu-bhava, one has to simultaneously perform the inner journey of yoga and the outer journey of yagna.

> Arjuna, those who cleanse themselves with contemplation and meditation discover me, embrace me, find shelter in me and are liberated from yearning, fear and anger.—*Bhagavad Gita: Chapter 4, Verse 10 (paraphrased).*

Two thousand years ago, hermits (shramanas) popularized the practice of yoga, but they did not care so much for the outer journey of yagna. They valued the inner fire of the mind (tapa), not the outer fire (agni) of the altar. While the word tapasya is used interchangeably with yoga, tapasya refers to the inner journey, while yoga refers to the inner journey that eventually leads to an outer journey. The hermits were tapasvis, who valued meditation and contemplation, not exchange. They can thus be differentiated from the yogis, who valued meditation and contemplation as well as exchange. Hermits valued withdrawal over engagement, celibacy over marriage, isolation over union and zero (shunya) over infinity (ananta). In other words, hermits caused a rupture between the inner and outer journeys.

Rupture of the Inner and Outer Journey

In the Puranas, this rupture is made explicit. The devas prefer yagna but not tapasya. The asuras prefer tapasya but not yagna. Both are the children of Brahma. Indra, leader of the devas, who is not committed to the inner journey, is eternally insecure: he fears those who perform yagna and tapasya, and considers them as rivals. So he disrupts the yagna of kings by stealing their horses. He sends damsels known as apsaras to enchant sages immersed in tapasya and irritates them by seducing their neglected wives. Asuras, on the other hand, are visualized as performing tapasya and obtaining, from Brahma, many powers that overpower Indra. Thus, devas are portrayed as entitled, insecure beings while asuras are portrayed as deprived, angry beings. Though half-brothers, these sons of Brahma do not like each other: the devas fear the asuras and the asuras hate the devas.

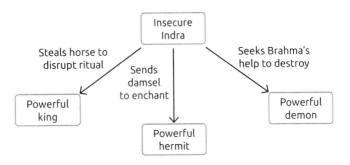

Stealing Horses, Seeking Brahma's Help and Sending Damsels

In the Vedas, the devas and asuras are celestial beings. But in the Puranas, they are clearly rivals. The Europeans identified asuras first as Titans, in line with Greek mythology, and later as demons, in line with Abrahamic mythology. This causes great confusion, as the asuras are neither 'old gods' nor 'forces of evil'.

My Gita

Both old gods and forces of evil are unwanted and need to be excluded, while in the Puranas, both are needed to churn the ocean of milk, and draw out its treasures. Since the devas were visualized as being surrounded by affluence and abundance in swarga, they were naturally preferred over the asuras as the devas had a lot that they could give, if made happy, while the asuras had nothing.

The visualization of asuras either as villains, anti-heroes or even wronged heroes persists even today amongst writers on mythology, who see asuras as old tribal units overrun, even enslaved and demonized, by yagna-performing Vedic people. Asuras are even seen as embodiments of our negative impulses and devas as personifying positive impulses. We overlook the fact that in popular Hinduism neither devas nor asuras are given the same status as ishwara or bhagavan. We need to see devas and asuras as our emotions that prevent us from completing the outer and inner journeys.

Puranic stories typically begin with Indra not paying attention to the yagna while an asura is deep in tapasya. Indra's power thus wanes while the asura's power waxes. The asura is able to invoke Brahma and get boons from him, using which he attacks, defeats and drives the devas out of their paradise, swarga. Dispossessed, Indra and the devas go to Brahma, not for boons but for help. Brahma then directs them either to Shiva, Vishnu or the Goddess, who form the foundation of the three major theistic schools of Hinduism.

In many ways, these stories echo the history of Indian thought: the decline of the yagna rituals of Vedic times, the rising popularity of monastic orders that practise tapasya, and eventually the triumph of theistic traditions. They also reflect the rise of the ritual known as 'puja' that forces the devotee to look at the divinity outside himself through images in the other, thus enabling the yoga of the self with the world around.

Vedic Period	Buddhist Period	Puranic Period (Gita)
Yagna	Tapasya	Puja yoga

Rediscovery of Atma

Puja

It is significant to note that the asuras seek Brahma's boons and the devas seek Brahma's help. The asuras are not interested in Brahma; only in his possessions. They perform tapasya not to attain wisdom that takes away insecurity, but to simply acquire powers known as siddhis. The devas are interested in Brahma and are directed to Shiva, Vishnu and the Goddess, a calling for the inner journey that grants wisdom, hence takes away insecurity. But the devas do not complete this inner journey.

As the Puranas remind us repeatedly, after either of the

gods or the Goddess vanquishes the asura and Indra gets back his paradise, he goes back to his old ways, feeling entitled and finding joy in material things, getting insecure with yajamanas who do too much yagna and tapasvis who do too much tapasya, unable to enjoy his prosperity as he feels his paradise is under siege, much like successful people in the world today, who think of God only in bad times and forget about God in good times. For them God is all about their own fortune, not everybody's fortune. For them there is no God within who enables the world without.

The asura is one who is striving for success. The deva is one who is, or has been, successful. A determination to be successful drives the asura to do tapasya. Fear of losing what they have or fear of never getting back what they lost makes the devas seek Brahma. The asura does not believe that anyone will help him. The deva believes that God exists only to help him while he does not exist to help anyone. In other words, the asura does not believe in atma whereas the deva believes in param-atma, but has yet to realize jiva-atma, the human potential.

The description of the condition of the asuras in The Gita is brutal and resonates with what we see in the world around us, where great value is placed on what you achieve and what you possess.

> Arjuna, asuras will say 'This I have gained, that desire of mine I have satisfied, that enemy of mine I have destroyed, by any means available; I am the master, the enjoyer, the successful, the strong, the happy; I am rich and I will donate; there is none like me.' Thus ensnared in his own net, addicted to satisfying his insatiable

desire, he tumbles into a hell of conceit and envy and rage; born again and again in similar wombs; trapped in the same context. Seeking more, getting angry when he does not get what he seeks and seeking more when he gets what he seeks, he is unable to escape the darkness and find the light of happiness.—*Bhagavad Gita: Chapter 16, verses 12 to 22 (paraphrased).*

The description above seems like judgement,or a wish, but is in fact observation: the inevitable outcome of what happens when we believe material things will bring us satisfaction, when we see humans as bodies who perform and accumulate, when we see the world in technocratic terms, devoid of meaning and a larger narrative. We expect things to give us pleasure but instead they fuel more yearnings, thus creating addiction, which fuels greed. We want more and more, and feel angry when we don't get what we desire.

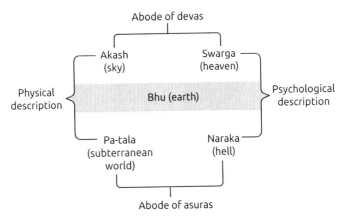

Swarga, Pa-tala and Naraka

In the Puranas, the residence of the asuras is called pa-tala, the subterranean realm; this is where they belong, just as the devas belong in the celestial realm, the sky above. But in The Gita, the residence of the asuras is called naraka, or hell. Pa-tala is a physical description but naraka is a psychological description: lack of faith results in hopelessness and rage and hence creates hell.

Victory over the devas does not bring the asuras satisfaction. Victory over the asuras does not provide enlightenment to the devas. Both are trapped in a merry-go-round, unable to break free. Yet, Vishnu ascribes greater value to the devas over the asuras, for the former look beyond the material, for some time at least. Both the Pandavas and the Kauravas are fighting over property, but at least Arjuna is listening to possibilities beyond.

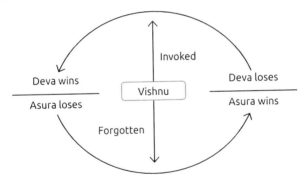

Cycle of Victories and Defeats

Yagna of the devas is good, as it forces us to look at the param-atma outside. Tapasya of the asuras is good, as it makes us discover the jiva-atma inside. But we need the two to inform each other. Only yagna is action without understanding. Only tapasya is understanding without action. When understanding impacts action and action impacts understanding, then it is yoga.

> Arjuna, yoga will enable you to perform action without expectation, and look upon success and failure equally. Action focussed on intent is better than action focussed on outcome. Such action liberates you from all dualities, so improve your skills with yoga.—*Bhagavad Gita: Chapter 2, verses 48 to 50 (paraphrased).*

We all ride waves of fortune and misfortune. If you and I believe we alone control the waves, then we are asuras. If you and I feel entitled in fortune and remember God only in misfortune or in fear of misfortune, then we are devas. We are not yet in touch with the atma within and without.

10.

You and I have potential

We mistrust fellow humans and so yearn for something beyond humanity, someone who comforts us, indulges our hungers, our insecurities and our inadequacies, without judgement. And so, two thousand years ago, The Gita introduced Hinduism to the concept of **bhagavan** that consolidates and personifies earlier, rather abstract, notions of divinity, such as brahmana, purusha and atma. This theme, elaborated from chapters 7 to 12 of The Gita, is what makes the Bhagavad Gita remarkable, challenging the ritual nature of the Vedas, the intellectual nature of the Upanishads and acknowledging the role of emotions in our life. We are not rational creatures who feel; we are emotional creatures who rationalize.

In The Gita, the idea of God begins in Chapter 2 itself, when Krishna identifies himself as a tool to tame the senses.

> Arjuna, the sage focusses on me to tame his senses and discover wisdom.—*Bhagavad Gita: Chapter 2, Verse 60 (paraphrased)*.

But the real discussion on God starts when, after having heard Krishna speak of yagna and yoga, Arjuna expresses his discomfort with introspection and the inner journey.

> Krishna, I feel the promise of sustaining equanimity through yoga is not easy as the mind is restless, fickle, turbulent like the wind while the senses are fixed and anchored.—*Bhagavad Gita: Chapter 6, verses 33 and 34 (paraphrased)*.

Arjuna's honest admission reveals how it is not enough to simply instruct a seeker or student. Unless the heart feels secure, the head will never receive new ideas. Arjuna needs an anchor, a support, someone to lean on, the comforting hand of God. And so Krishna introduces himself as God: the invisible beyond the visible, the immortal beyond the mortal, the infinite beyond the finite, the metaphor beyond the literal. The idea of Krishna as God accelerates from Chapter 7 through chapters 8, 9 and 10 until there is a veritable explosion in Chapter 11, which leaves no doubt in Arjuna's mind that Krishna is indeed God.

The word used for God in The Gita is bhagavan, a departure from the word 'devas' used in the Vedas. The word 'bhagavata' was used in Vedic times to mean 'benefactor' or 'bearer of fortune', a title for kings and sages. But The Gita transformed it. Thus, 2,000 years ago, it came to refer to God, especially visualized as Krishna or Vishnu, marking a shift in the dominant theme of Hinduism. While every living creature is apportioned a slice of reality that is its lot in life, God is master of every slice.

When the Europeans came to India, they tried long and hard to equate the devas of the Vedas with the Greek gods and the bhagavan of The Gita and the Puranas with the Abrahamic God. They argued that just as Christians had shifted from polytheism to monotheism thanks to Christianity, Hindus did so thanks to The Gita. But such forced comparisons failed, as the lines between polytheism and monotheism were blurred in Hinduism. While the Abrahamic God expressly considers Greek gods to be false, the Puranic bhagavan sees the devas as a part of his being. This is not appropriation or inclusion; this is evolution, a journey from the limited to the limitless. It is also a journey from the physical to the psychological. God is not 'out there'; God is also 'in us' and 'in others'.

The Hindu God resists the finiteness of history and geography that attracted Western mythologies, but embraces the infinity offered by psychology, a subject that Europeans took seriously only in the twentieth century after the works of Freud and Jung.

> Arjuna, at the end of many lives, the rare wise man finally realizes: Krishna is everything.—*Bhagavad Gita: Chapter 7, Verse 19 (paraphrased)*.

Greek mythology had no concept of a singular almighty God. It had many gods. First, there were the Titans who violently separated the earth goddess, Gaia, from the sky god, Uranus, and became the rulers of the world. Then came the Olympians, the children of the Titans, who overthrew them. The Olympians feared that the humans would overthrow them, and so kept them in place through the Fates. But occasionally, grudgingly, they admired a truly independent and defiant being: the hero, whom they gave a special place in the afterlife. The pattern here is overpowering, absorbing and appropriating the conquered. This mythology also shaped the worldview of the Romans who controlled the Mediterranean 2,000 years ago.

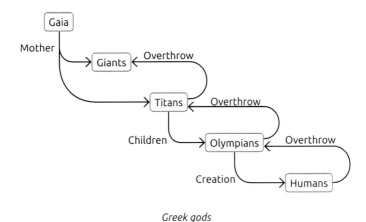

Greek gods

But then 1,700 years ago, in order to unify an increasingly divided empire, the Roman Emperor Constantine converted to Christianity and rejected all old gods in favour of the God of Abraham, who allowed worship of none other but Him. This God of Abraham was the creator of the world, distinct from the world He had created, who laid down rules of how humans should behave if they wished to return to heaven. This idea formed the basis of Islam as well. But the Muslims rejected the

Christian claim that Jesus was the Son of God; they believed that Jesus was a prophet, like Abraham and Moses before him, but the final prophet who really mattered was Muhammad. The question of who is the true prophet continues to divide those who subscribe to Abrahamic mythology.

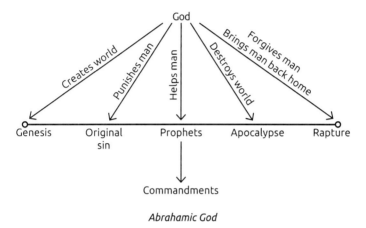

Abrahamic God

The God of Abrahamic mythology is constantly described as jealous and possessive, someone who does not tolerate false gods. The God of Hindu mythology does not create such divisions, and is seen present in diverse local and folk deities, who serve as portals of a larger singular divine entity.

One can say that the Abrahamic idea of God seeks purity, and so shuns contamination by the 'false', while the Hindu idea of God seeks completeness, and so keeps including many incomplete ideas of the divine in the journey towards infinity. This could account for why the legacy of pre-Christian Europe, America and Arabia has been completely wiped out or hidden, while various Vedic, pre-Vedic, post-Vedic and extra-Vedic practices continue to thrive and influence each other in India, under the large umbrella term called Hinduism.

> Arjuna, those who exchange knowledge in order to venerate me, discover me inside themselves or outside, in multiple forms or as a singular universal whole.
> —*Bhagavad Gita: Chapter 9, Verse 15 (paraphrased).*

The earliest word for God in the Rig Veda is 'ka', which is the first alphabet in Sanskrit, from which come all the interrogative pronouns such as what, when, where, why, how. Thus, divinity had something to do with enquiry. The kavi, or poet, enquired about ka. He later came to be known as the rishi, the observer.

The rishis also used the word 'brahmana' to refer to divinity. The earliest meaning of brahmana is language—for it is through language that humans make sense of the world around them. In fact, language is what gives humans their humanity and distinguishes them from animals that communicate observation, but have no language to analyse and contemplate abstract thoughts. Brahmana also means expanding the mind, for language expands the mind.

The Vedic rituals invoke one purusha, a multi-headed and multi-limbed being, who permeates every aspect of the cosmos and whose division creates the world. In the Aranyakas, early speculative texts, there is reference to prajapati, the mind-seed whose union with matter-womb creates the diverse world. Thus, division, and union, of divinity lead to creation. In the Upanishads, later speculative texts, brahmana, purusha and prajapati are equated with atma, the immortal, located inside all beings as jiva-atma, and around all beings as para-atma. If jiva-

My Gita

atma is what one is and para-atma is what the other is, then param-atma is what one and the other can become. The identification of God with humanity starts being passionately debated. From an abstract and mystical concept, God increasingly becomes a psychological concept.

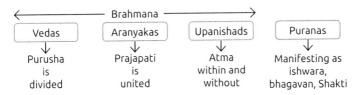

History of Hindu God

Two thousand years ago, in the Puranas, divinity was finally personified and given the form that we are very familiar with now. In fact, The Gita plays a key role in the shift. In the pre-Gita period, God was a concept. In the post-Gita period, God became a character in human affairs.

The old abstract words—purusha, brahmana, prajapati, atma—were gradually overshadowed by two new words: ishwara and bhagavan. Ishwara referred to the seed of divinity and bhagavan referred to the fully developed tree of divinity, laden with fruits and flowers. Ishwara is associated with Shiva, the hermit, whose marriage to Shakti creates the world. Bhagavan is associated with Vishnu, the householder, whose awakening results in creation and whose slumber results in dissolution. Between awakening and sleeping, Vishnu takes many forms to walk the earth, including that of Krishna. The Puranic Shiva and Vishnu presuppose the existence of the Goddess, who is nature, hence mother of humanity, as well as culture, daughter of humanity.

Ishwara, Bhagavan and Shakti

The God of Abrahamic mythology shies away from form. The God of Hindu mythology is both formless (nir-guna-brahman) and embodied (sa-guna-brahman), as described in Chapter 12 of The Gita. Without form, He is neither male nor female. With form, He may be birth-less and deathless, as in the case of Shiva, Vishnu and the Goddess, who are described as self-created (swayam-bhu) and not born from the womb (a-yonija). Or He may experience birth and death, as any womb-born (yonija), as in the case of Ram and Krishna.

Though formless, the God of Abrahamic mythology is addressed, even visualized, in masculine terms. The God of Hindu mythology is visualized as sometimes male, sometimes female, sometimes both and sometimes neither. Thus, Krishna refers, in Chapter 7, Verse 6, to the world of matter and mind as his two wombs (yoni), while also speaking of how he places his seed in the womb of Brahma, in Chapter 14, Verse 3. Krishna also describes himself in feminine terms. In Chapter 10, he identifies himself as the Ganga River and the wish-fulfilling cow

My Gita

Kamadhenu. Naturally, in Maharashtra, the poet-saints had no problem referring to the local form of Krishna, Vitthal, as Vittha-ai or Mother Vitthal.

The God of Abrahamic mythology has no family or any such human relationships. In Christian mythology, He has a son, but no wife. The God of Hinduism is visualized as a householder who deals with mundane human issues in temples and tales. Although the word 'brahma' remains sacred throughout Hinduism, referring to the divine potential in all things, the god Brahma in the Puranas is not worshipped, as he is visualized as the unenlightened householder, who seeks to control the Goddess, chasing her relentlessly against her will, and so loses a head to Shiva. Shiva is worshipped as the enlightened hermit who is turned into an enlightened householder by the Goddess. Vishnu is worshipped as the enlightened householder who takes responsibility for the Goddess and adopts various forms to protect her while she provides for him, becoming Ram when she is Sita, and Krishna when she is Radha, Satyabhama and Draupadi.

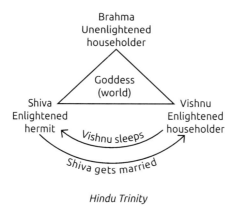

Hindu Trinity

From Chapter 7 of The Gita, the idea of God takes centre stage.

> Arjuna, your senses experience eight parts of my manifested form: the five elements, emotions, intelligence and identity. Beyond is my unmanifested form, that supports all this as a string holds a necklace of pearls together.—*Bhagavad Gita: Chapter 7, verses 4 to 7 (paraphrased).*

In Chapter 8, Krishna connects the impersonal mind (brahman) and impersonal matter (adi-bhuta) to the personal mind (adhyatma) and the personal body (adi-daiva), via impersonal action (karma) and personal connection (adi-yagna). Thus, divinity is connected with the individual, param-atma with jiva-atma. Krishna declares himself as the ultimate source and destination of all things, from where all things come and to which they return.

> Arjuna, at the hour of death, he whose mind is yoked by devotion, breath stilled, attention focussed, thinks of me, comes to me.—*Bhagavad Gita: Chapter 8, Verse 6 (paraphrased).*

In Chapter 9, Krishna says that he is accessible to all, even those considered bad or inferior.

> Arjuna, even those you consider villains should be respected if you find them walking my path, for they too will eventually find peace and joy. None of my devotees

My Gita

are lost, not even those generally held in disdain by the royal warriors: women, traders, labourers and servants, even those considered illegitimate.—*Bhagavad Gita: Chapter 9, verses 30 to 32 (paraphrased).*

In Chapter 10, Krishna says that he is present in all things, manifesting as excellence.

Arjuna, I am the life existing in all things. I am the beginning, the middle and the end. Amongst Adityas, I am Vishnu; amongst lights, the sun; amongst winds, the mirage; amongst constellations, the moon; amongst the books of knowledge, the melodies; amongst devas, Indra; amongst senses, the mind; amongst organisms, the awareness; amongst rudras, Shiva; amongst yakshas and rakshasas, Kubera; amongst elements, fire; amongst mountains, Meru; amongst priests, Brihaspati; amongst commanders, Kartikeya; amongst waterbodies, the ocean; amongst seers, Bhrigu; amongst chants, aum; amongst rituals, recitation; amongst the immobile, the Himalayas; amongst trees, the fig; amongst messengers, Narada; amongst gandharvas, Chitraratha; amongst yogis, Kapila; amongst horses, Uchhaishrava; amongst elephants, Airavata; amongst people, the leader; amongst weapons, the thunderbolt; amongst cows, the wish-fulfilling cow; amongst lovers, Kama; amongst earthly serpents, Vasuki; amongst celestial serpents, Ananta; amongst ocean-dwellers, Varuna; amongst forefathers, Aryaman; amongst regulators, Yama; amongst asuras, Prahalada; amongst reckoners, Yama; amongst beasts, the lion; amongst birds, the eagle; amongst cleansers, the wind; amongst warriors, Ram; amongst fish, the dolphin; amongst rivers, Ganga; amongst metres, Gayatri; amongst months, December; amongst seasons, spring; amongst deception, gambling; amongst my people, me; amongst your people, you; amongst storytellers, Vyasa; amongst poets, Shukra. I am the staff of the guardians, the strategy of the ambitious, the silence of secrets, the wisdom of the wise. I am the seed, without me there can be no element, no plant, no animal. There is no end to my manifestations. These are but samples of infinity—*Bhagavad Gita: Chapter 10, verses 20 to 40 (paraphrased).*

In Chapter 11, Krishna shows his expansive form (virat-swarup), on Arjuna's request and Arjuna discovers God as the infinite container (vishwa-rupa), cause and consequence of all things, at all times, and more.

Arjuna, behold my forms, hundreds, thousands, of myriad colours and shapes. Behold the thirty-three Vedic gods: eight vasus, twelve adityas, eleven maruttas, two ashwins and many more things never known before. See the entire universe in my body, the animate and the inanimate. Let me give you special eyes so that you can see this special sight.—*Bhagavad Gita: Chapter 11, verses 5 to 8 (paraphrased).*

After Krishna describes himself, Sanjaya describes what Arjuna saw.

> King, so saying, that great master of yoga revealed his divine form to Arjuna. Many mouths, many eyes, many adornments, many weapons, facing all directions, brilliant as a thousand suns rising, thus did Arjuna see the diverse world in one body. His hair stood on end and he bowed reverentially.'—*Bhagavad Gita: Chapter 11, verses 9 to 14 (paraphrased).*

And finally, Arjuna describes what he sees.

> Krishna, I see you and in you all deities, serpents, sages and Brahma seated on a lotus. You are everywhere, resplendent, the original one, the goal, the anchor, the defender, without beginning, middle or end, of infinite arms and of infinite strength. The sun and moon are your eyes, blazing, fire in your mouth, filling the void between earth and sky with your infinite limbs, infinite trunks. All beings enter you, admire you, venerate you. In your mouth, between your teeth, you grind entire words, all warriors too, those on that side and this.—*Bhagavad Gita: Chapter 11, verses 15 to 30 (paraphrased).*

In Chapter 12, after Krishna returns to his original form, he speaks of how he can be perceived in different forms, or even without form.

Some realize me by worshipping my form. Some realize me formless through meditation. For most people, it is easier to worship form than the formless.—*Bhagavad Gita: Chapter 12, verses 2 to 5 (paraphrased)*.

This God of Hindu mythology, churned out of Vedic hymns, declares that He is the very source and destination of the Vedas and everything else, in The Gita. In other words, language reveals the idea of God and the idea of God declares it gave birth to language. The form reveals the formless, which makes the form meaningful. The Hindu idea of God, presented through language and the liberal use of metaphors, is located inside humanity, not outside. It is what makes humans yearn for, and find, meaning. It is what makes humans outgrow fear and expand the mind to discover immortality, infinity. It is what enables humans to care for others. It is what everyone can be. This rather psychological understanding of God is unique to Hinduism, and distinguishes it from Western mythologies.

I want you to be bhagavan: see my slice of reality, my insecurity and my vulnerability, and comfort me, without making me feel small. You have that potential. So do I. If not you and I, then surely there is somebody else.

11.

You and I can include

To discover God within, we have to go beyond our slice of reality and appreciate the hungers and fears of those around us. For that we have to discover **brahmana** by expanding our mind, an idea that is best explored through the character of Hanuman, the monkey god who plays a key role in the epic Ramayana, and whose image flutters on Arjuna's flag. Hanuman became a popular deity in the ten centuries after the writing of The Gita, when Hindu monastic traditions waxed while Buddhist monastic traditions waned.

Arjuna's flag is known as kapi-dhvaja, as it has the image of a monkey (kapi) on it. Monkeys have long represented the human mind, as like the mind they are restless, dominating and territorial, clinging to the source of comfort, their mother, until they grow up. Another word for kapi is va-nara, meaning less than human. It is derived from vana-nara, meaning forest (vana) people (nara).

But the monkey atop Arjuna's flag is no ordinary one. It is Hanuman, the mightiest of monkeys, whose story is told in the epic, Ramayana. He is always visualized at the feet of Ram, who appears human (nara) but is actually God (Nara-yana, the refuge of nara). Nara and Narayana also refer to a pair of inseparable Vedic sages, avatars of Vishnu. The inseparable Arjuna and Krishna are considered Nara and Narayana reborn.

Va-nara, nara and Narayana represent three aspects of our existence: animal, human and divine. Scientists now speak of how the human part of the brain is a recent development and sits on top of the older animal brain. The animal brain is rooted in fear, and focusses on survival, while the human brain is rooted in imagination, and so seeks to understand itself by understanding nature.

Between survival and understanding comes judging—the state when everything and everyone around is evaluated based on imagined benchmarks, in order to position oneself. The animal wants to identify the other as predator or prey, rival or mate. The judge wants to classify the world as good or bad, innocent or guilty, right or wrong, oppressor or oppressed, based on his or her own framework. The observer wants to figure out what exactly is going on.

The journey from animal to judge to observer is the journey

of va-nara to nara to Narayana. It involves the uncrumpling of aham, the frightened mind, and the eventual discovery of atma, the secure mind. This is what it means to be brahmana.

	Narayana	God	Other realization
	Nara	Human	Self-realization
	Va-nara	Animal	Self-preservation Self-propagation

Expansion of Mind

The word brahmana has two roots: expansion (brah) and mind (manas). In the Rig Veda—depending on usage—it refers to language, the power of language to expand the mind, and the expanded mind. The student was referred to as a brahmachari, one who was expected to behave such that his mind expanded. Later, it came to refer to ritual manuals (brahmana texts), and eventually to keepers of these texts (the brahmana caste, more popularly known as Brahmins). Even later, it became a character in the Puranas, Brahma, the creator of the world, who is so consumed by his creation that he forgets his own identity and becomes unworthy of worship. Vishnu enables the many sons of Brahma to expand their mind. Some succeed, some don't. In the Ramayana, Ram enables the transformation of Hanuman from the servant, Ram-dasa, to Maha-bali, a deity in his own right. In the Mahabharata, Krishna struggles to transform the Pandava brothers and partially succeeds. Unlike in Greek epics, where the human protagonist transforms into something extraordinary, in Hindu epics, the human protagonist is God, who enables the transformation of those around.

The Gita uses the words 'brahmana' and 'brahma' to refer to

the sacred: the human ability to expand the mind and discover divinity and find meaning everywhere, as elaborated in the following hymn often chanted by Hindus before meals.

> Arjuna, the one who offers food is divine, the food that is offered is divine, the one who receives the food is divine, the one who consumes the food is divine. Everything will surely become divine to one willing to expand the mind.—*Bhagavad Gita: Chapter 4, Verse 24 (paraphrased)*.

This idea takes the shape of a story in the Puranas where the people of Ayodhya are amused to see Hanuman biting into the pearls given to him by Sita. 'What's the use of these pearls,' says Hanuman, 'if they do not contain Sita's Ram?' Hanuman then tears open his chest to reveal Sita's Ram. Hanuman thus reveals his deep understanding of dehi—what is located within the deha. He seeks dehi everywhere and thus expands his mind and finds brahmana.

Hanuman's Dehi

Brahmana represents a state when humans have totally overpowered the animal brain; in other words, outgrown fear. We do not look at the other as predator or prey, mate or rival. We do not seek to judge the other in order to position ourselves. Our identity is not dependent on the other. It is independent, devoid of the need for props. We either withdraw as Shiva does, or engage as Vishnu does, in order to enable the insecure other, who is entrapped in a crumpled mind.

> Arjuna, to expand your mind, use intelligence to draw your mind away from sensuality, so that there is no self-obsession, aggression, arrogance, desire, anger, possessiveness, attraction or repulsion. You are content in solitude, consuming little, expressing little, connected with the world and aware.—*Bhagavad Gita: Chapter 18, verses 51 to 53 (paraphrased).*

How will a man with expanded mind behave? We learn this from the Ramayana, the epic that tells the story of Ram, a prince exiled to the forest following palace intrigues. In the forest, he encounters rakshasas and vanaras, traditionally described as demons and monkeys, essentially creatures yet to expand their mind. The king of the rakshasas, Ravana, kidnaps Ram's wife, while the vanaras help him get her back.

Ravana, king of the rakshasas, is a Brahmin's son, well versed in the Vedas. Yet he shows all traits of an alpha male such as domination and territoriality. He makes himself king of Lanka by driving out his brother, Kubera. He tries to make Sita his queen and is quite infuriated, and bewildered, when she rejects his advances and stays faithful to Ram.

Sugriva, king of the vanaras, agrees to help Ram provided he helps him overthrow Vali, who has kicked him out of the kingdom of Kishkinda, following a misunderstanding, rather than sharing the throne, as their father wished. Ram kills Vali, but Sugriva promptly forgets his promise, until Lakshmana threatens him with dire consequences.

Like Ravana, Hanuman is well versed in the Veda. Like Sugriva, Hanuman is also a vanara. But he is very different. He observes and understands. He serves Sugriva because he is obliged to: Sugriva's father, the sun god Surya, is his guru. He protects Sugriva from Vali's excesses, but does not fight Vali as Vali is no enemy of his. Of his own volition, he serves Ram. He joins the fight against Ravana, even though Ravana is no enemy of his, because he realizes that Ram also does not see Ravana as his enemy. In Ram's eyes, there are no villains, or victims, or heroes, just humans who continue to indulge in animal-like behaviour out of fear, thereby following adharma rather than dharma. Ram fights Ravana because Ravana does not listen to human reason, and prefers animal force. No one but Hanuman recognizes that Ram is no nara; he is Narayana. This discovery enables Hanuman to expand his mind, make choices and take responsibility, transform from animal to God. This is why there are independent temples dedicated to Hanuman.

> Arjuna, the wise let go of the fruit of action, and so break free from the cycle of rebirths. Their wisdom cuts through formal hymns and official words, for yoga connects them with who they really are.—*Bhagavad Gita: Chapter 2, verses 51 to 53 (paraphrased).*

When Hanuman follows Ram back to Ayodhya, he observes how Ram casts out a pregnant Sita, following street gossip about her soiled reputation due to contact with Ravana. But he does not judge Ram. He observes how Ram, as scion of a royal clan, cannot break clan rules and must uphold clan reputation at all costs. He observes how Ram never abandons his people, even though they are being petty, nor does he try to convince them of his wife's innocence. Ram refuses to be Ayodhya's judge or Sita's lawyer. He simply refuses to remarry: he may have abandoned the queen, but he will never abandon his wife.

> Arjuna, he who sees the divine as present equally in all things does not hurt himself by hurting others and so attains the ultimate state.—*Bhagavad Gita: Chapter 13, Verse 28 (paraphrased).*

Hanuman also observes how Sita refuses to return to Ram's Ayodhya, though not even for a moment does she doubt his love for her and her love for him. In a world of rules, everyone makes choices and every choice has consequences. Karma applies to Ram and Sita too. No matter what the circumstances, neither Ram nor Sita abandons dharma. Hanuman thus realizes what it takes to be Narayana: to be independent, yet dependable.

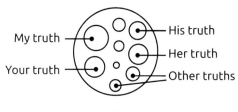

God's Truth

Hanuman serves Ram, God without, and discovers the God within. Krishna serves Arjuna and displays his divine form, so that Arjuna feels reassured and secure enough to make the inner journey, which will enable his outer journey.

Hanuman enters the Mahabharata when the Pandavas are in exile. Unlike Ram who is at peace despite being exiled for no fault of his own, the Pandavas feel like victims even though it is they who gambled away their kingdom.

Other Truths   His Truth   My Truth   Her Truth   Your Truth

Expanded Mind

Hanuman encounters Bhima as he walks through the forest like an entitled prince, refusing to go around rocks or trees, walking straight, expecting animals to stay clear of his path, so different from the caring and accommodating Ram. In the form of an old monkey, Hanuman reclines on Bhima's path and refuses to make way. 'Kick my tail aside and go ahead. I am too weak to

My Gita

move it myself.' Bhima tries to do so, even uses all his legendary strength, but fails to move the monkey's tail by even an inch. Thus humbled, he recognizes the monkey is Hanuman teaching him a lesson. Hanuman then displays his gigantic form, the one he took to leap over the ocean to find Lanka, a reminder never to underestimate the potential of things around.

Hanuman also encounters Arjuna just before the war, when Arjuna wonders aloud why Ram did not build a bridge of arrows to cross the ocean into Lanka. 'Maybe such a bridge would not hold the weight of a monkey,' says Hanuman. To prove him wrong Arjuna builds a bridge of arrows across the sea. As soon as Hanuman steps on it, it collapses. This happens again and again, until Krishna advises Arjuna to chant Ram's name while releasing his arrows. This Arjuna does and now the bridge is so strong that even when Hanuman takes his giant form, the bridge does not break. Thus the power of faith in the divine is demonstrated over skill and strength.

'When you were Ram, I was at your feet,' says Hanuman to Krishna. 'Now can I be on top of your head?' Krishna agrees. Arjuna is shocked: a monkey on Krishna's head? 'What is wrong, Arjuna?' asks Krishna, 'Wherefrom comes your assumption of superiority? I sit at your feet. Can Hanuman not be atop your head?'

> Arjuna, he who does not hate anyone, is friendly and compassionate always, is not possessive and self-indulgent, stable in pleasure and pain, forgiving, contained, controlled and firm in his love for me, in heart and head, is much loved by me.—*Bhagavad Gita: Chapter 12, verses 13 and 14 (paraphrased).*

The difference between the Pandavas and Ram is thus repeatedly demonstrated. Ram is not a great king because he is a king or a hero, but because his mind has expanded and he hates no one. The Pandavas are insecure, despite having strength and skills, and constantly seek validation. In their fear, they fail to see the love around. By observing Ram, Hanuman discovers the love of the atma beyond the fears of aham. By listening to The Gita, Krishna hopes that Arjuna will discover the same.

When I feel that you acknowledge, appreciate and accommodate my worldview, rather than dismissing, tolerating, adoring or even following it, I know you are expanding your mind and walking the path of brahmana.

12.

You and I can accommodate

An expanding mind can contract to accommodate the limited view of others. A mother, for example, can display mock rage to delight her child. Thus the limited worldview of the child is indulged, and emotionally nourished. At the same time, the mother is nourished by meaning and realization of potential. A healthy relationship, like a yagna, is always two-way, not one-way. That is why an **avatar** is not just a teacher or a saviour, as we shall discover through the character of Radha, who appeared in the Hindu landscape eight centuries ago as the flower of the Bhagavata plant whose seed was planted by The Gita. Radha replaced devotion with affection, made God both lover and beloved, and completed the divine with femininity.

There are over forty names by which Krishna is addressed in The Gita, but only one refers to his pastoral roots: Govinda, which means the cowherd.

Specific to Krishna	Specific to Vishnu	Generic names for the divine
Govinda (1.32)	Achyuta (1.21)	Adideva (11.38)
Hari (11.9)	Adhiyajna (8.2)	Amitavikrama (11.40)
Hrsikesha (1.15)	Adikarta (11.37)	Aprameya (11.17)
Janardana (1.35)	Ananta (11.37)	Apratimaprabhava (11.43)
Keshava (1.30)	Ananta-rupa (11.38)	Bhutabhavana (9.5)
Kesinishudana (18.1)	Ananta-virya (11.19)	Bhutabhrun (9.5)
Krishna—(1.28)	Arisudana (2.4)	Bhutesha (10.15)
Madhava (1.14)	Bhagavan (10.14)	Deva (11.14)
Madhusudana (1.34)	Jagannivasa (11.25)	Devadeva (10.15)
Sakha (11.41)	Jagatpati (10.15)	Devavara (11.31)
Varsneya (1.40)	Kamalapatraksha (11.2)	Devesha (11.25)
Vasudeva (7.19)	Mahabahu (6.38)	Isha (11.44)
Yadava (11.41)	Purushottama (8.1)	Ishvara (4.6)
	Sahasrabahu (11.46)	Kala (11.32)
	Vishnu (10.21)	Mahatma (11.12)
	Visvamurti (11.46)	Mahayogeshvara (11.9)
	Visvarupa (11.16)	Parameshvara (11.3)
	Visvesvara (11.16)	Prabhu (9.18)
	Yajna (3.9, 4.23)	Prajapati (3.10)
		Prapitamaha (11.39)
		Ugrarupa (11.31)
		Yogesvara (11.4)
		Yogi (10.17)

We cannot imagine Krishna today without cows, cowherds and milkmaids (gopikas). But the lore of his childhood amongst pastoral communities was elaborated and put down in writing

My Gita

only after the composition of the Mahabharata and The Gita, in the fourth-century Harivamsa, the fifth-century Vishnu Purana, the tenth-century Bhagavata Purana (also known as Shreemad Bhagavatam, or simply Bhagavata) and finally, the twelfth-century Gita Govinda by the poet Jayadeva, which introduces us to Radha.

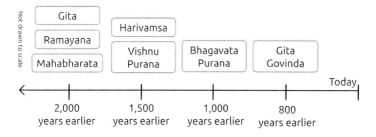

Bhagavata in Historical Timeline

In the Harivamsa, great value is placed on Krishna's parents, Nanda and Yashoda, who are cowherds, and his secret dalliances with gopikas. We are introduced to the rasa-mandala, the circular dance formation. But here, Krishna is not exclusive to any one gopika; he dances with all. In the Gita Govinda, which was written a few centuries later, Radha appears and demands exclusive attention. In both, Krishna ultimately leaves the cowherd life and moves to Mathura, and thereafter gets involved in the events described in the Mahabharata. Many regional works that followed etched this pastoral Krishna, son of Yashoda, beloved of Radha, in the Hindu mind. Collectively, we may call all of this Bhagavata lore. Whatever be the historical timeline, in terms of narrative, and psychologically, the Bhagavata is located between the Ramayana and the Mahabharata.

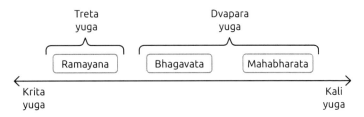

Bhagavata in Narrative Timeline

The Bhagavata is distinct from the Ramayana and the Mahabharata. The Ramayana and the Mahabharata focus a lot on masculine anxiety over power and property. The Bhagavata focusses on feminine anxiety about abandonment and affection. Anxieties stem from our desire to survive. In nature, the quest for survival gives rise to sex and violence. Hermits, however, seek to give up sex and violence completely, through practice of celibacy and non-violence, in order to be rid of all anxiety. Householder traditions seek to minimize anxiety by regulating sex and violence through rules of marriage and property. The Ramayana elaborates this. The Mahabharata reveals how rules can be manipulated with clever logic, and how this can take us away from the path of dharma. The Bhagavata elaborates on the emotions (bhava) that underlie rules, sex and violence, and places primacy on emotions over rules. If Buddhism speaks of shunning desire to break free from suffering, if the Ramayana and the Mahabharata speak of regulating desire with responsibility, the Bhagavata qualifies desire with love.

The Bhagavata creates an emotional highway between the devotee (bhagata/bhakta) and the deity (bhagavan), transforming intellectual and pragmatic Vedic conversations (Upanishad) into effusive adoration (upasana). Here, the self (jiva) can be

My Gita

the parent, like Yashoda, to the divine other (param), who is the child. Here the self can also be a lover, like one of the gopikas who pines for the divine other, who is the beloved. When Radha comes along she even transforms the divine into a lover who pines for her, the beloved. The seed of the Bhagavata traditions can be traced to The Gita itself.

> Arjuna, the one who offers me, with affection, a flower, a fruit, some water, a leaf, I accept.—*Bhagavad Gita: Chapter 9, Verse 26 (paraphrased).*

Here, the devotee is expected to be active in devotion and cling to the deity like a baby monkey clings to its mother. In other verses, the devotee is expected to be passive in devotion, like a kitten trusting that its mother will take care of it.

> Arjuna, give up all that you are doing and have full faith in me. I will free you from all fetters. Do not worry. —*Bhagavad Gita: Chapter 18, Verse 66 (paraphrased).*

Cat Mother and Monkey Mother

In both cases, God is placed on a pedestal: God is the parent and saviour. In the Ramayana, Sita has no doubt that Ram will find a way to rescue her from the clutches of the mighty Ravana. In the Mahabharata, when her husbands fail to protect her, Draupadi turns to Krishna, who prevents her public disrobing at the hands of the Kauravas. The emotional highway between devotee and deity moves one way—the devotee is dependent on God; God is not dependent on the devotee.

> Arjuna, I know that those who existed in the past exist in the present and will exist in the future. None know me.—*Bhagavad Gita: Chapter 7, Verse 26 (paraphrased).*

But there is a festering incompleteness in the Ramayana and the Mahabharata. At the end of the Ramayana, Ram abandons Sita. Despite being faultless, she finds herself the subject of street gossip and is cast out of the palace, forced to fend for herself in the forest. At the end of the Mahabharata, Krishna grants Draupadi her revenge by ensuring that all the Kauravas and their commanders are killed. But revenge comes at a price: all of Draupadi's children, her five sons, are killed too. The jiva-atma feels abandoned. Has the saviour failed?

Bhagavata traditions take this conversation forward. The one-way emotional highway becomes two-way, involving not merely transaction but transformation. The Bhagavata shifts the balance of power.

In the 1,000 years that followed The Gita, the doctrine of Bhakti was elaborated. It took two distinct routes—the masculine route, based on submission, celibacy and restraint, embodied in

Hanuman; and the feminine route, based on affection, sensuality and demand, embodied in Yashoda and Radha. The masculine route was favoured by the mathas, the Hindu monastic order. The feminine route was favoured by the devadasis, temple dancers who used the performing arts to connect the masses with the divine.

One can say that the masculine route, grounded in celibacy, was the route of Vedanta, and the feminine route, grounded in pleasure, was the route of Tantra. These two thoughts emerged as distinct branches from the seventh century onwards. This happened because the old division between the Buddhist hermit and the Hindu householder was collapsing. The Hindu householder started adopting hermit practices like vegetarianism, while Hindu hermits began reaching out to the masses through song and dance, practices previously associated only with the household.

More importantly, knowledge transmission was no longer top-down. It did not just come from priests who performed rituals and kings who rode chariots and controlled the land. Ideas were even coming from the bottom upwards, even from cowherds who wandered the countryside with their cattle in search of pastures. In the new discourse, God was not a feudal overlord to whom one submitted. God was a commoner who sought affection and returned affection. The distant Ram was overshadowed by the more accessible Hanuman. Krishna, the cowherd, beloved of the gopikas, overshadowed Krishna, guardian of the Yadavas and guide of the Pandavas.

	Achievement	Submission Devotion
Masculine		
Feminine	Abandonment	Affection
	Anxiety	Comforts

Masculine Submission and Feminine Affection

The story of Krishna's childhood mimics a Greek epic until we start considering the role of the women. It begins with a prophecy that Kansa, the dictator of Mathura, will be killed by his own nephew, the eighth son of his sister, Devaki. Kansa imprisons Devaki and kills all the sons she bears. To save the eighth child, Devaki's husband, Vasudeva, takes the newborn across the river Yamuna to the village of cowherds, Gokul, and switches babies, bringing back a cowherd girl child born the same night. Years later, when Krishna returns to Mathura and kills Kansa, his true identity is revealed. But many still refer to him as the son of a cowherd, rather contemptuously, an indicator of social hierarchy. But family name and honour, so important to Ram, do not matter to Krishna. He has discovered something deeper—love—that conquers all anxieties.

Krishna owes this discovery to the milkmaids of Gokul and Vrinda-vana. They collectively raised Krishna as their own child, showered him with affection, indulged his pranks, suffered his mischief, admonished him when he crossed the line and loved him as a mother would, even though none of them had given birth to him. This is parental love (vatsalya bhava), embodied in Yashoda.

My Gita

Krishna and Yashoda

When Krishna becomes a youth, his relationship with the gopikas changes. Pranks give way to flirtation. The child is forgotten as the man takes over. The women now quietly slip out of their homes at night when their family is asleep and go deep into the forest (vana), unafraid to dance in a circle around Krishna, who plays the enchanting flute. There are passionate disagreements, demands, separations and reunions. He is not their brother, father, son or husband. Theirs is not a relationship governed by niti (law) or riti (tradition). Yet, in his company, they feel alive and secure. It is a relationship that springs from within, and is not forced from without. Everything is authentic but private, for it is beyond the comprehension of the public. This is love evoked by presence (madhurya bhava), union (shringara bhava) and even absence (viraha bhava), embodied in Radha.

When Krishna leaves the village of Vrinda-vana for the city of Mathura, he promises he will be back. But he cannot keep that promise. He sends his friend, Uddhava, to inform his village of his decision to stay in the city, and to comfort them in heartbreak. Uddhava's advice is intellectual in approach and monastic in spirit: he speaks of the impermanent nature of things and the importance of letting go. Radha replies with a smile—she is not afraid of pain and suffering and abandonment. In fact, she relishes it, for it reminds her of Krishna. 'He is the black bee who moves from flower to flower, but I am the flower that cannot leave its tree. He has transformed me, enabled me to turn into a fruit that contains the seed of love.'

Krishna and Radha

The abandoned women of Gokul and Vrinda-vana, be it the mother, Yashoda, or the lover, Radha, express what the abandoned women of the Ramayana and the Mahabharata do not: love, not anger. They do not judge Krishna. They don't expect him to ask for forgiveness, because there is nothing to forgive. They do not begrudge him his ambitions, his compulsions and his adventures. They don't want him to turn back. They accept the nature of nature: nothing lasts forever, everything changes. They want their beloved to move on his outer journey, just as their love for him inspires them to undertake their inner journey. They are no longer dependent on him. But they will always be dependable for him.

This attitude of the womenfolk has a huge impact on Krishna. Being God is not about being limitless, it is about allowing the limited and including the limited, despite all their shortcomings, as a wise parent allows a child to grow up and go on his or her own path. Krishna acknowledges his indebtedness to the gopikas of Gokul when despite being male, he always strikes a very female pose, the tri-bhagna. This makes him the purna-avatar, the complete incarnation of Vishnu to walk the earth.

In the Bhagavata Purana, we find the story of how Yashoda once found baby Krishna eating dirt. She scolded him and forced him to open his mouth so that she could wash the dirt away. But within his mouth she beheld a vision of the whole universe, similar to the one Arjuna sees in Chapter 11 of The Gita. It terrified her. For a moment she realized the awesomeness of her child. But then she resumed her maternal duties, bathing him, feeding him, educating him, admonishing him when the neighbours complained about his pranks, even punishing him when he disobeyed. He might be God, but she was his mother. For her sake, the deity became a child. For his sake, the devotee stayed a mother.

Yoga may expand our mind, but love demands that we contract ourselves so that our lover does not feel inadequate or inferior. This conscious contraction of divinity is why the infinite bhagavan descends on earth as the finite avatar, experiencing death as Ram and Krishna for the benefit of his devotees. In Chapter 11, Arjuna wants to see Krishna in his cosmic form. A curious child, the thought excites him.

> Krishna, I have heard in detail the grand nature of the world, how things fold and unfold. I am curious to see your divine form that you describe. Show me, if you feel I can handle it.—*Bhagavad Gita: Chapter 11, verses 2 to 4 (paraphrased).*

But when Krishna does display his form, its awesomeness ends up intimidating Arjuna, for it suddenly makes him aware of his insignificance in the cosmic canvas.

> Krishna, I am happy to see your secret form, but it frightens me. Return to your original form, please. —*Bhagavad Gita: Chapter 11, Verse 45 (paraphrased).*

The thousand-armed God becomes the two-armed friend and charioteer once again. If devotion to Ram makes Hanuman expand and become bhagavan, then affection for Arjuna makes Krishna contract to become an avatar. He is like the mother who pretends not to see the child while playing a game of hide-and-seek. Though limitless himself, he submits to the limited truth of those around him. These are the games (leela) the deity-parent plays with the devotee-child. The aim of bhagavan's contraction (avatarana) is to uplift the devotee (uddhar). For bhagavan can see all slices of reality and can make the bhakta see more than just the one.

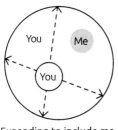 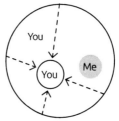

Expanding to include me	Contracting to comfort me
Brahmana	Avatar
Bhagavan	

Expanding and Contracting

Ram uplifts Hanuman, but Krishna realizes that Arjuna does not have the same capacity and capability as Hanuman. However, he does not make Arjuna feel small. Like Yashoda and Radha, he never judges the Pandavas, never makes them feel guilty for gambling away their kingdom. He simply prepares them to face the consequences of their action.

Darshan of the other enables us to acknowledge and accept their inadequacies. This makes them neither small nor helpless. It just makes them different. A student may not learn because he does not have the capacity, or because he does not have the will or because he does not have the resources. None of these makes the wise teacher unhappy, for he knows that teaching is about the student's benefit, not for his aggrandizement. He cannot control the karma of the student; he can only focus on the svaha of his yagna, plant the karma-bija and not seek control over the karma-phala.

Likewise, a wise man never argues when a less learned man argues with him. He knows when to expand and when to contract, when to give and when to receive. Darshan of the limited other enables the self to gain insight into the human condition and further expand the mind. By submitting to the truth, the yajamana experiences brahmana.

A hermit does not want to do yagna. A saviour is only a benefactor (yajamana). But a lover is both benefactor (yajamana) and beneficiary (devata). In The Gita, Krishna identifies himself with the input to the yagna.

> Arjuna, I am food for the child, exchange for the adult, offering to the dead, medicine to the sick, the chant, the butter, the fire, the libation.—*Bhagavad Gita: Chapter 9, Verse 16 (paraphrased).*

Then, in another verse, Krishna becomes the recipient of the output.

> Arjuna, offerings made with affection to other deities eventually reach me. I am the recipient of all libations. Most do not recognize me, and so falter.—*Bhagavad Gita: Chapter 9, verses 23 and 24 (paraphrased).*

Ram may be the saviour of the downtrodden (patita-pavana), stoically bearing the burden of royal responsibilities and suffering personal tragedy, but Krishna is also a lover. He gives and receives. He is not complete without Radha. In Radha-bhakti, the jiva-atma may seek param-atma in the forest and dance around him, but Krishna also yearns for her, filling the forest with his lovelorn chant, 'Radhe! Radhe!' And while Sita and Ram are separated by social laws and remain heartbroken in separation, Krishna and Radha move on with their respective lives—Krishna always carries Radha in his heart, and Radha always carries Krishna in hers. For Krishna, his time in Gokul may be limited, but his love for Radha is limitless.

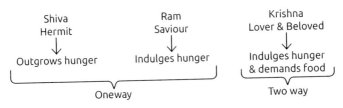

Hermit, Saviour and Lover

Radha, however, is excluded from many Krishna-bhakti traditions, such as those of Shankardev in Assam and the Mahanubhav panth of Chakradhara Swami in Maharashtra. There is no Radha image in most major temples of Krishna outside the Gangetic plans, such as those in Puri, Pandharpur, Udupi, Guruvayur or Nathdwara. Radha's unabashed eroticism and the rather Tantric approach of mutuality was not universally accepted, especially suggestions that Radha was older and was Krishna's aunt (either Nanda's younger sister or married to Yashoda's brother), metaphors that sought to intensify the social inappropriateness, so as to amplify the genuineness of the emotional connection. Preference was given to the nameless milkmaids of the Bhagavata Purana whose love (prema) is seen as pure, uncontaminated by eroticism (kama). Or the entire Bhagavata lore came to be dominated by Yashoda, whose maternal love is not as discomforting as Radha's love.

For centuries, the devadasis of Hindu temples sang the song of the cowherd ('Gita Govinda') that describes the intense emotions of Krishna and Radha revealed secretly, at night, outside the village, in the forest. The voice of the devadasis was silenced in the early twentieth century as they were deemed prostitutes. Greater value was placed on the Hindu monastic order that preferred the celibate Hanuman and the song of God (Bhagavad Gita).

Mahabharata	Bhagavata	Gita Govinda
Masculine	Feminine	Erotic and Transgressive

Shifts in Bhakti Literature

The Gita speaks of bhakti as devotion, with God occupying a higher position and the devotee submitting to him. However, in Chapter 18, Verse 65, he does refer to Arjuna as 'one very dear to me' (priyo-si-me), indicating love. Gita Govinda wipes out the hierarchy and transforms bhakti into affection. In it, Krishna begs Radha to place her feet on his head to cure him of the poison of longing, lines that, legend has it, Jayadeva himself hesitated to write, but Krishna wrote for him, thus indicating the power of love.

Sometimes, you can see more than me, but you pretend to know less so that I don't feel intimidated by you. I do the same for you. We do not feel superior when the other is vulnerable; or inferior when we feel helpless. This is what sustains our relationship.

My Gita

13.

You and I have no control

As the mind expands, you and I will accept how helpless we really are, how limited our control over the world is. We will discover how every organism has little control over his or her own capabilities and capacities that are dependent on their natural material tendencies, or **guna**, which in turn is shaped by karma. It will dawn on us that we are not agents who can change the world, we are merely instruments of the world, that is constantly changing. In this chapter we shall explore the three guna. From here onwards, the conversation becomes less emotional and more intellectual: we venture from bhakti yoga to gyana yoga as we understand the role of insecurity and identity in shaping our choice of action. Krishna elaborates on the guna in chapters 14, 17 and 18 of The Gita.

In Chapter 3, Arjuna speaks of the inability to control the mind.

> Krishna, how is it that despite unwillingness, humans
> do bad things?—*Bhagavad Gita: Chapter 3, Verse 36
> (paraphrased).*

He was perhaps thinking of his eldest brother, the upright Yudhishthira, who could not stop himself from gambling away their kingdom, his brothers, their wife and even himself. Or perhaps he was thinking of his elder brother, the mighty Bhima, who could not stop himself from killing Kichaka, the lout who tried to abuse Draupadi while they were hiding disguised as servants in the palace of Virata, despite Yudhishthira's express instructions to resist every urge to reveal their secret identities, for if any Pandava was recognized before the end of the stipulated period, they would have to go back into exile for another thirteen years. Or perhaps he was wondering why his grand-uncle Bhisma and tutor Drona were fighting on the Kauravas' side. Krishna attributes this inability to guna, the tendency of matter.

> Arjuna, in your conceit you may declare that you do
> not want to fight but your nature will compel you to do
> so, shattering all resolve.—*Bhagavad Gita: Chapter 18,
> verses 59 and 60 (paraphrased).*

Krishna mentions guna early in his discourse in Chapter 2 of The Gita, but elaborates on it only later in chapters 14, 17 and 18. In between, he takes Arjuna on a detour: the inner journey of discovering the divine nature of dehi. This exploration of bhagavan and bhakti in the middle third portion of

The Gita marks an acknowledgement of the role emotion plays in cognition. Unless the heart feels secure, the head will not accept the reality revealed by darshan: the reality that humans are helpless before the force of nature, that karma determines the circumstances of our life and guna determines the personality of people around us. We can, at best, understand these, but we cannot control them. Attempts at control only contribute to inescapable and often dreadful consequences that haunt us lifetime after lifetime, generation after generation.

> Arjuna, mind and matter have always existed and from tendencies of matter all forms that exist have come into being.—*Bhagavad Gita: Chapter 13, Verse 19 (paraphrased).*

Darshan reveals that humans are propelled by desire, animals by fear, plants by hunger, but what eventually manifests depends on the guna that constitutes each individual. Even elements and minerals that have no internal or external drive, no hunger or fear, are continuously transforming because of guna. Guna is what causes clouds to expand, temperatures to shift, rivers to cascade, volcanoes to explode, the sun to rise and set, tides to ebb and flow and winds to blow even when there is no life around. Guna is the nature of nature, the root of its diversity and dynamism. The atma within observes the dance of guna.

> Arjuna, the truly wise can see that restless nature is the agent, not the immortal one within, but all diverse forms depend on, and emanate from, that one.—*Bhagavad Gita: Chapter 13, verses 29 and 30 (paraphrased).*

Guna Underlies All Actions

The guna are three (tri-guna): tamas, rajas and sattva. The tendency towards inertia comes from tamas guna, the tendency towards activity from rajas guna and the tendency towards balance from sattva guna. The three guna cannot exist without the other. They are like three phases of a wave: tamas being the movement downwards towards the nadir, rajas being the movement upwards towards the crest and sattva being the balance, the point at which there is a pause.

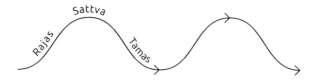

Tri-guna as Parts of a Wave

In the elements, tamas guna dominates, which is why they have a tendency towards inertia, unless acted upon by an external force (first law of motion). In plants and animals, rajas guna dominates, which is why they grow and run to overcome hunger and fear in order to survive. In humans, the sattva guna dominates, which is why only humans are able to trust and care

My Gita

for strangers, empathize and exchange. But it does not mean that all humans are sattvik. While humans have a strong sattvik component compared to animals, plants and minerals, amongst humans there is a differential distribution of all three guna.

> Arjuna, when sattva shines through all body gates, there is happiness and understanding; when rajas shines through, there is greed, restlessness and lust; when tamas shines through, there is confusion and indolence. At the time of death, if sattva dominates, rebirth takes place in happy and knowledgeable realms; if rajas dominates, rebirth takes place in action-filled realms; if tamas dominates, rebirth takes place in lost, decaying realms. From sattva comes knowledge, from rajas desire and from tamas ignorance.—*Bhagavad Gita: Chapter 14, verses 11 to 17 (paraphrased).*

Guna impact not just matter but also the mind. Thus, thought and emotions also display the three tendencies. Therefore some people are lazy followers, some are driven leaders who want to change the world and some decide when to follow and when to lead, and know that the world can be changed only cosmetically with technology, but not in essence, at a psychological level. Tamas guna stops us from thinking, so we follow the trend. Rajas guna stops us from trusting anyone but ourselves. Sattva guna makes us care for those who are frightened, intimidated by the diverse and dynamic reality of the world.

Different guna dominate at different times. Tamas guna is dominant in a child who follows the adult parent. Rajas guna is dominant in a doubting, fiercely independent, energetic youth who strives to make his own path. Sattva guna is dominant in the mature, who understand when to be silent and when to speak, when to follow and when to lead.

The guna can be seen literally or metaphorically. They explain the diversity of nature, the diversity of ecosystems, plants, animals and humans, the diversity displayed by each living creature in various stages of his or her life. When we react unconsciously or involuntarily, unaware or unable to control our impulses, we are being governed by our guna. Guna results in karma and karma creates guna. This creates the fluid material world: the complex canvas of our existence.

> Arjuna, there is none born on earth or in heaven who is free of the influence of the three tendencies.
> —*Bhagavad Gita: Chapter 18, Verse 40 (paraphrased).*

Chapter 17 informs us how the three guna can express themselves as external activities: faith (shraddha), food (ahara), exchange (yagna), austerity (tapasya) and charity (daan). In tamas, the tendency is to be lazy and confused, and so there is mimicry of the other. In rajas, the tendency is to achieve, dominate and impress, and so there is initiative and aggression towards the other. In sattva, the tendency is to understand and be happy, and so there is gentleness and affection for the other.

> Arjuna, everyone's faith is in line with their nature. They are what they believe. The satvik worship those who give on getting; the rajasik worship hoarders and grabbers; the tamasik worship ghosts. Worship need not be based on scriptures, and can involve harrowing

penance and torture for self-aggrandizement, hypocrisy and passion. Different is the food we like. Different is also the reason for exchanging, being austere or charitable.—*Bhagavad Gita: Chapter 17, verses 4 to 7 (paraphrased).*

Chapter 18 takes things further and classifies even internal aspects of our being, from knowledge to activity to personality to intelligence to willpower to happiness, to the three guna. Each time, tamas involves backward movement and no thought, rajas involves forward movement with self-absorbed thought and sattva involves appropriate movement, forward or backward, taking even the other into consideration.

Arjuna, the tamasik gives up action fooled by others; the rajasik gives up action in fear; the sattvik never gives up action, only the fruits of action, doing not just the nice, shunning not the nasty.—*Bhagavad Gita: Chapter 18, verses 7 to 10 (paraphrased).*

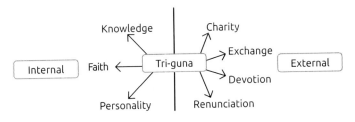

Tri-guna Within and Without

In Chapter 18, Krishna attributes human aptitude and talent (varna) to the guna.

Arjuna, it is these tendencies that create the four aptitudes: scholarship, leadership, entrepreneurship and servitude.—*Bhagavad Gita: Chapter 18, verses 41 to 44 (paraphrased).*

Our talents come from our guna. This does not mean that every talent can be mapped to a particular guna. It does not mean that scholarship comes from sattva guna, or leadership and entrepreneurship come from rajas guna or servitude comes from sattva guna. It means that the three guna, in different proportions, manifest as scholarship, leadership, entrepreneurship and servitude. We will find scholars who are rajasik, sattvik or tamasik; leaders who are rajasik, sattvik or tamasik; entrepreneurs who are rajasik, sattvik or tamasik; servants who are rajasik, sattvik or tamasik.

		Tendencies (guna)		
		Tamasik	Rajasik	Sattvik
Talent (varna)	Intellectual	✓	✓	✓
	Managerial	✓	✓	✓
	Entrepreneurial	✓	✓	✓
	Service provider	✓	✓	✓

Mapping Varna to Guna

From around 2,000 years ago, we find in Indian society a discomfort with fluidity and a great desire to fix things with rules. Genetic studies have shown us that India's infamous caste system, which began as professional guilds, became increasingly rigid from this time onwards. This was the time when the Manu

Smriti and other such books, that reduced dharma to a set of rules (niti) and traditions (riti), came to be written. Rules were aimed to create predictability and so greater value was placed on gender and lineage, than talent. Communities (jati) started following a particular profession that maintained their fidelity by insisting that the sons follow the father's trade and daughters not marry outside the community. The Manu Smriti mapped these jatis to the varnas: thus it was assumed that children of priests would be scholars, children of kings would be leaders, children of traders would be entrepreneurs and children of servants would be servile. Further, these varnas were mapped to guna: Brahmin jati was mapped to sattva guna, Kshatriya jati and Vaishya jati to rajas guna and Shudra jati to tamas guna.

The Manu Smriti, and other such law books, are more political and prejudiced than accurate, for every community has members of all three guna. And in every community there will be those who think, those who get things done, those who calculate and those who follow. The Manu Smriti reveals the human attempt to control the world and make nature predictable by forcing people to follow the vocation of their fathers. It is all about trying to fix a fluid world, a futile effort according to The Gita.

The Mahabharata, for example, speaks of Karna, whose talent as archer overrides the social demand that he follow his father's vocation and stay a charioteer. No matter how hard we try to fix things, nature will break all boundaries and rules. Varna will always overshadow jati. Duryodhana appreciates Karna's talent while Draupadi, the Pandavas, Bhisma and Drona reject and mock Karna. Duryodhana sees in him an opportunity and the rest see him as a threat. Nobody is a yogi. They are either attracted (raga) or repelled (dvesha) by him. No one sees Karna for himself, beyond his varna and jati, that he cannot stop himself from pursuing his passion for archery, logical arguments notwithstanding, for such is the power of one's guna.

		Tendencies (guna)		
		Tamasik	Rajasik	Sattvik
Classical categories of caste (jati)	Brahmin	✓	✓	✓
	Kshatriya	✓	✓	✓
	Vaishya	✓	✓	✓
	Shudra	✓	✓	✓

Mapping Jati to Guna

Likewise, marriage rules are designed to regulate the desires of humanity. But guna will force us to challenge these rules. Thus in Ramayana, though married, Parashurama's mother Renuka desires Kartaviryarjuna, Gautama's wife Ahalya desires Indra and Ravana's sister Surpanakha desires Ram. Renuka is beheaded, Ahalya turned to stone and Surpanakha's nose is cut off. None of these brutal actions stops nature from changing its course. Guna will continuously make people take decisions that even their mind opposes.

A judge tends to see sattva guna as superior and tamas guna as inferior, but the observer knows that sattva guna is the most desirable simply because it is least threatening while tamas guna is least desirable because it is burdensome. Rajas guna is glamorous and seductive, for it is associated with ambition and determination and is seen as far more proactive, compared to the reactive sattva guna.

The observer also distinguishes the sattvika from the yogi—

My Gita

the sattvika's tranquillity is effortless and inborn, while the yogi's tranquillity is the outcome of learning and effort. The yogi pays attention to the other, which distinguishes him from the sattvika.

> 'Arjuna, the wise observer does not hate what is there and seek what is not there amidst light or activity or delusion. He knows that it is the tendencies of matter at work, and so is always indifferent to the shifts around, always at peace, amidst pleasure and pain, gold or clay, when loved or unloved, when treated as friend or foe, in honour or disgrace, if praised or blamed.'—*Bhagavad Gita: Chapter 14, verses 22 to 25 (paraphrased).*

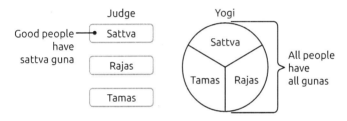

Views on Tri-guna

Krishna points to rajas guna for all desires (kama) and anger (krodha); tamas guna for all laziness and confusion; sattva guna for a balanced, responsible view. The moment we say that the agent is the guna, we don't take credit or blame, nor do we give credit or blame. In other words, we don't judge. We are able to connect with atma. The moment we judge, attribute agency to others or ourselves, for fortune or misfortune, we disconnect from atma and give rise to aham. In aham, we don't accept the power of guna and blame people for our problems. We then seek leaders if we are tamasika, followers if we are rajasika or simply disconnect if we are sattvika.

> Arjuna, the lord resides in everyone's hearts, deluding them with a sense of control while making them go round and round like cogs in a wheel.—*Bhagavad Gita: Chapter 18, Verse 61 (paraphrased).*

A yogi accepts that the stubbornness of Ravana in the Ramayana, Kansa in the Bhagavata Purana and Duryodhana in the Mahabharata are the results of their guna, which is beyond their control. As bhakta, he attributes their behaviour to the games (leela) of God. This makes it easier to make even the undesirable part of a yagna, rather than simply exclude them.

Threat	Tamas	'I will do as others do.'
	Rajas	'I will destroy him.'
	Sattva	'I will withdraw from him.'
	Yogi	'I will engage with his fears and hungers.'

Response of Different People to Villains

We are all a masala box of guna, with one guna dominating at different times. We can all be lazy, assertive, detached or engaged. Yoga makes us aware of the guna at work.

My Gita

14.

You and I value property

Guna may determine our body and our personality. Karma may determine the circumstances of our life. But humans have the power to create their own identity by creating and claiming property, or **kshetra**. Society values people more as proprietors, than as residents of the body, for property is visible and measurable. As a result, 'mine' becomes more important than 'me'. The gaze shifts from the inside to the outside. Krishna speaks of kshetra before he speaks of the tri-guna, in Chapter 13 of The Gita, but in *My Gita* kshetra is discussed after guna, as it flows better into the following chapters by introducing us to the social body, the artificial expansion of the body, found only in human society.

To stay alive, animals need to know the identity of the other: whether the animal around them is a predator (can it eat me?) or prey (can I eat it?); mate (can we produce offspring?) or rival (can it grab my food or mate?). They need to locate the other, and thus themselves, precisely in the food chain and pecking order.

Humans do not have to bother about food chains and pecking order. But we wonder who we are, and about our relationship with those around us. What is our purpose? How are we valued?

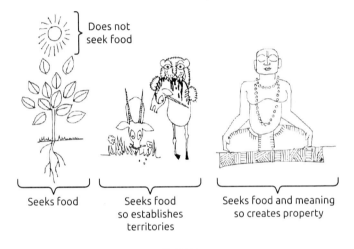

Purpose

A thing in nature has value only if it can be consumed as food. The sun, the rain and the earth did not have any value until trees came along and sought sunlight, water and soil as food. Likewise, plants had no value until animals sought them as food. Animals had no value until other animals sought them as food. Who seeks humans as food? Can humans be of value without being consumed?

My Gita

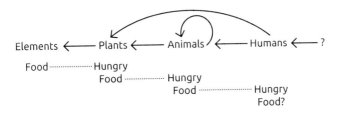

Value Chain = Food Chain

Speculation along these lines led to the composition of the Rig Vedic hymn of humanity (purusha sukta), which speaks of the consumption of man, and the Yajur Vedic ritual of dismemberment of the human-animal (purusha-medha). Both hymn and ritual were composed a thousand years before the composition of The Gita. Both can be taken literally or metaphorically. The literal approach associates them with human sacrifice: this idea appealed to the nineteenth-century European Orientalist notion of exotic India, of the 'noble savage'. The metaphorical approach draws attention to the human ability to give meaning to each other, and nourish each other emotionally and intellectually. In the Upanishads, it is common to equate food (anna) with meaning and identity (atma): food is what all living creatures seek; meaning is what only humans seek. The same idea is visualized in Chapter 11 of The Gita, when Arjuna notices Krishna's universal form consuming humans.

Krishna, I can see the warriors of their side and ours rushing into your mouth, being crushed between your teeth, entering your blazing mouth like rivers running into the ocean. Entire worlds hurry to your mouth to be destroyed, like moths to flame. You devour all the worlds with your many fiery mouths.—*Bhagavad Gita: Chapter 11, verses 26 to 30 (paraphrased).*

This vision taken literally can be terrifying, as Krishna appears as a predator, even a villain. But when the blindfold of judgement is removed, Arjuna understands the metaphor: by consuming the Pandavas and Kauravas, Krishna is giving them value. He is declaring that they nourish him, thus extending the logic. Arjuna realizes that he exists as 'food' for those around him. He brings value to his brothers, to his cousins, to the world at large. They are also 'food' for him. They nourish him, give him value and purpose. This consumption is both material and psychological. Withdrawal from the battle would mean denying the others meaning.

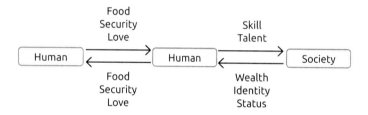

Man as Food

But while Krishna eats, he is not really hungry. He declares that he is immortal, and so does not fear death, and does not need food. He declares he is infinite, and so he cannot be separated from the other—he is both the eater and the eaten. He eats, not because he is hungry, but to make the other feel valued. And he allows himself to be eaten to nourish the other. In other words, he is a yogi who does not seek meaning from outside; he gets his identity from within, from the atma.

> 'Arjuna, I am the ritual, I am the exchange, the offering, the herb, the chant, the butter, the fire, all that is offered.'—*Bhagavad Gita: Chapter 4, Verse 24 (paraphrased)*.

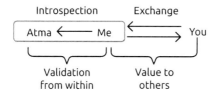

Meaning From Within and Outside

Before the start of the Kuru-kshetra war, the Pandavas and the Kauravas once came to Krishna for help. Krishna offered them all that he had: one could have Narayani, his fully equipped army, and the other could have Narayana, his own unarmed self. The Kauravas chose Narayani while Pandavas chose Krishna. Narayani is Krishna's resources, all that he has. Narayana is all that he is. The former is tangible and measurable, and even outlasts death, hence preferred by the Kauravas over the latter.

The Kauravas mimic the behaviour of the asuras in the Puranas who prefer Brahma's boons to Brahma. The Kauravas and the asuras seek material nourishment, not emotional or intellectual nourishment. They seek 'his' not 'him'.

During a yagna, Narayani is exchanged: 'mine' becomes 'yours'. If this is done with consideration of the hungers and fears of the devata, then the yajamana has a relationship with the devata. If, the yajamana, is only focussed on his hungers and fears, then it is simply a transaction with the devata where more value is given to 'what you have' rather than 'who you are'.

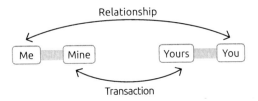

Relationships and Transactions

Economists value the Narayani called wealth. Educationists value the Narayani called literacy. Politicians value the Narayani called power. Feminists value the Narayani called gender. Employers value the Narayani called skill. Physicians and surgeons value the Narayani called the body. Society is not interested in Narayana—what a person is: his hungers, his fears, or his potential. Things matter more than thoughts. Property becomes a substitute for feelings. Hence the purpose of life has become all about acquiring more and more Narayani. In The Gita, the concept of Narayani is presented in Chapter 13 as kshetra.

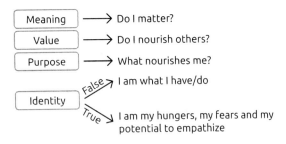

Meaning (artha)

My Gita

Kshetra literally means a farm, a manmade space created by domesticating nature. In nature, there are no farms. Humans turn forest into farms to produce food. They mark out the boundaries, uproot the trees, clear the land, till the soil, sow the seeds, permit growth of crops and get rid of weeds. The farmer protects the farm and the produce fiercely. Born of his effort, he claims ownership of the farm: 'It is mine'. Other humans acknowledge it: 'It is yours.' Thus, the farm becomes his property. The property nourishes him, physically and psychologically. Physically it gives him food. Psychologically it gives him an identity of a farmer. He feels entitled. The property also grants him immortality, since he can bequeath it to his family, who are also his own.

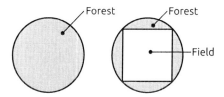

Field versus Farm

In nature, there is no property. There is territory that animals fight over to ensure they have enough food supply. Territories cannot be inherited; they go to the strongest. Properties, however, can be inherited. The son gets the estate, the title and all the accompanying wealth, power and status from the father.

In the Ramayana, during the forest exile, when Lakshmana draws a line (rekha) around Sita's hut, he very publicly defines what is Ram's kshetra. Within the Lakshmana-rekha, Sita is Ram's wife; outside she is just a woman for the taking. Kshetra thus is an artificial construction, not a natural phenomenon.

Me and Mine

In Chapter 2, Krishna speaks of deha and dehi, the body and resident of the body. In Chapter 13, he speaks of kshetra and kshetragna, the property and proprietor. Another word used for kshetragna is kshetri. The resident transforms into the proprietor as the body expands to include titles and estate.

> Arjuna, the wise know the body as a farm and the mind as its farmer. This body, your farm, is constituted by the five elements that make up your flesh, your notion of who you are, your intelligence, your emotions, your sense organs, your response organs and the pastures that your senses graze upon, and all that causes pain and pleasure, attraction and revulsion.—*Bhagavad Gita, Chapter 13, verses 1 to 6 (paraphrased).*

In the Upanishads, kshetra is seen as the third layer of deha. It is the outermost layer, known as the social layer (karana-sharira). Then comes the physical layer (sthula-sharira) and finally the mental layer (sukshma-sharira). Social body refers to property inherited at birth or earned through effort. Physical body, container of beauty, skills and talent, is the flesh, which is acquired at birth. The mental body comprises our sensations, our feelings and our ideas and, most importantly, how we imagine ourselves. The mental body is the resident-owner, dehi-kshetragna. When the mind outgrows its dependence on kshetra and deha, it discovers atma. When we die, the deha is cremated. We live behind kshetra. The dehi/kshetragna/atma move on to the next life if still dependent on deha and kshetra, else it breaks free entirely from the unending waves of rebirths and re-deaths.

	Karna	Arjuna
Mental body	Ambitious	Insecure
Physical body	Archer	Archer
Social body	Servant	Prince

Three Bodies

In the Mahabharata, both Arjuna and Karna are talented archers. In fact, Karna has the distinct advantage of being born with celestial armour and earrings that cling to his body like flesh. But society respects Arjuna more than Karna, because Arjuna is seen as a prince of the Kuru clan and legal heir of Hastinapur, while Karna is seen as a charioteer's son, even after he is made a warrior and king by Duryodhana who admires his talent with the bow. For society, kshetra is more important than deha. No one cares about dehi.

So much value is given to the external that neither Arjuna nor Karna look within for identity. Arjuna derives his identity from his talent (archery), his inherited title (Pandu's son) and the estate he cultivates (Indra-prastha). Karna also derives his identity from his talent (archery), but he distances himself from his inherited title (charioteer's son) and strives to earn new titles (Duryodhana's friend) and estates (Anga). Identity based on what we have is aham, not atma.

The karana-sharira is an outcome of karma—past karma and present karma. What we attract naturally towards us is based on past karma. What we bring forcibly towards us is based on current karma. Arjuna's royal status is based on past karma, as is Karna's association with charioteers. Neither of them chose this. It was an accident of birth. Archery is their inborn talent that they inherited and honed with effort. Arjuna's association with Indra-prastha, and Karna's association with Anga, are the outcome of effort. Or are they? Were these properties supposed to come into their lives after a struggle? It is not easy to answer these questions. Karana-sharira remains mysterious. It travels with us from our previous lives into our next lives, gathering impressions of karma, keeping a record of debts that we are obliged to repay.

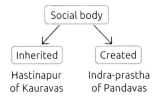

Two Types of Social Bodies

Property and proprietors exist only in culture (sanskriti), not nature (prakriti). The divide between nature and culture, forest and field, is a consistent theme in Hinduism. In the Sama Veda, where hymns of the Rig Veda are put to melody, songs are classified into two: songs of the forest (aranya-gana) and songs

My Gita

of the settlement (grama-gana). What applies to the forest does not apply to the settlement: in the forest, the rules of man are meaningless, not so in the settlement. The Pandavas realize this during their exile.

In the forest, Arjuna shoots a wild boar and discovers it has been struck by another arrow, that of a tribal, or kirata. As entitled prince, he claims the boar as his. But the kirata does not recognize him as prince, and demands that the two fight over it like two alpha males fighting over a territory or a mate: the winner takes the prize. In the forest, Arjuna realizes his social body does not matter. Only his strength and skill do.

In the final year of exile, the Pandavas have to hide, keep their identities secret. As per the agreement with the Kauravas, if discovered in this year, they would have to go back to the forest for another twelve years. During this period, they take employment as servants in the palace of Virata, king of Matsya. They discover for the first time what it means to be a servant, when one has nothing to offer other than skills and so become the objects of constant abuse and exploitation.

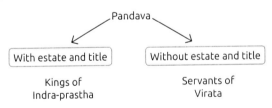

The Pandavas as Princes and as Servants

Without their titles or estates, the Pandavas had no value. To get back their kshetra from the Kauravas naturally became the purpose of their life. Krishna's conversation with Arjuna, however, is not to enable this. It is to teach Arjuna that while society may value him for his kshetra, while securing that kshetra for his family should be his purpose as property is vital for his family's survival, he must not derive his identity from property. Identity comes from within, not without: from kshetri, not kshetra, from dehi, not deha.

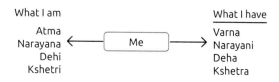

What I am		What I have
Atma		Varna
Narayana	Me	Narayani
Dehi		Deha
Kshetri		Kshetra

Source of human meaning

You may value me for what I have and what I do. But I am not what I have or what I do. If you love me, focus on who I am: my hungers and my fears, and my potential to focus on who you are.

15.

You and I compare

Animals and plants do not measure or compare. They fight for as much territory as they need to survive. But humans can measure the size of their property and hence compare. This ability to measure and delimit reality is called **maya**. Maya establishes the structures, divisions and hierarchies of society, in which we locate our identity and the identities of those whom we compare ourselves with. We can qualify these yardsticks as unwanted illusions, or necessary delusions, that imagination can easily overturn. While the word maya is used a lot in the Vedas and The Gita in the sense of the magical powers of the human mind, its role in measurement and construction of human perception was elaborated much later in the Vedantic tradition that flowered about a thousand years ago.

Kshetra demands clear demarcation of what is mine and what is yours. In the Mahabharata, the Kauravas do not consider the Pandavas to be theirs, which is why Dhritarashtra refers to his sons as 'mine', and refers to his nephews not as his brother's sons but merely as 'Pandu's sons'. He considers both Hastinapur and Indra-prastha as Kuru-kshetra, belonging to the Kauravas, and sees the Pandavas as intruders.

The Pandava brothers consist of two sets of brothers borne by Pandu's two wives—three sons from Kunti and the twins from Madri. During the gambling match, Yudhishthira first gambles away Nakula, the son of Madri, indicating that he considers his stepbrother a little less his than Arjuna and Bhima. Later in the forest, when his four brothers die after drinking the water of the poisoned lake, and he is given the option of bringing only one of his brothers back, he chooses Nakula over Kunti's sons, indicating a shift in mindset: he realizes that a good king is one who expands his boundaries and turns even half-brothers, cousins and strangers into relatives.

In the Bhagavata, Krishna never talks to Balarama as his half-brother. There is no division between them. He does not treat his biological parents, Devaki and Vasudeva, as different from his foster parents, Yashoda and Nanda. In the Mahabharata, however, Karna never identifies himself with his foster parents, as they are charioteers and he aspires to be an archer.

This ability to create a boundary, and shift boundaries, between what I consider mine and what I do not consider mine comes from maya, the unique human ability to measure, delimit and apportion. The word maya is commonly translated as illusion, or delusion, but its root 'ma' means to 'to measure'. Maya is the delusion when we look at the world through the filter of measurement.

Measurement helps us to label and categorize all things around us in order to make sense of the world. We organize the world into understandable units, such as the periodic table of all elements in chemistry, or the various taxonomies of plants and animals and diseases in biology. Measurement is key to science, to understanding nature. However, with measurement also comes judgement—we not only classify, we also compare, create hierarchies, hence compete. This gives rise to conflict.

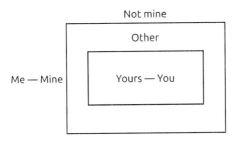

Mine and Not Mine

The kshetragna cannot be compared to anything, as it is infinite and immortal. The atma within you is the same as the atma within me. But if you and I are not in touch with our atma, and we do not empathize with each other's hungers and fears and potential, we will compare our respective kshetras to locate ourselves in a hierarchy and give ourselves an identity.

When value comes from what I have, then the more I have, the more valuable I become. And so I want to ensure that I have more than you. That is why in the Ramayana, conflict begins with comparison. Kaikeyi hates being junior queen. So she wants her husband, Dasharatha, king of Ayodhya, to crown her son as heir, so that as queen mother she can dominate over the senior queen, Kaushalya.

The Mahabharata also speaks of conflict generated by comparison. Pandu, king of Hastinapur, retires to the forest following a curse that prevents him from mating with his wives and fathering children. His two wives, Kunti and Madri, follow him to the forest and Kunti tells him of a way to bypass the curse. 'I have a mantra by which I can invoke a deva and compel him to give me a child.' Pandu does not use this way out until he hears that Gandhari, the blindfolded wife of his blind elder brother, who is now regent of Hastinapur, is pregnant. The competitive spirit kicks in. He tells Kunti to take advantage of her mantra. She calls upon Yama, Vayu and Indra and begets Yudhishtira, Bhima and Arjuna. Pandu asks for more sons, but Kunti says she cannot use the mantra more than three times. So Pandu begs her to share it with his second wife, Madri. Kunti does as advised but is quite irritated when, using one mantra, Madri begets two children by simply calling the Ashwin Kumars, who always come in a pair. She refuses to give Madri the mantra again as she wants to be the mother of more children than Madri. On learning of the birth of Pandu's children, Gandhari is so upset that she gets her midwife to strike her pregnant belly with an iron bar and force the child out. What she delivers instead is a ball of flesh, cold as iron. She divides and transforms this, with the aid of Rishi Vyasa, to get a hundred sons, ninety-eight more than Madri, ninety-seven more than Kunti, to establish her superiority, and hence her husband's.

Humans very instinctively evaluate and compare. In The Gita, when Krishna distinguishes between asuras and devas, we position devas as better than asuras. When Krishna speaks of the three yogas, we wonder which is superior: karma, bhakti or gyana. When Krishna speaks of the three guna, our minds position sattva as better than rajas and rajas as better than tamas. When Krishna speaks of the four varnas, we place Brahmins over Kshatriyas, Kshatriyas over Vaishyas and Vaishyas over Shudras. This is all because of maya.

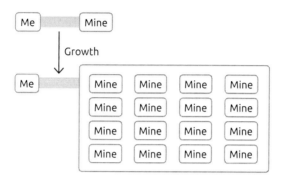

Materialism

In nature, there is a pecking order. But animal domination is not aspirational; it is necessary for survival. Domination ensures they get access to more food. Humans dominate to grant themselves value, and feel good about themselves. Social structures are designed to grant humans identity. They are invariably based on comparsion of the social body, what we have: wealth, knowledge, contacts and skills. Kaikeyi, Gandhari, Kunti, Pandu, all compete on the basis of their sons. Who has more children? Whose children are stronger, or smarter? Whose son is king? I am better than you because what I have is bigger or better or faster or richer or prettier or cheaper or nicer or nastier than yours. By comparing our titles and estates we validate ourselves, make ourselves feel significant and relevant.

Arjuna, the veil of measurements and hierarchies deludes all those who try to make sense of this material world with its three innate tendencies, unless they accept the reality of me, who cannot be measured or compared. Those trapped in this delusion of imagined boundaries behave like demons.—*Bhagavad Gita: Chapter 7, verses 13 to 15 (paraphrased).*

Maya distracts us from infinity and immortality, from the feeling that the world can continue without us. Maya makes us feel important.

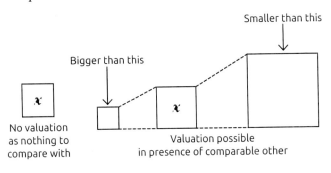

Measurement

In the Puranas, there is a sage called Narada who travels from house to house comparing people's talents, titles and estates: his wife is more beautiful, his son is more talented, his daughter is married to a richer man, he has more followers, his kingdom is larger, she has more jewellery... This comparison evokes feelings of inadequacy and jealousy in people. It fuels ambition and ignites conflicts. Having created the tension, Narada walks away chanting, 'Narayana! Narayana!' But no one hears this. They are too consumed by Narayani (kshetra) to worry about Narayana (kshetragna).

Narada did not want to marry and produce children. He wanted to be a hermit. This annoyed his father, Brahma, who cursed that Narada would wander in material reality forever. This is why Narada spends all his time mocking householders who value themselves on the basis of Narayani, rather than paying attention to the Narayana within.

Once, Narada came to Dwaraka and tried to spark a quarrel in Krishna's house. Krishna's wives asked him what he wanted. 'I want you to give me your husband,' said the mischievous quarrel-monger. The queens said that they could not give their husband. 'Then give me something that you value as equal or more than him.' The queens agreed. Krishna was put on a weighing pan and the queens were asked to put something they valued equal to or more than Krishna on the other pan. Satyabhama put all her gold. But it made no difference; Krishna was heavier. Rukmini then placed a single sprig of tulsi on the pan and declared it to be the symbol of her love for Krishna. Instantly, the weighing scale titled in her favour and Narada had to be satisfied, not with Satyabhama's gold but with Rukmini's tulsi sprig, symbol of devotion.

This story does not make logical sense: how can a sprig of tulsi weigh more than Krishna? But it makes metaphorical sense. When the sprig is given meaning by human imagination, it becomes heavier than anything else. Human imagination can attribute any value to anything. A dog does not differentiate between gold and stone. But humans see gold as money and can turn a rock into a deity. This is the power of imagination. We cannot measure infinity, as Satyabhama realized when she tried to weigh Krishna against gold. But we can lock infinity in a symbol, as Rukmini did.

Measuring Krishna

Arjuna, I am infinite and immortal and yet, respecting the ways of nature, I bind myself in finite and mortal measurable existence.—*Bhagavad Gita: Chapter 4, Verse 6 (paraphrased).*

Thus in temples, a rock (pinda, linga) or a fossil (shaligrama) can represent the formless divine. It is our imagination that gives value to things, purpose to an activity and identity to a thing. We can give meaning or wipe it away. That is the power of maya. It is the power of God bestowed upon us humans. Maya is often called magic, for it has the power to make the world meaningful, transform every word into a metaphor, every image into a symbol.

Human Ability to Attribute Value

Maya can divide and separate, cause conflict by comparison. It can also turn anything around, change reality for us, for our mind can give meaning to anything. For example, a hermit may see sex and violence as horrible, while a householder may see sex and violence as necessary, even pleasurable. Maya can divide the world. It can also unite the world, serve as the glue to a relationship, as we expand our boundaries to include whoever we wish. Duryodhana's inclusion of Karna, a charioteer's son, but exclusion of Arjuna, his royal cousin, is a case in point. That is why, in colloquial parlance, maya also means 'affection', that which binds relationships together.

When people say in Hindi, 'Sab maya hai,' it is commonly translated as 'the world is an illusion or a delusion'. What it means is that the world can be whatever we imagine it to be—valuable or valueless, fuelling ambition or cynicism.

In Vedanta there is a popular Sanskrit phrase, 'Jagad mithya, brahma satya!' It is translated as 'the world is a mirage and only divinity is real'. 'Mithya' means a measured limited truth created through maya. So the phrase can also be translated as 'the material world is an incomplete reality, made complete by imagination and language'. We can manufacture depression and joy in our lives by the way we measure, delimit and apportion the world. The world itself has no intrinsic measurement.

> Arjuna, the wise look at a learned man, an outcaste, a cow, an elephant or a dog with an equal eye. A person who sees equality in all, and is equanimous in all pleasant and unpleasant situations, has realized the divine for the divine is impartial too.—*Bhagavad Gita: Chapter 5, verses 18 to 20 (paraphrased).*

Do you derive your identity by comparing yourself with me? This is maya, a necessary delusion without which society cannot function. It can uplift you with inspiration, depress you with jealousy or grant you peace by revealing how different you are from me.

16.

You and I cling

If I am what I own, then I cling to what I have to secure my value in the world. And when you try to take it from me, I feel violated, for my identity is attached to my property. In this chapter we shall explore **moha**, an attachment to boundaries that separates 'mine' from 'not mine' and transforms violence into violation. Violation is psychological violence, that may or may not be associated with physical violence, and the pain is even more searing, for it involves the very invalidation of our identity. It is directly proportional to our relationship with all that we consider 'mine'. The idea of attachment flows through The Gita and plays a key role in Hindu hermit and householder traditions, meriting a separate chapter.

All his life the Buddha spoke about the impermanence of things (anikka, in Pali) and the notion of non-self (anatta, in Pali). Yet, after he died and his body was cremated, the remains of his body (tooth, hair, nails, bones) were collected by his disciples and worshipped as relics placed in stupas. Chaityas were built to enshrine the stupas and around the chaityas came up the viharas where monks lived. The monks could not let the Buddha slip away into oblivion. They clung to his physical remains, despite his explicit instructions not to do so, seeking permanence of the mortal remains of the teacher who expounded on life's impermanence. The story goes that when the Buddha was dying, his disciples wept and wondered how they would live without their master. The Buddha then realized that he had hoped to be a raft that takes people across the river of sorrow, but people chose to make him a palanquin that they wanted to carry around and be burdened with forever. He wanted to liberate them; they wanted to fetter themselves.

This is one of the ironies of Buddhism. This irony exists even in Hindu monastic traditions, where monks cling to the bodily remains of their teacher, and rather than cremate the corpse, they mummify it with salt, bury it and build a memorial over it, so that the teacher can be venerated forever. This memorial is called a samadhi, encasing the mortal remains of the hermit who voluntarily gave up his property (kshetra) initially and his body (deha) eventually.

In nature, there are natural forces of attraction and repulsion, even between two objects. Plants and animals are drawn to food and shun threats. Over and above this, humans cling (raga) to property (kshetra) that grants them value in society. We convince ourselves that our social body defines our identity. To be told that

My Gita

our true identity is intangible and immeasurable (kshetragna) seems quite unbelievable, as it can never be proven, only believed. So we cling to goals or rules, to property or relatives, to titles or ideas, and fight over them as animals fight over territory. Animals fight because the survival of their body depends on it. Humans fight as the survival of their identity (aham) depends on it. Clinging is comforting. Insecurity fuels desire (kama) for more, and so acquiring more becomes the purpose of life. We get angry (krodha) when we don't get them, become greedy (lobha) once we get them, get attached (moha) to them, become intoxicated with pride (mada) because we possess things, feel jealous of those who have more and insecure around those who have less (matsarya). Material reality thus enchants us and crumples our mind several times over. These are called the six obstacles (ari-shad-varga) that prevent the mind from expanding, the aham from transforming into atma and discovering bhagavan.

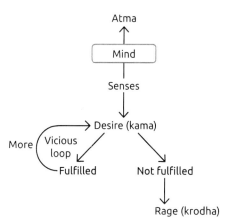

Kama and Krodha

Arjuna, from aggressive material tendencies is born desire in the senses, in the heart and the head. Desire is insatiable and if not indulged can result in rage. Desire and rage can block all wisdom, as smoke masks fire, dust masks mirrors and the womb masks a baby.—*Bhagavad Gita: Chapter 3, verses 37 to 40 (paraphrased).*

We also shun (dvesha) things out of fear. We avoid taking ownership, responsibility or proprietorship in fear. We are terrified of heartbreak, and so refuse to fall in love. We are terrified of failing, and so avoid struggles. We are terrified of the outcome, and so refuse to take any action. We clearly demarcate what is mine and what is not mine. If attraction of things makes us householders, and revulsion of things makes us hermits, then neither is actually wise, as neither accepts reality. As householders, we wish we expand the mine, sometimes at the cost of yours. As hermits, we want to shun even what is mine and reject all that is yours.

Reality is allowing things to come to us naturally and not seeking things that do not come to us naturally. Wisdom is bearing the fruit we are supposed to bear and not wanting to bear fruit that we cannot bear. Depending on its guna, a tree bears mango fruit; this is not ambition or desire, it is simply realization of potential. If we expect a mango tree to bear apples, then problems start. We do not respect guna. A human being can become a king, a warrior, a merchant, a servant or a poet, depending on his qualities and potential. If we try to change a warrior into a poet because we are revolted by war or attracted to poetry, then we cause tension and suffering. Hinduism therefore does not talk of conversion, only realization of potential. To let our potential be realized without deriving our identity from it, or without denying its existence, is the hallmark of wisdom.

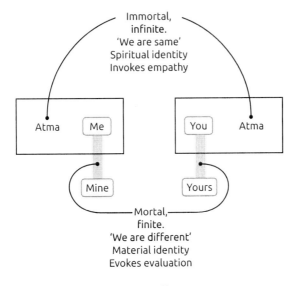

Same or Different

Arjuna, all beings follow their nature. Even the wise act according to their nature. What is the value of restraint then? Your senses will naturally be drawn to or revolted by things around the body. Do not let them beguile you and distract you from discovering yourself.—*Bhagavad Gita: Chapter 3, Verses 33 and 34 (paraphrased).*

To want nothing (shunya) is as delusional as to want everything (ananta). The wise want nothing but accept whatever comes their way, letting it pass when it is time to part ways. Ram is not Ram because of what he has on account of his birth (royal status) or because of what he has achieved (killing Ravana). Even without these possessions or achievements, he would still be Ram.

> Arjuna, he who identifies himself with the atma engages with the material pleasures without attachment or revulsion, and so is always at peace.—*Bhagavad Gita: Chapter 2, Verse 64 (paraphrased).*

In nature there is violence. In culture there is also violation, for things are not just things, they are markers of identity. Animals do not feel violated when their territories are invaded, or their bodies attacked. They fight back for survival, but there is no morality attached to the violence. Amongst humans, since we identify ourselves through things, an attack on what we consider ours becomes a violation of our identity. This is unique to the human species.

Humans can violate another human by attacking their social body (kshetra) without even touching their physical body (deha). The pain is felt in the mind. The damage is done to the mental body (aham) that gets its value from the external body. Thus, when a passerby scratches our car, we feel hurt. The scratch on the car does not physically hurt us, but we feel emotionally disturbed. We are violated, even though there is no violence, for our car is our property, a part of our social body, that contributes to our identity. Human society conditions us to cling to things around us, gain identity through relationships, titles and estates. In other words, culture celebrates moha and mada.

Mada refers to the fluid that oozes out of the temples of a sexually aroused bull elephant. This state is called 'musth', when the animal seems fully aroused and intoxicated and can attack anything that comes in its way. It is determined to get what it wants. From mada comes the word madira, which means wine. From mada comes the word Madan, which refers to Kama, god of lust.

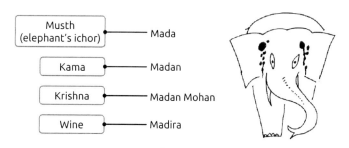

Mada: Literal and Metaphorical

But Krishna is also called Madan Mohan. He even turns into the enchantress Mohini. Vishnu and all his incarnations are associated with a lot of sexual and violent behaviour. But these are distinguished from attachment and revulsion, for Vishnu's actions are designed to give value to those around him, not derive value for himself.

In the Ramayana, Ravana demonstrates this mada when he refuses to give up Sita, even after Ram kills his son, Indrajit, and his brother, Kumbhakarna, and Ram's army of monkeys set Lanka aflame. He clings to Sita and refuses to turn to Ram. He finds meaning in Sita because he sees her as Ram's property. He wants to violate Ram by claiming Sita, whom he views as Ram's property. Ram, though, does not see Sita as his property, but as his responsibility. Ram, however, does not seek to violate Ravana; he simply wants to rescue Sita, for her security is the responsibility of the Raghu clan, into which she was given in marriage. He fights not because he wants what is 'his' back, but because he refuses to value 'her'. In fact, after the battle is over, he does not expect her to follow him; he offers her a choice to go wherever she wishes and she chooses to return with him to Ayodhya.

In the Mahabharata, when Krishna kills Kansa, he simply kills a man who threatens his life. It is an act of defence, not offence. This is violence, not violation. There is no desire to dominate Kansa, to hurt or humiliate him. However, Jarasandha feels violated, because Kansa to him is his social body, his property, on whom his self-esteem rests. He attacks Mathura, intent on killing Krishna, and burns the city to the ground. This act is violation, adharma. Later, with the help of Bhima, Krishna gets Jarasandha killed. Again the desire is not to hurt or humiliate Jarasandha or dominate him, but to enable Yudhishthira to be king, make him sovereign, something that Jarasandha would not have allowed.

Duryodhana's decision to disrobe Draupadi and not return Pandava land comes from the desire to violate the Pandavas. By violating them, he nourishes his aham. Krishna does not want Arjuna to do the same. He wants Arjuna to fight without seeking to violate his enemies. He does not indulge Bhima's bloodlust. Violence is unavoidable in the world, for it enables the living to nourish themselves, but violation is nothing but a vulgar indulgence of aham for its own self-aggrandizement.

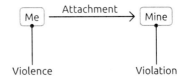

Violence and Violation

In the Bhagavata Purana, there is the story of Gajendra, the king of elephants, who in a state of 'musth', enters a pond of lotus flowers to sport with his harem of cow elephants, when suddenly a crocodile grabs his leg and drags him underwater. Gajendra tries to escape, but in vain, as no one comes to his rescue. Lost, helpless, he prays to Vishnu, who appears and strikes the crocodile away.

This is a metaphor for a mind consumed by passion, seeking gratification in the material world and suddenly finding the world turning against it, becoming even more hostile. The solution is not to fight harder, for that only leads to the crocodile tightening its grip. The solution is to stop fighting and have faith that another force will intervene.

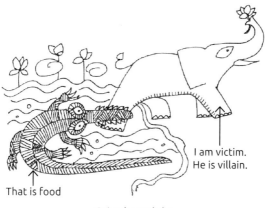

That is food

I am victim.
He is villain.

Gajendra Moksha

In the story, Gajendra chooses to see himself as a victim and the crocodile as a villain. If he wins, he will be hailed as a hero and if he loses, he will still be hailed as a martyr who died trying. But the observer can see that the crocodile is no villain: it looks upon

Gajendra either as threat, or as food. The crocodile's violence is not violation. But Gajendra sees it as violation, as he is in a state of mada, seeing himself as the king of elephants, master of all the cow elephants, loved and feared by all, and not as an animal, prey to a predator. Rather than imagining violation, being heroic or acting like a martyr, Vedic wisdom suggests that we recognize maya, moha and mada at work, stop struggling over imagined boundaries, and have faith that life is shaped by many other forces, not just the ones we have control over.

As long as we don't have faith, we carry the burden of solving all problems. We will be impatient and fight and cling. Wisdom is enjoying things that drift in and letting go of things that drift away, like watching the waves drift in and out of the beach.

> Arjuna, those who keep thinking of property get attached to it and crave it relentlessly, which causes frustration, which leads to anger, then confusion, then loss of memory, then loss of intelligence, and eventually destruction.—*Bhagavad Gita: Chapter 2, verses 62 and 63 (paraphrased).*

There is no violation in nature. Only violence. Violation follows when we grant meaning to things and derive our identity from them. We are attached to property as long as we are disconnected from atma.

17.

You and I can be generous

Moksha is liberation from the fear that makes us cling. Only when we let go can we be materially and emotionally and intellectually generous. This alternative to the trap of rebirth is offered by Krishna in Chapter 8 of The Gita. The tug-of-war between the inner world of liberation and the outer world of entrapment is elaborated in Chapter 15 of The Gita. In Chapter 18 of The Gita, Krishna clarifies whether letting go involves giving up of action itself, or giving up the expectation for a particular reaction.

Chapter 15 begins with a spectacular visual to explain the world we live in.

> Arjuna, there is a banyan tree that grows upside down, its roots in the sky and its trunk below. The wise know that Veda constitutes its leaves. The branches go up and down, as a consequence of nature's tendencies, nourished by experiences. The aerial roots that grow down are actions born of desire that bind it to the realm of men. Wisdom alone can cut these downward roots, enabling discovery of the reverse banyan tree, with its primal roots, before enchantment of the senses began and obscured the view.—*Bhagavad Gita: Chapter 15, verses 1 to 4 (paraphrased).*

The banyan tree is sacred to the Hindus. It symbolizes immortality (akshaya). But it is unique in that it has primary roots and secondary roots. The latter grow from its branches and eventually become so thick that it becomes impossible to distinguish them from the main tree trunk.

In this verse, Krishna visualizes a banyan tree growing from the sky, its primary roots rising up into the sky, its secondary roots growing down to the earth. Thus, it is being nourished from above and below. The primary root rising from the sky is nourished by inner mental reality. The secondary roots going down to the earth are nourished by external material reality.

The tree is who we are. We are nourished from within as well as without. Within is the atma that is immortal and infinite, and so does not suffer from the anxieties of the mortal and the finite. It is neither hungry nor frightened, nor does it yearn for validation.

My Gita

Without is the world of things, people, our relationships, our desires and frustrations. When we derive value from the outside, we assume that our identity is the anxious aham. So Krishna advises Arjuna to use the axe of knowledge (gyana) to cut down all secondary roots, take refuge in the primary root of atma and liberate himself. This is moksha, liberation, where we no longer seek validation from the outside, but feel eternally validated from the inside. Moksha is liberation from fear.

> Arjuna, he who truly understands the truth of mind, matter and material tendencies is liberated from rebirth, no matter what his lifestyle.—*Bhagavad Gita: Chapter 13, Verse 23 (paraphrased).*

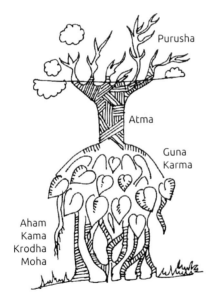

Upside-down Banyan Tree

You and I can be generous

219

The Buddha spoke of desire (tanha, in Pali) as the cause of all suffering. Hence he advised people to shun desire by accepting the truth of life—nothing is fixed or permanent, not even identity.

The Gita, however, speaks of two kinds of identity: external identity or aham, based on property, and internal identity or atma, based on wisdom. Aham is the fruit of fear. Atma is the fruit of wisdom. Aham is the seed of kama, krodha, lobha, moha, mada and matsarya. Atma results in moksha. With atma, we don't cling. We don't seek control. We simply let go. We become generous. And we allow.

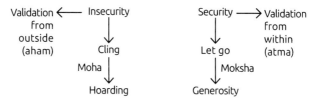

Mada to Moksha

> Arjuna, one who gives up conceit and ownership and craving, in other words the sense of 'I', 'mine' and 'me', will always find peace.—*Bhagavad Gita: Chapter 2, Verse 71 (paraphrased).*

How we give things away to others is a good indicator of moksha. In a yagna, a svaha can be either dakshina, bhiksha or daan. Dakshina is payment for service received. In other words, with dakshina we repay a debt (rin), complete a transaction and are free from all obligations. Bhisksha is charity, a good deed (punya) for which we expect something in exchange—respect, admiration, acknowledgment or blessings. Daan is giving away things without expecting anything in return. There is no expectation from the devata. No obligation is imposed upon him. There is no talk of debt, or fruit of action. In The Gita, daan can be sattvik, rajasik or tamasik. Dakshina and bhiksha are equated with rajasik daan.

> Arjuna, charity that is given to a suitable candidate at the right time and place without expecting him to give anything in return is sattvik; charity given unwillingly or to get something in return is rajasik; charity given without thought, at the wrong time and place to unsuitable candidates out of contempt and disrespect is tamasik.—*Bhagavad Gita: Chapter 17, verses 20 to 22 (paraphrased).*

This is elaborated in two stories, one from the Mahabharata and one from the Bhagavata. Both stories have the same beginning but very different endings.

Two childhood friends, out of affection for each other, promise to share all that they possess even when they grow into adulthood. One is the son of a nobleman, the other the son of a priest. Fortune favours the nobleman's son, not the priest's son. Reduced to abject poverty, the desperate but hesitant priest's son decides to approach his rich friend.

In the Mahabharata, Drupada, king of Panchala, insults the pauper Drona for assuming that promises of childhood matter in adulthood. He tells Drona to earn a service fee, or beg for alms, as befits a priest, rather than demand a share of the royal fortune in the name of friendship, as if it was his right. Friendship can only exist between equals, he is told. A furious Drona leaves the palace, determined to become Drupada's equal—a decision that leads to a spiral of vendetta that culminates in the bloody carnage at Kuru-kshetra with Drona supporting the Kauravas and Drupada supporting the Pandavas.

In the Bhagavata, however, the pauper is Sudama and the king, Krishna. He is warmly welcomed and showered with lavish gifts by his rich friend.

Drupada does what a king is supposed to: lay down the law, tell Drona not to curry personal favours and advise him to behave instead in keeping with his role in society. As a priest, Drona can either ask for a fee (dakshina) if services are rendered, or for alms (bhiksha) if no services are rendered. Drupada, unfortunately, does not do darshan: he does not see that Drona is embarrassed by his need to ask for help, so hides his awkwardness by reminding Drupada of his childhood promise and 'demanding' his share. Drona also does not do darshan: he is too consumed by his poverty to notice that Drupada is a changed man, not the friend he once knew.

Sudama, on the other hand, despite being poor, is sensitive to the change of status over the years. He does darshan of Krishna and realizes his childhood friend may not recognize him, considering that years have passed and fortunes have changed. Despite his poverty, he carries a gift for Krishna: a packet of puffed rice saved by denying himself a few meals. Krishna also does darshan of Sudama, does not gloat over the latter's poverty but instead demands affection, even a gift, making Sudama realize he is still remembered and much loved. Sudama, overwhelmed by Krishna's generosity, asks for nothing, only to discover he is given everything.

Daan creates neither obligations nor expectations. It is an

indicator of moksha. Moksha follows when we do not feel we have to cling to our wealth or dominate people around us, because we do not derive our identity either from our wealth or our power. Wealth and power are just tools to make our life comfortable, and enable those around us.

Types of Charity

Another indicator of moksha is allowing, which is essentially emotional generosity. We notice that the Ramayana ends in tragedy, with Sita being banished. The Bhagavata also ends with heartbreak, with Krishna promising Radha, the gopikas and his mother, Yashoda, that he will come back, but not returning because of his obligations in Mathura. Even the Mahabharata ends with the realization of the curse hurled by Gandhari at Krishna for not preventing the death of her children, or those of Draupadi.

However, a sad Sita is not angry at Ram. She knows him and understands him well, his wisdom, his love, as well as the burdens of kingship that limit him. A heartbroken Radha is not angry at Krishna. She too understands that Krishna has to walk his path, and even she cannot be his companion, as she has familial obligations. A thoughtful Krishna is not angry at Gandhari. He understands her rage, her inability to take responsibility for her blindfold that contributed to her children's insecurity. Sita does not derive her identity from Ram. Radha does not derive her identity from Krishna. Krishna does not derive his identity from Gandhari. All three are immersed in dehi, atma, kshetri, brahmana and bhagavan. Each one is an inverted banyan tree, forever nourished by the sky, and forever nourishing the earth.

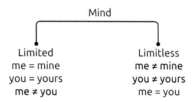

Limited | Limitless
me = mine | me ≠ mine
you = yours | you ≠ yours
me ≠ you | me = you

Limited to Limitlessness

Am I aware of my fears that make me greedy, stingy and controlling? What stops me from being generous materially, emotionally and intellectually? Liberation, essentially, is letting go of our insecurities that disconnect us from others.

18.

You and I matter to each other

Generosity presupposes the other. Monastic traditions focus on isolating the self from the other. The Gita, however, is the doctrine of the householder, not the hermit, the one who does not withdraw from the battlefield but fights without attachment or hatred, and so is neither violated nor violates. So while Buddhism speaks of anatta (absence of atma) and nirvana (oblivion of self), The Gita speaks of **atma-rati**, the joy of the immortal within, and **brahma-nirvana**, discovery of the other. This relationship between the self (jiva-atma) and the other (param-atma) forms the theme of this, our final chapter. Krishna introduces this idea early on in The Gita, as samadhi, in Chapter 2.

The Gita ends twice. First, with Krishna concluding his discourse.

> Arjuna, thus have I passed on the most secrets of
> secrets. Reflect on it and do as you wish. If you trust
> me completely and forsake all other paths, know that I
> will liberate you. Do not share this knowledge with the
> cynical, disdainful or disinterested. Those who share
> my words, I adore. Those who hear my words, even
> without understanding, are blessed with joy. I hope you
> have focussed on what I said. I hope this knowledge has
> shattered all delusion.—*Bhagavad Gita: Chapter 18,
> verses 63 to 72 (paraphrased).*

Arjuna confirms that his delusion is shattered and perspective
has been replaced by focus. He stands firm, with clear resolve and
no doubts, ready to do as told.

Sanjaya then concludes The Gita once again, expressing his
gratitude towards Vyasa for giving him the telepathic sight
that enabled him to hear Krishna's wise words and see Krishna's
magnificent form. Finally, in the last paragraph of The Gita, he
gives his personal take on Krishna's discourse.

> Where Krishna yokes the mind and Arjuna bears
> the bow, there is always fortune, success, dominion,
> stability, and law. That is my opinion.—*Bhagavad Gita:
> Chapter 18, Verse 78 (paraphrased).*

The difference between the two conclusions is stark. Krishna's
conclusion is rather psychological. Sanjaya's conclusion is very
material. Krishna offers Arjuna liberation from worldly fetters

(moksha) if Arjuna demonstrates faith in him by performing his role as a warrior, for the benefit of others, without any expectation of reward. Sanjaya believes Krishna's discourse holds five promises: fortune (shri), success (vijaya), dominion (bhu), stability (dhruva) and law (niti).

Arjuna's problem concerned only him, but Krishna's solution made him consider the other. Sanjaya is the other: the embodiment of the people of Hastinapur, who are overlooked in the war between the Pandavas and the Kauravas. For Sanjaya, The Gita is clearly a discourse meant for kings, who are expected to rule, take responsibility for their subjects and usher in peace and prosperity, rather than fight wars in self-indulgence. It is Sanjaya's appeal to Dhritarashtra to listen to The Gita and outgrow his own victimhood, that blinds him to the plight of others.

> Arjuna, whatever a noble person does, the world follows.
> —*Bhagavad Gita: Chapter 3, Verse 21 (paraphrased).*

Sanjaya's conclusion connects The Gita to Vaishnava mythology, for Shri and Bhu are proper nouns, referring to the two consorts of Vishnu, who is also known as Vijaya, the victorious one. Vishnu is visualized as the king of the universe, dressed in regal attire, attended by his queens: Shri, who embodies intangible fortunes such as sovereignty, glory, fame and charisma; and Bhu, who embodies tangible fortune like the earth and its treasures. Dhruva and Niti are Vishnu's devotees. Dhruva embodies the Pole Star, a child who wants to sit on Vishnu's lap, the only seat from which no one can pull him down, so that he can enjoy forever the affection of his divine father. Niti means law, that is of value only when it submits to the idea of Vishnu, which is dharma. With dharma, law will help the helpless and provide justice (nyaya) to all. Without dharma, law will be a tool for control, oppression and even sabotage.

We must remind ourselves of the period when the Ramayana and the Mahabharata came to be written. It was a time when kinship was giving way to kingship, meaning that communities included not just members of the same extended family or tribe (kin), but also members of other families, tribes and clans. Thus, the Ramayana is the story of the descendants of Ikshvaku engaging with outsiders—va-naras and rakshasas, who follow the jungle way. The Mahabharata is the story of tension within the Kuru clan itself, between two branches of the same family. The central issue in both epics is property: the thrones of Ayodhya, Kishkinda and Lanka in the Ramayana and the throne of Hastinapur in the Mahabharata. A good king was supposed to be one who took care of those he called his own (mama) as well as the rest (para). Ram is considered the greatest king, as he was more concerned about his kingdom and his family's reputation than his personal happiness. Krishna is considered the greatest kingmaker, as he shows the Pandavas that war is not about vengeance or ambition, it is about governance.

> Arjuna, there is nothing in the three worlds that I need to do or gain. Yet I work, for if I don't, others won't, and I will be the cause of confusion and destruction of all that has been created.—*Bhagavad Gita: Chapter 3, verses 22 to 24 (paraphrased).*

Vishnu reclines on the coils of a serpent. The image of a man seated under the hood of a serpent was typically used to depict leaders of monastic movements, such as the Buddha, for example, and the Jain tirthankara Parsva-nath. By making Vishnu occupy the same seat, the Puranas were communicating the message that a great man did not have to be a monk; he could also be king. The Gita is Vedic wisdom customized to the needs of king and kingdom. The kingdom needs the king but the king also needs the kingdom.

Under the Serpent Hood

The Gita introduces a subtle tension between the concepts of dharma and moksha. Dharma demands social engagement, while moksha is about social disengagement. Dharma is about building relationships. Moksha is about abandoning relationships. Dharma binds people to society. Moskha enables them to break free. In Vedic times, dharma was seen as appropriate for the youth, while moksha was seen as appropriate for the old, until followers of Buddhism and Jainism popularized the hermit culture and made it part of the mainstream, 2,500 years ago. In Vedic Hinduism, dharma is valued over moksha. But in Puranic Hinduism, moksha starts being valued over dharma, indicating the growing influence of Hindu monastic orders for the past 1,000 years.

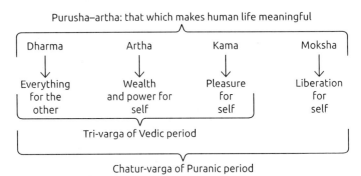

Inclusion of Moksha

Today we tend to see moksha as aspirational, almost the goal of Hindu life. But the concept of 'goal' makes sense only in one-life cultures, where existence has an expiry date. In rebirth cultures there are no expiry dates, hence no goals, only pursuits that make our endless life meaningful (purusha-artha). Originally three categories (tri-varga) of pursuit were identified: dharma, artha and kama, or social obligations, power and pleasure. Later, moksha was included as the fourth category (chatur-varga). A judge finds moksha to be the best of the three, while an observer is able to see the contextual appropriateness of each varga. While artha, kama and moksha focus primarily on the self, dharma alone is about the other. This is why Krishna keeps speaking about action, not inaction, engagement, not withdrawal.

Arjuna, when doing your duties, surrender yourself to me, offer all actions to be, and demonstrate equanimity no matter what the reaction—you will be liberated and at peace. Fix your mind on me and you will overcome all obstacles. Rely on your conceit and you will perish.—*Bhagavad Gita: Chapter 18, verses 56 to 58 (paraphrased).*

In Buddhist mythology, Siddhartha Gautama walks away from wife, child, father and kingdom, and goes into the forest to solve the problem of suffering. In the forest he encounters and defeats Mara, the demon of desire, to become the Buddha. In Hindu mythology, Mara is Kama, god of desire, and he is a friend of Indra, king of the devas. In Indra's abode, Amaravati, all desires are indulged. That is why it is called swarga, which means 'paradise'.

But Indra is insecure and restless; he fears that all his treasures will be taken away. He has no faith. No temples are built for Indra. Temples are built for Shiva instead, who opens his third eye and burns Kama to a heap of ash. Shiva's abode, Kailasa, is a mountain of stone covered with ice. Nothing grows here. Nothing can survive here. But it does not matter, for in Shiva's abode there is no desire, no hunger, hence no need for food.

In Shiva temples, Shiva is always associated with Shakti, the Goddess. She manifests as the trough (yoni) in which the solitary stone pillar (lingam) representing Shiva is made to stand. Shiva may withdraw from the world as a hermit, but she binds him to the earth, transforms him into a householder and makes him descend from the lofty inhospitable icy peaks of Kailasa to the riverside city of Kashi, full of markets and crematoriums. Here, the Goddess makes him aware of, and attentive to, the desires, hungers and fears of those who are not as resourceful, capable and accomplished as he. The self is made to empathize with the inadequacies of the other and feel love, not disdain. She is Kamakshi, whose eyes evoke desire. Through her desire is reborn, but located in the other. She is Paramita, the one who completes the self through the other (para/param). She is Annapoorna, who provides food for all, and he becomes Bhikshatan, the beggar, who begs for others. They create two children: the corpulent elephant-headed Ganesha and the mighty lance-bearing Kartikeya, embodiments of Shiva's grace as he acknowledges the human struggle with meaning and validation.

When Siddhartha Gautama finally returns from the forest, he is an enlightened teacher, not a wise husband, father, son or king. His wisdom causes detachment. In other words he returns, but does not reconnect. But in Hindu epics, return from the forest is always about reconnection. In the Ramayana, palace intrigues force Ram to go to the forest, where he discovers, and rejects, the ways of the jungle and returns to be a great king. In the Mahabharata, the Pandavas are born in the forest, and they return to the forest for the first time when their lives are threatened by the Kauravas, the second time after they gamble away their fortune and the third time after having ruled Hastinapur successfully for a very long time. With each return, they are wiser in the ways of society. While the forest teaches the Buddha to disconnect from all relationships, it enables the protagonists of the Ramayana and the Mahabharata to connect and be better at relationships.

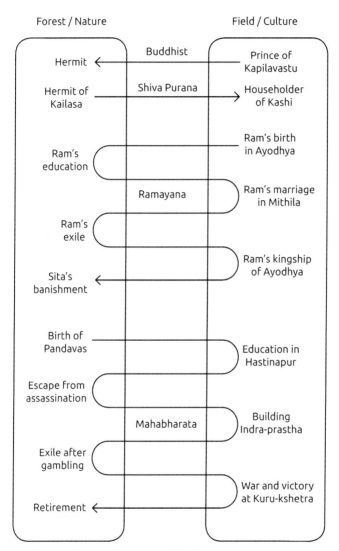

Forest / Nature   Field / Culture

Hermit ← Buddhist ← Prince of Kapilavastu

Hermit of Kailasa — Shiva Purana → Householder of Kashi

Ram's birth in Ayodhya

Ram's education

Ramayana — Ram's marriage in Mithila

Ram's exile

Ram's kingship of Ayodhya

Sita's banishment ←

Birth of Pandavas — Education in Hastinapur

Escape from assassination

Mahabharata — Building Indra-prastha

Exile after gambling

War and victory at Kuru-kshetra

Retirement ←

Return of the Buddha, Ram and the Pandavas from the Forest

You and I matter to each other

In Patanjali's Yoga-sutra, there are eight steps, which involve gradual withdrawal from society through the body, breath, senses and mind towards the atma. The final step is called samadhi, and is said to be a union with the infinite. For a hermit, samadhi refers to the ability to voluntarily leave his physical body and merge with the infinite. For the householder, it means something else. And the clue lies in the structure of the word itself.

The word 'samadhi' is based on two words: 'sama' that means the first beat of the musical cycle in Hindustani classical music and 'adi' that means primal origin. The hermit's journey begins by withdrawing from the other. The householder's journey ends by returning to the other. It is the return to the first beat. It is the return to the primal origin. It is about returning from the forest liberated (moksha) to reconnect (yoga) with those we left behind, those who are very different from us (brahma-nirvana).

The hermit may seek zero (shunya), hence withdrawal and oblivion (nirvana). But the householder can seek infinity (ananta), hence participation, which leads to expansion of the mind to accommodate the infinite truths of those around (brahma-nirvana). Krishna thus makes moksha an outcome of dharma.

> Arjuna, he who is at peace with himself, happy with himself, illuminated by the knowledge of the resident within all beings, finds supreme bliss everywhere. He does not see himself as separate and disconnected and finds happiness in the happiness of all creatures. This state of being exists everywhere for the wise one who has outgrown desire and rage.—*Bhagavad Gita: Chapter 5, verses 24 to 26 (paraphrased)*.

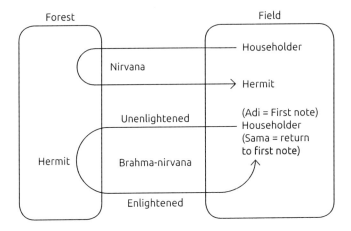

Return to the Origin

If Indra's heaven, swarga, is about indulging desires, hungers and fears, and Shiva's heaven, Kailasa, is about outgrowing desires, hungers and fears, then Vishnu's heaven, Vaikuntha, is about outgrowing desires, hungers and fears of the self by gaining perspective on the desires, hungers and fears of others.

Vaikuntha is located on the shore-less ocean of milk. This ocean of milk is a metaphor for nature (prakriti), its shore-less state indicating that it has no purpose or destination, and milk indicating that all wealth is ultimately churned out of nature. Here Vishnu lies in deep slumber until the cries of the earth goddess wake him up and force him to watch the rise and fall of human societies, the alternating victories and defeats of the devas and the asuras who seek control over the world. Vishnu descends in various mortal forms (avatars) to help everyone appreciate the reality of nature (prakriti) and the potential of humanity (purusha).

Besides being a saviour, Vishnu is also an enjoyer (rasika) of the various flavours (rasa) of existence. His temples contain dancing halls (natya-mandapa), food halls (bhoga-mandapa), assembly halls (jaga-mohana) and wedding halls (kalyana-mandapa). They are associated with fine music, fragrances and garments.

Unlike the independent Shiva made dependable by Shakti, Vishnu displays vulnerability and dependence on the other when he descends as Ram and Krishna, for the other also wants to feel powerful and valued, and this can only happen when the self 'consumes' the other. I want you to need me. If you do not need me, and only give me, without taking anything from me, I feel inadequate, meaningless, valueless and purposeless. In wanting me, you illuminate me and contribute to my fulfilment. Likewise, you want me to need you. If I do not need you, if I am dependable but detached, you will feel insulted, hurt, unwanted, and I will appear patronizing.

Wisdom for both that
neither receives

Boons for
asuras

Saviours for
devas

Brahma

Vishnu stories in the Ramayana, Bhagavata and Mahabharata reveal how he experiences birth, death and even heartbreak. Both Ram and Krishna display human emotions, yearning for the beloved. Though God, Ram cannot be with Sita, Krishna cannot be with Radha. Yet they do not turn bitter, angry or vengeful. They love unconditionally.

This idea of a vulnerable god, who gets as much as he gives, is unique to Hinduism. While the transformation of the wise Buddha of old Buddhism into the compassionate Bodhisattva of later Buddhism mirrors the transformation of the hermit Shiva into the householder Shankara, the idea of Vishnu, who is at once king and hermit and lover, who not only cares for but needs the other, is unique to Vaishnava mythology.

Hermit to Householder

Neither Sita, who Vishnu abandons as Ram, nor Radha, who he abandons as Krishna, begrudges him. They also love him unconditionally. Love, in either case, does not guarantee happiness. Love, in either case, does not manifest as control. Loving is its own reward, the ultimate human possibility. This is

atma-rati, feeling fulfilled in doing the deed without expecting
a reward, referred to in Chapter 3, Verse 7. This is the outcome
of brahma-sthithi, being firm in the understanding of human
imagination, referred to in Chapter 2, Verse 72. It follows
accepting oneself as nimitta-matra, instrument of a larger
narrative, referred to in Chapter 11, Verse 33.

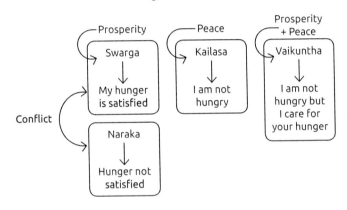

Swarga, Kailasa, Vaikuntha

Buddhism popularized the hermit practice of shutting the
eyes and contemplating (dhyana) while Puranic Hinduism
popularized the householder practice of opening the eyes and
seeing the deity in the temple (darshan). In one, there is focus
on the inner journey. In the other, the inner journey is meant to
facilitate the outer journey.

The Buddhist concept of nirvana offers freedom from suffering
by realizing that even the idea of the self is manufactured by the
mind. The Gita's concept of brahma-nirvana offers awareness of,
and empathy for, the manufactured anxieties of the other, their
need to control and dominate and cling, their inability to let go

despite being enabled and empowered to do so. The more we observe the other, without judgement, the more we see ourselves mirrored in them. We realize our manufactured anxieties that indulge our manufactured selves.

> Arjuna, he who is always aware of the divine, and unites with the divine, within and without, will always be at peace and blissful.—*Bhagavad Gita: Chapter 6, Verse 15 (paraphrased).*

Typically, we are trapped in a world where there is conflict between my kshetra and your kshetra. I compare what I have with what you have and this leads to conflict and competition as between the Pandavas and the Kauravas. Darshan begins when I look at your aham, the hungers and fears that constitute your imagined identity, and discover my aham, fears and hungers that constitute my imagined identity. This is what Krishna asks Arjuna to do. Only then do we discover the atma that permeates all beings and all things, that is infinite, immortal and at peace.

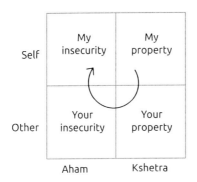

The Journey of The Gita

In other words, darshan of the other leads to darshan of the self. Darshan without leads to darshan within. This is atma-gyana, self-awareness that enables us to accept, maybe even outgrow, our own anxieties and be kinder to ourselves, and others, even in a fight.

This is the promise of The Gita, revealed through me to you.

Can you and I participate in a relationship without seeking to control the behaviour of the other? Can we help each other outgrow our hungers and fears? Then we are on the path of brahma-nirvana. When we derive joy from within, not from achievements outside, we are on the path of atma-rati.

My Gita

After My Gita:
Yet Another Discourse by Krishna

After The Gita, there was the Kama Gita, the song of the god of desire, and then the Anu Gita, the follow-up Gita, both narrated by Krishna. This is how they come about.

Kama Gita

As he concludes the Bhagavad Gita, Krishna asks Arjuna if he has heard what has been said and if he is free of confusion. Yes, says Arjuna.

> Krishna, by your grace, I am no longer deluded or confused. I remember what I am supposed to do. I am firm. I have no doubts. I shall do as you say.—*Bhagavad Gita: Chapter 18, Verse 73 (paraphrased).*

Arjuna then blows his conch shell, announcing the start of the war, and lets Krishna take him into battle. Krishna's perspective brings back Arjuna's focus; confusion is replaced by clarity, paralysis with action. All is well that ends well.

At least, so we think.

But as the days of the war progress, Arjuna shows repeated moments of doubt, despair and dilemma. He is unable to bring himself to kill Bhisma who is like a father to him, Drona who is his teacher and Karna who stands before him unarmed, despite Krishna goading him on to do so.

After the war too, doubts persist.

In Ashwamedika Parva, Book 14 of the Mahabharata, Arjuna overhears Krishna present the very short Kama Gita to his eldest brother:

'Yudhishthira, hear what Kama, god of craving, says about himself. He who seeks to destroy craving with weapons ends up craving those very weapons. He who seeks to destroy craving with charity ends up craving charity. He who seeks to destroy craving with scriptures ends up craving scriptures. He who seeks to destroy craving with truth ends up craving truth. He who seeks to destroy craving with austerities ends up craving austerities. He who seeks to destroy craving with renunciation ends up craving renunciation. Craving cannot be destroyed, but it can be put to good use by locating it in dharma. So seek to destroy craving with the pursuit of dharma. You will ends up craving dharma! And that will be good for the whole world, for you will then conduct more and more exchange, bring prosperity to the world, liberating yourself in the process from all obligations, enabling others to give without expectations.'

Arjuna then approaches Krishna, just when he is about to leave for Dwaraka, with a request to repeat what he had said at the start of the war. 'Really!' replies Krishna, surprised, even a little irritated, by the request. 'You want me to recollect all that I had said then? That was a tense and inspired moment. I was in a state of full awareness, fully connected with the world and my faculties. That moment has passed.'

But still Krishna presents the Anu Gita, or the follow-up Gita, which is also located in Ashwamedika Parva, Book 14 of the Mahabharata. The knowledge provided in the Anu Gita is secondary. Krishna recalls three conversations: the first one between a sage called Kashyapa and a learned Brahmin, the second one between the Brahmin and his wife and the third one between the Brahmin and his student. The conversation is long: thirty-six chapters, double that of the Bhagavad Gita, and far less lucid. Here, the quest for wisdom is described as journeying from one forest of metaphors to another. As in the Vyadha Gita and the Bhagavad Gita, reference is made to the wise King Janaka of Mithila, who was seen as the champion of the Upanishads, Sita's father in the Ramayana. When this discourse ends, Krishna hopes that by sharing these three conversations of ancient sages, Arjuna has regained his knowledge of the Bhagavad Gita. Then he leaves.

As in most other Gitas, the Anu Gita elaborates on karma and gyana, not bhakti. Perhaps Arjuna's emotional breakdown on the battlefield created the need for an innovation: an emotional anchor, faith in someone outside, someone bigger than everyone and everything around, someone who supports and cares unconditionally. In other words, God! Krishna does not present himself as bhagavan in the Anu Gita, though Arjuna does identify and venerate Krishna as bhagavan in the final chapter of the Anu Gita, as the two ride out to Dwaraka.

As the Mahabharata draws to a close, we are told that Arjuna, recipient of multiple discourses of Vedic wisdom from Krishna himself, lands up in hell (naraka) after his death, because of demerits accumulated owing to his insecurity and arrogance. He has to stay there until he is cleansed and only then can he rise to swarga, the paradise of his father, Indra. Even here, stay is impermanent, only as long as his merits last. Vishnu's Vaikuntha remains elusive.

Arjuna may be the hero of the Mahabharata, Krishna's companion and recipient of The Gita. He may be Nara to Krishna's Narayana. But that does not make him perfect. Even the state of the world after the war at Kuru-kshetra is far from perfect. In fact, traditionally, it marks the dawn of Kali yuga, the final era of a culture, before collapse. So much for Krishna's intervention!

The yearning for perfection stems from the desire to control and organize the world to our taste, to create a cocoon where everything makes sense to us. It demands that we judge the world as a problem that needs fixing, chaos that needs to be organized, a disease that needs to be cured, a polluted space that needs purification. It assumes that the world needs to have a climax, a happy ending, or else life is a tragedy. These are typical of finite narratives, where there is only one life to lead.

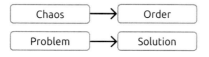

Climax of Finite Narratives

The word 'perfect' cannot be translated in Sanskrit, or any Indian language. The closest we come to it is excellent (uttam) and complete or comprehensive (purnatva), a reminder that Eden is not a Hindu concept. There is no fall from perfection, as in Abrahamic mythology. Nor is culture a journey out of chaos into order, as in Greek mythology. We can at best keep expanding our mind, keep getting more understanding, as we make the journey from limited reality (mithya) to limitless infinite reality (satya). Wisdom comes with the realization that other people's karma that impacts our life cannot be wished away. And this is most evident in the concept of Ram Rajya, the 'perfect' kingdom of Ram described in the Ramayana.

In Ram Rajya, everything is predictable, everything is pure, all wishes are fulfilled and everyone is taken care of. But then a Brahmin's son dies prematurely, because a 'low-caste' man called Shambuka wants to be a hermit and so has abandoned his vocation. And people gossip about Sita's stay in Ravana's palace, and a washerman (dhobi) calls it a 'stain' on the reputation of the Raghu clan. The desires and meanness of others are beyond Ram's control. To restore perfection, Ram has to do terrible things: kill an innocent hermit and banish an innocent wife. Aspirations are crushed and people are abandoned, in order to create predictability and purity for the rest. The horrific price of perfection is thus demonstrated. The physical and psychological violence generates more karmic ripples that end up as turbulent waves lashing against the perfection created. Shambuka's cry and Sita's anguish haunt Ram Rajya from without. Ram Rajya turns into rana-bhoomi, under siege by those excluded, like Indra's swarga surrounded by angry asuras.

Eventually the Treta yuga gives way to Dvapara yuga, where upright men like Bhisma and Karna allow the Kauravas to thrive while honest men like Yudhishthira gamble their kingdom and their wife away, even when Krishna walks the earth.

Does that make the Ramayana and the Mahabharata tragedies, since they do not have happy endings? Attempts to classify the epics so are themselves judgemental, against the very spirit in which they were composed. The epics simply end with the death of their protagonists: Ram dies in Book 7 of the Ramayana while Krishna dies in the Mausala Parva, Book 16 of the Mahabharata; Arjuna dies in Book 17. Ram walks into the river Sarayu, and a stray arrow kills Krishna. Both have a smile on their lips when they die for they know death is not the end: another life awaits. Arjuna on the other hand slips while climbing a mountain and dies in disappointment, having failed to reach swarga.

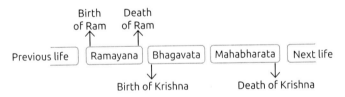

Beginning and End of Hindu Epics

My Gita

The Gita does not aspire for perfection. Hence, there are no rules in The Gita, only three paths to establish relationships: karma yoga, bhakti yoga and gyana yoga that deal with human conduct, human emotions and human identity. These three routes are interdependent. One cannot exist without the other. Without karma yoga, we have nothing to give, or receive from, the other. Without bhakti yoga, we are machines that feel nothing for the other. Without gyana yoga, we have no value, purpose or meaning. There can be no bhakta who does not do or understand. There can be no gyani who does not do or feel. There can be no karmi who does not feel or understand. The optimal functioning of the hands (karma) depends on the head (gyana) and the heart (bhakti). A yogi simultaneously does, feels and understands.

Interdependence of the Three Yogas

Krishna presents these three paths to Arjuna like a mother lays out food. Arjuna has the option of eating what he feels like, what his body craves for. No matter what he eats, he has no control over the digestion, what his body will finally assimilate. The final outcome is dependent not just on his will (sankalpa) but also his natural tendencies (guna) and, of course, whatever he is supposed to experience (karma). Hence, Krishna is not disappointed when Arjuna's doubts and despair resurface again and again. It is how it is supposed to be.

> Arjuna, some discover the divine through meditation and introspection, others decipher it through logic and analysis, others experience it through activity, and still others are introduced to it by listening to others. All are able to overcome the fear of mortality.—*Bhagavad Gita: Chapter 13, verses 24 and 25 (paraphrased).*

Krishna knows that in a world without boundaries, there will always be another chance, and then another.

Recommended Reading

For a literal, readable translation of The Gita without commentary:

- Debroy, Bibek. *The Bhagavad Gita*. New Delhi: Penguin Books India, 2005.
- Nabar, Vrinda and Tumkur, Shanta. *The Bhagavad Gītā*. Hertfordshire, UK: Wordsworth Classics, 1997.
- Menon, Ramesh. *The Shrimad Bhagavad Gita*. Delhi: Rupa Publications, 2004.
- Miller, Barbara. *The Bhagavad-Gita*. New York: Bantam Press, 1986.

For a readable translation that also captures the poetic spirit of The Gita:

- Rao, Mani. *Bhagavad Gita*. New Delhi: Fingerprint, 2014.
- Mitchell, Stephen. *Bhagavad Gita*. London: Random House, 2000.

For a verse-by-verse translation of The Gita with commentary:

- Easwaran, Eknath. *The Bhagavad Gita*. Mumbai: Jaico Publications, 1997.
- Sivananda, Swami. *Bhagavad Gita*. Divine Life Society Trust, 2008.
- Radhakrishnan, S. *The Bhagavadgita*. Delhi: HarperCollins India, 2008.

For appreciating the history of The Gita:

- Davis, Richard. *The 'Bhagavad Gita': a Biography*. Princeton, USA: Princeton University Press, 2016.
- Desai, Meghnad. *Who Wrote the Bhagavadgita: a Secular Inquiry into a Sacred Text*. Delhi: HarperCollins India, 2014.

For appreciating the Vedas, the Puranas and other Hindu literature:

- Agarwal, Satya P. *Selection from the Mahabharata: Reaffirming Gita's call for good of all.* New Delhi: Motilal Banarsidass, 2002.
- Dange, Sadashiv Ambadas. *Encyclopaedia of Puranic Beliefs and Practices, Vol: 1–5.* New Delhi: Navran, 1990.
- Flood, Gavin. *An Introduction to Hinduism.* New Delhi: Cambridge University Press, 1998.
- Frawley, David. *From the River of Heaven.* New Delhi: Motilal Banarsidass, 1992.
- Jaini, Padmanabh S. *The Jaina Path of Purification.* New Delhi: Motilal Banarsidass, 1979.
- Mani, Vettam. *Puranic Encyclopaedia.* New Delhi: Motilal Banarsidass, 1996.
- Stall, Frits. *Discovery of the Vedas.* New Delhi: Penguin Books India, 2008.
- Zimmer, Heinrich. *Myths and Symbols in Indian Art and Civilization.* New Delhi: Motilal Banarsidass, 1990.

For appreciating how imagination and language (brahmana) play a key role in human development:

- Coupe, Lawrence. *Myth [The New Critical Idiom Series].* London: Routledge, 1997.
- Harari, Yuval Noah. *Sapiens: A Brief History of Humankind.* London: Harvill Secker, 2014.
- Pagel, Mark. *Wired for Culture.* London: Penguin Books UK, 2012.

My

HANUMAN
CHALISA

Reflecting on one of Hinduism's most popular prayers for positive energy

Every time I experience negativity in the world, and in myself, every time I encounter jealousy, rage and frustration manisfesting as violation and violence, I hear, or read, the Hanuman Chalisa. Composed over four hundred years ago by Tulsidas, its simple words (in Awadhi, a dialect of Hindi) and its simple metre (dohas and chaupais) musically evoke the mythology, history and mystery of Hanuman, the much-loved Hindu deity, through whom Vedic wisdom reaches the masses.

As verse follows verse, my frightened, crumpled mind begins to expand with knowledge and insight, and my faith in humanity, both within and without, is restored.

Why *My Hanuman Chalisa?*

One of the things that catch your eye in the middle of a horrifyingly crowded Mumbai local train is the sight of people sitting or standing in a corner, reading from a tiny chapbook sold in roadside shops near temples. Most popular of these chapbooks is the Hanuman Chalisa. In the midst of the crushing inhumanity that is urban life, you see a glow on the reader's face. It is the most powerful expression of personal Hinduism that one can encounter on India's streets.

I have always wondered what the Hanuman Chalisa is and what is in it that makes it so popular. Its language—Awadhi—is an old dialect of Hindi, one of the many languages of India. Do people reading it understand what they are reading? Or does the gentle poetic rhythm calm the nervous heart, as it prepares to face the day? Or is it simply a ritual exercise, where the point is to do, not think or feel?

So I decided to explore this popular religious work through which a Hindu god is made accessible to the masses. I realized that reading this chapbook is completely voluntary, as in all things Hindu. It is neither a commandment of a guru, nor a prescription of a priest. Its popularity is organic. Its ordinariness makes it sublime.

As I explored this work, I realized each line allows us to leap into the vast body of Hindu thought, a heritage of over 4,000 years ago, much as Hanuman leapt from his cradle to the sun, or across the sea towards Lanka, or over land towards the mountain bearing the Sanjivani herb, always returning to find Ram. From the particular, we traverse the universal, and finally return to the personal.

As you go through the forty-three verses in this book, you will notice how sensitively the poet has structured his work, how it creates a temple in the mind, and enshrines a deity in that temple, and how the verses take us from ideas of birth, through ideas of adventure, duty and glory, to the ideas of death and rebirth.

In my work, I have always avoided the academic approach, as scholars are too busy seeking 'the' truth while I am interested in expanding 'my' truth and the truth of my readers. If you seek 100% perfection, you often lose 99% of readers in cantankerous and often self-serving debates; but if you seek 90% perfection, you are able to reach out to over 90% of readers through thought-provoking elaborations that seek not to convince but to enrich. And that is good enough for me. Hence I present to you my Hanuman Chalisa, firmly anchored in the belief that:

Within infinite myths lies an eternal truth
Who sees it all?
Varuna has but a thousand eyes
Indra, a hundred
You and I, only two.

The Text

Shri guru charan saroj-raj nija manu mukura sudhaari.
Baranau Raghubara Vimala Jasu jo dayaka phala chari.

Buddhi-heen tanu janikay sumirow Pavanakumara.
Bala-buddhi bidya dehoo mohee harahu klesha vikaara.

1. *Jai Hanuman gyan gun sagar. Jai Kapish tihun lok ujagar.*

2. *Ram doot atulit bala dhama. Anjani-putra Pavan-sut nama.*

3. *Mahabir Bikram Bajrangi. Kumati nivar sumati ke sangi.*

4. *Kanchan baran biraj subesa. Kanan kundal kunchit kesa.*

5. *Hath bajra aur dhvaja biraje. Kaandhe moonj janehu sajai.*

6. *Sankar suvan Kesari nandan. Tej prataap maha jag bandan.*

7. *Vidyavaan guni ati chatur. Ram kaj karibe ko aatur.*

8. *Prabhu charitra sunibe ko rasiya. Ram Lakhan Sita man basiya.*

9. *Sukshma roop dhari Siyahi dikhava. Vikat roop dhari Lank jarava.*

10. *Bhima roop dhari asur sanghare. Ramachandra ke kaj sanvare.*

11. *Laye Sanjivan Lakhan jiyaye. Shri Raghuvir harashi ur laye.*

12. *Raghupati kinhi bahut badai. Tum mam priye Bharat-hi-sam bhai.*

13. *Sahas badan tumharo jasa gaave. Asa-kahi Shripati kanth lagaave.*

14. *Sankadhik Brahmaadi muneesa. Narada-Sarad sahita Aheesa.*

15. *Jam Kubera Digpaal jahan te. Kavi kovid kahi sake kahan te.*

16. *Tum upkar Sugrivahin keenha. Ram milaye rajpad deenha.*

17. *Tumharo mantra Vibhishan maana. Lankeshwar bhaye sub jag jana.*

18. *Yug sahastra jojan par Bhanu. Leelyo tahi madhur phal janu.*

19. *Prabhu mudrika meli mukh mahee. Jaladhi langhi gaye achraj nahee.*

20. *Durgam kaj jagath ke jete. Sugam anugraha tumhre tete.*

21. *Ram dwaare tum rakhvare. Hoat na agya bin paisare.*

22. *Sub sukh lahae tumhari sarna. Tum rakshak kahu ko darna.*

23. *Aapan tej samharo aapai. Teenhon lok hank te kanpai.*

24. *Bhoot pisaach nikat nahin aavai. Mahabir jab naam sunavae.*

25. *Nase rog harae sab peera. Japat nirantar Hanumat Beera.*

26. *Sankat se Hanuman chudavae. Man, kram, vachan dhyan jo lavai.*

27. *Sab par Ram tapasvee raja. Tin ke kaj sakal tum saja.*

28. *Aur manorath jo koi lavai. Sohi amit jeevan phal pavai.*

29. *Chaaron jug partap tumhara. Hai persidh jagat ujiyara.*

30. *Sadhu sant ke tum rakhware. Asur nikandan Ram dulhare.*

31. *Ashta-sidhi nav nidhi ke dhata. As bar deen Janki mata.*

32. *Ram rasayan tumhare pasa. Sada raho Raghupati ke dasa.*

33. *Tumhare bhajan Ram ko pavai. Janam-janam ke dukh bisraavai.*

34. *Ant-kaal Raghuvir-pur jayee. Jahan janam Hari-bhakt kahayee.*

35. *Aur devta chit na dharehi. Hanumat se hi sarve sukh karehi.*

36. *Sankat kate mite sab peera. Jo sumirai Hanumat Balbeera.*

37. *Jai Jai Jai Hanuman Gosain. Kripa karahu gurudev ki nyahin.*

38. *Jo sat bar path kare koi. Chhutehi bandhi maha sukh hoyi.*

39. *Jo yeh padhe Hanuman Chalisa. Hoye siddhi sakhi Gaureesa.*

40. *Tulsidas sada Hari chera. Keejai Nath hriday mein dera.*

Pavan tanay sankat harana mangala murati roop.
Ram Lakhana Sita sahita hriday basahu soor bhoop.

The Exploration

Doha 1: Establishing the Mind-Temple

श्रीगुरु चरन सरोज रज निज मनु मुकुरु सुधारि ।
बरनऊँ रघुबर बिमल जसु जो दायकु फल चारि ॥

Shri guru charan saroja-raj nija manu mukura sudhaari.
Baranau Raghubara Bimala Jasu jo dayaka phala chari.

Having polished my mind-mirror with the pollen-dust of my guru's feet.
I bask in the unblemished glory of the lord of the Raghu clan (Ram), bestower of life's four fruits.

Thus begins the Hanuman Chalisa, composed by Tulsidas four centuries ago in Awadhi, a dialect of Hindi spoken in the Gangetic plains around the cities of Awadh, or Ayodhya, and Kashi or Varanasi.

Chalisa means a poem of forty verses (chalis means forty in Hindi). Hanuman Chalisa, however, has forty-three verses. The main forty verses are chaupai, or quatrains (verses with four short, rhythmic segments). Framing these are three dohas, or couplets (verses with two long, rhythmic segments)—two at the beginning and one at the end—which serve as the entry and exit points into the 'mind-temple' that is created by the Chalisa.

Hindus have always believed that a temple can be created in the mind using words and verses, just as brick, wood and stone can be used to construct a temple in the material world. The psychological world exists parallel to the physical world; these are the two worlds inhabited by all living creatures (jiva in Sanskrit) according to Hindu scriptures. Only the non-living (ajiva) exist solely in the physical world.

In Hinduism, mind and matter are seen as interdependent, and their complementary nature was expressed using many words such as dehi-deha, atma-sharira, purusha-prakriti, shiva-shakti. The value placed on the psychological world is the reason why sacred Hindu writings are full of symbols and metaphors. The literal is for those who cannot handle the psychological, and prefer to see the physical as real. This yearning for the literal is indicative of insecurity, for the insecure mind finds it easier to control matter, which is measurable, than the mind, which is not.

The verse refers to the mind as a mirror that reflects the world. We think we engage with the real world, when in fact we engage with the world reflected in the mind-mirror. A dirty mirror will distort our view of the world, so we need to clean it. The cleansing agent is the dust of the guru's feet, who is so realized that the dust of his feet has the potency of pollen (saroj).

Our dirty mind-mirror is contrasted against the pure (vimala) glory of Ram who offers the four fruits (phala chari) that come from God, that nourish human existence: dharma (social order), artha (wealth and power), kama (pleasure) and moksha (freedom from material burdens).

Is there a relationship between the pollen of the guru's feet and the fruit bestowed by God? There could be. The mind which is a mirror (mukura) can also be seen as a flower (mukula), similar sounding words when we think about it. Is that deliberate device used by the poet? We can surely speculate. By the use of pollen-flower-fruit metaphors a connection is established between the guru's wisdom, a clear human mind, and the glory of the divine, which together will give us what we desire.

Having sought the blessings of the guru and invoked God, and polished the mind-mirror, it is time to declare the intention behind this enterprise we are embarking upon. It is time for the sankalpa.

Doha 2: Statement of Desire

बुद्धिहीन तनु जानिके सुमिरौं पवनकुमार ।
बल बुद्धि बिद्या देहु मोहिं हरहु कलेस बिकार ॥

Buddhi-heen tanu janikay sumirow Pavanakumara.
Bala-buddhi bidya dehoo mohee harahu klesha vikaara.

*Aware that I lack intelligence, I recollect the son of the wind
god (Hanuman),*
*He will surely grant me strength, intelligence, knowledge
and take away all problems and afflictions.*

Sankalpa is the statement of purpose that marks the beginning of
any Hindu ritual. We clarify who we are, and why we are doing
what we are doing. This verse is the sankalpa that we are invoking
Hanuman—identified here as the son (kumara) of the wind god
(pavan)—to get what we want but don't have, and to rid ourselves
of what we have but don't want. Thus the seed of desire is planted,
with the hope of germination and fructification. Perhaps, the
poet wants Hanuman to take care of him as Hanuman was taken
care of by his divine father, the wind god Vayu, which is why he is
addressing Hanuman using his father's name.

We identify ourselves as lacking intelligence (buddhi). In
colloquial language, the one without buddhi is buddhu, a fool,
and one with buddhi is either the intelligent (buddhiman) or the
awakened one (buddha).

The Buddha is a title that was given to a prince who lived
2,500 years ago after he came to the conclusion that where there
is life there is desire, and hence suffering. Suffering ends when we

realize that nothing is permanent, neither the world, nor our sense of self. The ultimate aim is oblivion (nirvana) of the self which exists by imagining the world is real and permanent. The Buddha propagated this idea of dhamma (which is Pali for dharma) by establishing monastic orders (the sangha).

By contrast, Hinduism is life-affirming. Desire (kama) is accepted as the force that creates the world, with destiny (karma) as the counterforce that limits the satisfaction of desires. If one wants to give purpose to life, then one must enjoy desire and accept destiny, without being addicted to either, and realizing there is more to life than satisfaction and suffering, desire and destiny. This can only happen when we have buddhi, complemented with strength (bala) and knowledge (vidya), which is what this chaupai refers to.

Strength without intelligence makes us dim-witted tools in the hands of others. Intelligence without strength, on the other hand, means we can never realize our dreams, for strength means a body that has stamina, a mind that has patience, and a life with access to resources and agency.

Knowledge without intelligence prevents us from being worldly. Intelligence without knowledge makes us narrow-minded, short-sighted frogs in a well. Knowledge is infinite, it has no boundaries, and in Hinduism, God is the personification of that infinite knowledge. Everyone has access only to a slice (bhaga) of reality; the one who knows all slices is God (bhagavan).

In the information age, as we move towards gathering data about everyone and everything, it is easy to assume we are moving towards infinite knowledge hence God-hood, through computers and databases. However, this data being gathered is material, not psychological. What is being measured is stimulus and its behavioural response. What is being manipulated by technology, is behaviour alone, not thought and emotions. What information is not being gathered is how the mind perceives and processes sensory stimuli. Science today is so focussed on the material, that it assumes measurable input (stimulus) and measurable output (behavioural response) is indicative of thought and emotion, and dismisses arguments to the contrary. Reality is seen as what we do (measurable), not what we feel (not measurable). At best, doing is seen as an indicator of feeling. At worst, doing is seen as relevant while feeling is considered of no consequence. When the West speaks of an intelligence quotient or an emotional index, it derives all understanding of the mind from measuring behaviour. Measurement limits science. This distinguishes the modern discourse, and disconnects it with traditional Indian wisdom where measurement is seen as establishing a delusion (maya) of certainty.

The obsession with quotients, and indices, hence mathematics, reveals the desire to control, regulate, manipulate human behaviour. Control, in Hinduism, is an indicator of fear. The intelligent seek control: the strong have the resilience to handle the lack of control, and the knowledgeable know the futility of control. Hence, we ask Hanuman for strength as well as knowledge, along with intelligence.

We also ask Hanuman to solve our problems: problems that bother our mind (klesha) and problems that bother our body (vikara). Colloquially, klesha simply means a problem of any kind, but in Sanskrit 'klesha' refers to the psychological root of all problems such as lust (kama), anger (krodha), pride (mada), obsession (raga), revulsion (dvesha), jealousy (matsarya), that exists within us or in those around us. In the Bhagavad Gita, these kleshas are identified as vikara, making the two words synonyms. In Ayurveda, vikaras refer to diseases arising from the imbalance of the humours (doshas). Hanuman is being evoked to restore balance and harmony, in our mind and in our body, within us as well as around us.

Note that everything that is being sought from Hanuman involves the mind and body: we want him to give us strength, intelligence, and knowledge. We are not asking for fortune or success. With a healthy mind, we know, we can cope with all of life's vagaries, and find happiness, always.

This doha marks the end of the introduction. Having paid obeisance to the guru and God, having made our statement of intent, we plunge into the main Chalisa, composed of forty chaupais.

Chaupai 1: Why Monkey as God

जय हनुमान
ज्ञान गुन सागर ।
जय कपीश
तिहुँ लोक उजागर ॥

Jai Hanuman
gyan gun sagar.
Jai Kapish
tihun lok ujagar.

Victory to Hanuman
who is the ocean of wisdom and virtue.
Victory to the divine amongst monkeys
who illuminates the three worlds.

In this verse, Hanuman is addressed for the first time by his most popular name, Hanuman, and identified as a monkey (kapi).

Classically, Hanuman means one with a wide or prominent or disfigured jaw, indicating a monkey. Colloquially, in the Hindi belt of India, the name means one without ego, pride and inflated self-image (maan), a meaning that makes sense when we appreciate the structure of the epic Ramayana, where Hanuman appears for the first time.

Some scholars have proposed that the word Hanuman comes from a proto-Dravidian word—an-mandi, which probably means male monkey—later Sanskritized to Hanuman. They also point to Hanuman being called Anuman in Thailand and Andoman in Malaysia, lands where Dravidian culture spread a long time ago. It has even been proposed that the Andaman Islands in the Bay of Bengal got its name from sailors who told stories of the great monkey who had the power to leap across the sea and reach distant islands. Those familiar with early Tamil Sangam literature dispute this theory.

The Ramayana reached its final form roughly 2,000 years ago, and is one of the first epics to be composed in India with the intention of communicating Vedic ideas to the masses. It marks the birth of a new phase of Hinduism known as Puranic Hinduism, which is also marked by the rise of temple culture.

Before the Ramayana, for over a thousand years, maybe more, Vedic ideas were communicated using chants, melodies, rituals and conversations, not stories. This had a limited audience, the intellectual elite, such as priests, philosophers and aristocrats, with ample time on their hands. To reach out to a larger audience, Vyasa—the man who is credited with organizing Vedic hymns— composed the stories and epics compiled in the Puranas, including the story of Ram.

Some say Vyasa composed the stories himself, some say he compiled stories he heard from other sages, like Markandeya, and still others say he heard it from Shiva, or from the birds and fish who in turn had overheard the conversation between Shiva and Shakti. Amongst the birds was a crow called Kakabhusandi who told the story of Ram to the sage Narad who passed it on to the sage Valmiki, who transformed the story into the world's first poetry, which is why the Ramayana, the maha-kavya, is also called adi-kavya.

In the Ramayana, we find three sets of characters. In the north are the humans (nara) in Ayodhya, led by sages (rishis) who seek to enable humans to expand their mind, discover their divine potential (brahmana), which is the essence of Vedic wisdom. In the south, beyond the sea, on the island of Lanka are the demons (rakshasas) led by Ravana, son of a rishi (Vaishrava, son of Pulastya), who uses Vedic knowledge for power, and fails to internalize Vedic wisdom. In between, live the monkeys (vanaras).

Words like 'north' and 'south' in the Ramayana need to be read metaphorically, not literally, because Vedic thought is all about the mind, and seeks to inform how we 'see' the world. Ram is a metaphor. So is Ravana. So is Hanuman. The Ramayana takes place in the landscape that is our mind.

In nature, animals, including monkeys, compete for food, and so dominate and mark territories to secure their food. All behaviour is aimed at ensuring the body survives. This is the jungle way (matsya nyaya). To outgrow these animal instincts is the hallmark of humanity; it is our divine potential. To walk this path is dharma. But when we indulge in competition, domination and territoriality, we become worse than animals; we become demons, who subscribe to adharma. Ram embodies dharma. Ravana embodies adharma. Hanuman, from amongst all the monkeys, makes the journey towards Ram.

The world is composed of the self (sva-jiva) who lives in the ecosystem of others (para-jiva). For animals, monkeys included, the other is predator or prey, rival or mate. But humans have the ability to outgrow these hardwired animal instincts. The 'north' in the Ramayana is the highest potential that we can realize—where the self is not consumed by its own hunger for, and fear of, the other, but by empathy for other people's hungers and fears. This caring world is the world of Ram.

The 'south' in the Ramayana is where there is so much hunger and fear that the other is seen only as food and enemy, and the self (jiva-atma) twists itself and transforms into the ego (aham), unable to appreciate the divinity in the other (para-atma), hence the continuum of divinity that permeates the whole infinite universe (param-atma). This self-indulgent world is the world of Ravana.

The rishis, who Ram defends, are sages who go from the north to the south to enable, empower and enlighten the hungry and the weak. They know that the other will see the sages from the north either as invaders or as patronizing benefactors, who seek to destroy their way of life. The rishis also know that should their wisdom slip, they will themselves be enchanted by the knowledge and power they are revealing.

Ravana, a son of one such rishi, embodies what can go wrong. Ravana uses his great strength, knowledge and intelligence to exploit those around him, be their lord and master, make them followers, rather than liberating them to find their own path. The liminal or in-between space between the north and the south is the land of the monkeys, our animal core, that can move either way, towards Ram or towards Ravana, towards empathy or towards exploitation, towards dharma or adharma.

The hungry and the frightened seek combat and conquest, hence vijay—victory where someone is defeated. The wise seek a different kind of victory, jai—where no one is defeated, where the self is able to conquer its own hunger and fear to acknowledge, appreciate, even accommodate the other. Both jai and vijay seem to mean the same thing, 'hail' or 'victory', but there is a nuance in the meaning, the preference for internal victory in the case of jai over external victory in the case of vijay. This jai is what we want for Hanuman, and from Hanuman, as we read the Hanuman Chalisa.

Many people are uncomfortable with such symbolic, structural, or psychological readings of the Ramayana and want it to be historical. So vanara becomes forest (vana) people (nara), or primitive (va) humans (nara). They see north as the Aryan homeland in the Gangetic plains and the south as the Dravidian homeland south of the Vindhyas. Such rationalizations are often seen in people who are unable to differentiate the physical from the psychological, the measurable (saguna) from the non-measurable (nirguna), the form (sakar) from the formless (nirakar). Since the world is diverse, diverse readings of the Ramayana must be appreciated with empathy so that we appreciate the diverse needs of the human mind.

Chaupai 2: Son of Wind

राम दूत
अतुलित बल धामा ।
अंजनिपुत्र
पवनसुत नामा ॥

Ram doot
atulit bala dhama.
Anjani-putra
Pavan-sut nama.

Agent of Ram
Bearer of great strength.
Son of Anjani (mother)
Also known as son of the wind god (father).

This chaupai focuses on the origin and role of Hanuman. He is described as the son of the god of wind (Pavan) and a monkey woman called Anjana or Anjani, and has immense strength and uses his strength to serve as Ram's agent.

In the Vedas, divinity was often personified as natural phenomena: Indra, the god of thunder and lightning; Agni, the fire; Soma, the juices within trees; Surya, the sun; Vayu, the wind. Pavan is a colloquial name for Vayu who is also known as Maruta, the god of storms. Pavan is also associated with prana (breath in the lungs) and vata (gases in the bowels), and so integral to life. The wind god who connects the earth with the sky is a companion and messenger of Indra, a role replicated by his son Hanuman, who is also known as Vayu-putra and Maruti.

If Hanuman gets his awesome strength from his father, his monkeyness comes from his mother, Anjana, a vanara woman. As the son of Anjana, Hanuman is often called Anjaneya, especially in South India. Not much is known about Hanuman's mother. In some stories, she was a nymph, an apsara, cursed to live on earth, after she upset a rishi. In other stories, she is the daughter of Gautama, the sage who discovers his wife, Ahalya, in the arms of Indra. She is cursed either by Gautama for not telling the truth about her mother or by Ahalya for not lying to her father. The curse involves her turning into a monkey. She marries Kesari, a vanara, who lives in Kishkinda.

The idea of a god making a human pregnant is often found in Greek mythology, where it is used to explain the existence of extraordinary heroes. Thus Hercules has a celestial father (Zeus) and a mortal father (Amphitryon) just as Hanuman has a celestial father (Vayu) and a mortal father (Kesari). Did this story of Hanuman have a Greek influence? At the time the Ramayana was being composed, Indian storytellers may have been exposed to Greek tales that had followed Alexander the Great to the East. We can only speculate as there is little by way of proof.

It is significant that Hanuman's father and mother are clearly identified. It means he is born of the womb (yonija). He is never referred to as self-created (swayambhu), indicating that his status is lower. In Hindu mythology, there are two kinds of gods: the greater ones who are self-created and are hence beyond space and time, immortal and infinite, and the lesser ones who are born to parents and are hence located within space and time, are mortal and finite. In the Puranas, all old Vedic gods—Indra, Agni, Vayu, Surya—are given secondary status by being described as children of Kashyapa and Aditi. Primary status is given to Shiva and Vishnu who are described as self-created. Vishnu voluntarily takes a mortal form as Ram, thus striding both categories. Hanuman, however, does not fit so neatly into the second category: yes, he takes birth on earth, but he is also described as immortal (Chiranjivi). There are no stories of his death.

In the Mahabharata, Vayu places his seed in the womb of Kunti, as a result Kunti becomes the mother of Vayu's son, Bhima. While Vayu had chosen Anjani, Kunti had chosen Vayu. Kunti had invoked Vayu with a mantra, and asked him to give her a child, but Anjani had not. This made Bhima a child of desire, whereas Hanuman was a child of destiny.

As sons of the wind god, both Hanuman and Bhima are brothers. Like Hanuman, Bhima is very strong. But unlike Hanuman, Bhima is not divine. Bhima may be his elder brother's loyal agent, but that is not the same as serving Ram. For in serving his elder brother, Bhima does his duty as a younger brother, and is serving his family; in serving Ram, Hanuman is fulfilling no obligation but acting of his own volition and love. Bhima is as strong as Hanuman, but he lacks Hanuman's humility. While Hanuman is content being a messenger (doot) for Ram, as he is born of a monkey, Bhima feels entitled because he is born of a princess.

In Hindu mythology, destiny determined our body, our family, hence our social role. Our desire makes us either want to change a social role or cling to a social role. Destiny makes Ram the eldest son of a royal family, hence he acts as king. He does not desire to be king. Destiny makes Hanuman a monkey, he *chooses* to serve Ram, not for wealth and power, but for wisdom—the realization of the divine potential. Hence, he serves but does not seek. Bhima not only fulfils his social role, he also uses it to dominate the world around him, and benefit from his birth-determined strength and status. Hanuman teaches him to change his ways as we learn from the following story.

In his royal arrogance, Bhima always walked straight and expected all things to move aside and make way for him, even mountains and trees. Those who blocked his path were simply hurled aside or crushed underfoot. In his path, one day, he found an old monkey sleeping. 'I am too old to get out of your way,' the monkey murmured. 'Just kick my tail aside and make your way.' But when Bhima tried to kick the old monkey's tail, he realized it was really heavy, so heavy that it could not be pushed or pulled, even when he used all his strength. Bhima realized this was no ordinary monkey. When Hanuman revealed himself, he showed Bhima his awesome form (virat-swarup), making Bhima realize the insignificance of his physical strength and social position.

A king uses his power to serve people and create an ecosystem where people can outgrow hunger and fear. When a king uses his power to dominate those around him, it reveals the king has not outgrown his hunger and fear; he is not yet Ram. Likewise, a king's agent uses his power to serve his master. When a king's agent uses his power to dominate those around him, it reveals he has not outgrown his hunger and fear; he is not yet Hanuman.

Chaupai 3: Thunder Body, Lightning Mind

महाबीर
बिक्रम बजरंगी ।
कुमति निवार
सुमति के संगी ॥

Mahabir
Bikram Bajrangi.
Kumati nivar
sumati ke sangi.

Great hero
valiant, with Lightning body.
Who drives away bad thoughts
and is always accompanied by good thoughts.

Having explained his origins and role, this verse presents the qualities of Hanuman that make him worthy of worship. Most villages in India worship a vira, or hero, who protects the village. Hanuman is identified as Maha-vira, or Mahabir, who also protects the mind. Hanuman not only vanquishes physical demons like rakshasas and asuras, but also psychological demons such as negative thoughts (kumati) and ushers in positive thoughts (sumati).

Hanuman stands on the frontier between the wilderness and the settlement, between the animal and the human world, and has the power to turn the negative into positive, poison into medicine. This is why in temples Hanuman is often offered special Arka (*Calotropis indica*, Bowstring Hemp, Giant Milkweed) leaves and flowers, which grow wild in the forest and are poisonous. This 'negative' offering becomes positive after contact with his body.

Hanuman's status as a special kind of hero is reaffirmed by being called vikram, which is both a common noun meaning valiant and a proper noun referring to a legendary king, Vikramaditya, king of Ujjain, who was renowned for his worldly wisdom. There is a famous Sanskrit work known as *Vetala Pachisi*, which tells twenty-five tales in which Vikramaditya takes difficult decisions. These questions are posed by a ghost, or vetala, feared by all mortals, but not the brave king of Ujjain. Hanuman is like this legendary king, brave enough to face ghosts, and wise enough to solve complex puzzles.

Hanuman is also being addressed as Bajrangi, which means one who possesses a body (anga) that is as powerful and radiant as the thunderbolt (vajra). In Hindu mythology, vajra is the weapon of Indra, the sky god who hurls thunderbolts against dark monsoon clouds to release rain. Indra once hurled this weapon at Hanuman and instead of being hurt by it, Hanuman simply absorbed and internalized his power. Hence he is also called Vajra-angi, one whose body is as powerful as a thunderbolt.

In Buddhist mythology, vajra refers to thunderbolt and diamond, and is a metaphor of incisive analytical abilities. Vajrapani is a guardian of the Buddha and a fearsome deity who strikes the ignorant down and grants the wise incisive, analytical abilities. He is visualized trampling the enemies of the Buddha and holding a vajra in his hand, much as Hanuman tramples demons and holds a mace in his hand, suggesting the overlapping roots of these two deities.

Vedic Hinduism, based on worldliness, thrived over three thousand years ago, but it was overshadowed, two thousand years ago, by Buddhism that valued other-worldliness. In order to spread, both Hinduism and Buddhism assimilated with folk beliefs and to stay relevant, both exchanged ideas. As a result both transformed—Vedic Hinduism became Puranic Hinduism, while Buddhism split into Theravada Buddhism and Mahayana Buddhism. Vedic Hinduism worshipped the vajra-wielding Indra who was assimilated with Vishnu of the Puranic tradition. The historical teacher, Sakyamuni Buddha, of Theravada Buddhism made room for mythological saviours known as Bodhisattvas of Mahayana Buddhism. When Islam came to India, Buddhism waned out of mainstream, but many Buddhist ideas and icons survived and were absorbed into the mainstream. Hanuman reflects many Buddhist ideals—he has no desires like the Buddha, yet he helps people by solving their problems like the Bodhisattva, and his form mirrors the form of the Buddhist guardian-god Vajrapani.

In pre-Buddhist, even pre-Vedic, times, it has been postulated that the blood of enemies and wild animals was offered to the village guardian-god by the warriors who defended the village frontier. Red became the colour of valour and fertility. Later, as the doctrine of ahimsa (non-violence) gained ground, blood was represented symbolically using sindoor (vermillion). Even later, the red colour was replaced by saffron colour, indicating celibacy and continence, a rejection of all things sensory. Buddhist monks were the first to use saffron, ochre, maroon and red robes to distinguish themselves from the robes of common folk, but eventually these colours were adopted by Hindu monks and saffron has now become the colour of choice of political Hinduism. Hanuman's orange-red body is often covered with silver and gold foil representing his Lightning-like body.

Chaupai 4: Darshan

कंचन बरन
बिराज सुबेसा ।
कानन कुंडल
कुंचित केसा ॥

**Kanchan baran
biraj subesa.
Kanan kundal
kunchit kesa.**

*Golden body
seated with elegant adornments.
Rings in the ears
curly locks.*

If the previous verse described the prowess of Hanuman, this verse focuses on his physical form: his golden complexion, his curly hair and his fine clothes, including the earrings.

The golden complexion reminds us that Hanuman is a monkey, with golden fur. But his earrings and curly hair draw attention to his humanity, as only humans wear ornaments and have hair on the head.

In some stories, Hanuman was born with earrings. The story goes that Vali, the king of monkeys, had heard that Kesari's wife Anjani was pregnant with a child who would be more powerful than him. So he cast a missile to hurt this child. However, instead of getting hurt, Vayu ensured the missile transformed into Hanuman's earrings, a symbol of Vali's, hence Indra's, defeat.

Earrings have a special significance in Hinduism. Piercing the ears of a child is a rite of passage (samskara). By piercing the ear, one creates a passage for sunlight through the body, making the body auspicious. Traditionally, men and women both wore earrings. So Vishnu is famous for his dolphin (makara) shaped earrings and Shiva is famous for wearing serpent (naga) shaped earrings. Hanuman's earrings connect him to fierce warrior-hermits known as Nath-yogi, of the ear-split (kan-phata) order (sampradaya), who were identified by their special earrings made of rhinoceros skin inserted by splitting the ear cartilage. Their gurus, Matsyendra-nath and Gorakh-nath, wrestled Hanuman and earned his respect.

Hanuman is described as well dressed. In folklore, he was born wearing an adamantine loincloth made of thunder, or diamond (vajra-kaupina), to reaffirm his celibacy, and his association with orders of ash-smeared, trident-bearing, warrior-hermits. This association with warrior-hermit orders starts only around a thousand years ago, following the institutionalization of the Hindu monastic orders, on one hand by wandering Tantrik mendicant jogis of the Nath order (such as Matsyendra-nath), and on the other hand by Vedantic acharyas such as Adi Shankara-acharya who established Hindu abbeys (mathas).

That the verse describes how Hanuman looks and what he wears indicates that we are gazing upon the deity. This is darshan, an integral ritual in Hinduism. The whole purpose of going into a temple is to see the deity and be seen by the deity, who invariably has large, shapely eyes that captivate the visitor even from afar. The devotee describes the deity's beauty, and hopes the deity will reciprocate, identify the devotee's needs and wants, and give them what they deserve and desire.

A Christian church, a Muslim mosque, a Buddhist monastery or a Sikh gurudwara are spaces designed to bring the community together and focus on a common goal—confess sins, reaffirm submission, awaken to desires and delusions and learn from the songs of the sages, as the case may be. But a Hindu temple is the house of a deity. We go to see them and be seen by them, no different from visiting a relative's or friend's house, or going to a king's court, with a petition.

The practice of invoking and adoring a deity and then petitioning him for material benefits informed the ancient Vedic ritual known as yagna. It continued to inform the later temple rituals known as puja. What makes puja different from yagna, however, is the value placed on darshan. The word 'darshan' has a double meaning: view as well as worldview, sight as well as insight. It is simultaneously about doing and thinking, action and introspection. It seeks to counter the purely intellectual approach of Buddhism where greater value is given to dhyan (meditation) wherein eyes are shut. It also seeks to appeal to the masses who are not interested in introspection. Deities in Buddhism are just tools to enable better meditation, while Hindu deities have elaborate form, their images, charged with hymn and ritual, are capable of responding to the prayers of the devotee. Darshan acknowledges the value of relationship, between deity and devotee, between self and other—in contrast to the isolation and individualism that informs Buddhist practices, and even Hindu monastic orders.

We prove that we have truly seen the deity on the basis of what offering we make. Every deity is unique and so seeks unique offerings. For Vishnu, there are tulsi leaves, for Shiva, there are bilva leaves. Hanuman is typically offered items sought by wrestlers and bodybuilders: til (sesame) oil, rai (mustard) oil, and urad (black gram) seeds, which build up muscle mass, and are traditionally considered 'hot' ingredients, firing up the body with energy.

Chaupai 5: Warrior, Servant, and Sage

हाथ बज्र
औ ध्वजा बिराजै ।
काँधे मूँज
जनेऊ साजै ॥

My Hanuman Chalisa

**Hath bajra
aur dhvaja biraje.
Kaandhe moonj
janehu sajai.**

*You hold a thunderbolt club
and a flag in your hands.
And have the sacred thread
on your shoulder.*

In the previous verse, the focus was on what Hanuman was born with—his complexion, his hair, even his earrings. This verse focuses on what he holds in his hands and bears on his body: a mace, a flag and a sacred thread (janehu) made of sabai grass (munja) on his shoulder. These are instruments (yantra) that embellish the icon (svarupa) of Hanuman and help refine our understanding of him.

The common word used for mace is gada, but the word used here is vajra, or the thunderbolt, which is Indra's weapon. In the Vedas, Indra is the greatest of gods, one who battles demons like Vritra, and releases the waters held by clouds. He is the patron of kings. Yet, in the Puranas, his role is reduced. He is the lord of Paradise (Swarga), leader of devas, who lives in celestial regions and enjoys worldly pleasures, but lacks wisdom. He needs the help of Vishnu to fight the demons (asuras) who lay siege to Paradise and declare war relentlessly. This shift in status indicates a shift from the older more materialistic Vedic way to the later Vedic (Upanishadic) way where greater value was placed on the mind (on meaning) than on riches and power.

In the Puranas, every deity has a flag (dhvaja) of his own—

Vishnu has a flag with the image of a hawk known as garuda-dhvaja, and Shiva has a flag with the image of a bull known as vrishabha-dhvaja—but Hanuman's dhvaja belongs to Ram, in keeping with his role as Ram's messenger and commander of his armies. Hanuman holds both Indra's weapon and Ram's flag, which endorses his status as mightier than the old Vedic celestial god-king, but serving the latter Puranic earthbound god-king.

Hanuman's janehu makes him a twice born (dvija). Hindus believe that we have two births: first there is physical birth and then there is the psychological birth. Physically, we are born out of the mother's womb into human culture. Our navel reminds us of our origin in the mother's womb. In Hindu culture, pierced earlobes are indicators of human culture, similar to the practice of tattooing, or tooth-filing, in other cultures.

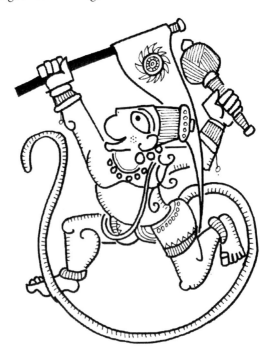

Our psychological birth takes place when we accept a guru who reveals to us the secrets of the Vedas. The mark of psychological birth is the sacred thread made of munja grass that hangs over the left shoulder. This thread has three strings representative of the Hindu trinity: Brahma, Vishnu, and Shakti. It also reminds us that while animals have only one body (physical), humans have three (physical, psychological and social). Hanuman accessed Vedic wisdom through Surya, the sun god, who also revealed Vedic secrets to Yagnavalkya, the sage whose words are captured in many Upanishads. Vedic secrets include knowledge of karma and dharma, of aham (our identity based on hunger and fear) and atma (our identity independent of hunger and fear).

Hanuman being given the janehu, despite being a servant of Ram and a wild forest creature, is not highlighted in the Valmiki Ramayana but becomes prominent in later texts, especially regional Ramayanas written in vernacular languages in the last five centuries, when caste excesses had peaked. People were asking: what makes a real Brahmin, effort or birth? Hanuman becomes Brahmin by effort and education, while Ravana is the son of a Brahmin named Vaishrava, who married a rakshasa woman, Kaikesi. The Vedas turn Hanuman from beast to human, giving him the wisdom and compassion to unconditionally help a man find his lost wife. By contrast, Ravana although human, and despite his Vedic knowledge, behaves like a brute, grabbing another man's wife for his own pleasure.

That Hanuman holds a weapon in his hand establishes him as a warrior (Kshatriya). That he holds Ram's flag establishes him as a servant (dasa, Shudra). That he has the sacred thread across his chest establishes him as a Brahmin, one who has accessed the Vedas. Thus the highest and the lowest stations of Vedic society (varna) are accommodated in Hanuman, a creature of the forest.

Chaupai 6: Rudra's Eleventh Form

संकर सुवन
केसरीनंदन ।
तेज प्रताप
महा जग बंदन ॥

Sankar suvan
Kesari nandan.
Tej prataap
maha jag bandan.

Shankara's (Shiva's) manifestation
Kesari's son
Your glory
is venerated by the whole world

This verse connects Hanuman to Shankara, which is another name for Shiva. For many devotees today, Hanuman is a form of Shiva. He is described variously as the son of Shiva, as the manifestation of Shiva, as an avatar of Shiva, as the eleventh Rudra form.

This connection between Hanuman and Shiva began roughly 1,500 years ago, a time that also saw Puranic Hinduism split between two schools of thought: the Vaishnavites who saw the world-affirming Vishnu as the supreme divine being and the

Shaivites who saw the world-renouncing Shiva as the supreme divine being.

When the Ramayana became popular, Vishnu-worshippers saw Ram as the mortal form (avatar) of Vishnu who kills Ravana, a devotee (bhakta) of Shiva. This turned the Ramayana into a tale of rivalry between Vishnu and Shiva. To counter this, Shiva-worshippers said that Hanuman was the form of Shiva. They pointed to Hanuman's status as brahmachari (celibate, continent and content, with no wants or needs) and his colour being as white as camphor (karpura-go-ranga) indicative of his being Shiva.

In some stories explaining the origins of Hanuman, it is said that when Shiva saw Vishnu in the form of Mohini, or Parvati, he began to sweat profusely. Vayu collected this sweat and poured it in the ear of Anjana, a vanara woman, who gave birth to Hanuman. Anjana's husband, Kesari, raised Hanuman as his own son and so Hanuman is also known as the son of Kesari. So besides a mortal father (Kesari) and a Vedic father (Vayu), Hanuman also has a Puranic father (Shiva). Besides a mortal mother (Anjani), Hanuman also has a celestial mother (Shakti).

According to Shaivites, Shiva himself descended as Hanuman to destroy Ravana, an errant Shiva-bhakta. According to them, Ravana had offered his ten heads to Shiva and obtained boons that made him very powerful. But as Rudra, Shiva has eleven forms. Ravana's offering of ten heads satisfied the ten forms of Rudra. The eleventh unhappy Rudra took birth as Hanuman to kill Ravana. Hence Hanuman is also Raudreya. In Maharashtra, the seventeenth-century saint Ramdas established eleven Maruti temples, reminding all of Hanuman's association with the eleven forms of Rudra.

To establish their superiority, Vishnu-worshippers argued that

Hanuman, hence Shiva, obeyed instructions given by Vishnu. To counter this, Shiva-worshipers said that without Hanuman's help, Ram would never have found Sita. In many retellings of the Ramayana, it is Hanuman who enables the killing of Ravana. For example, in one Telugu retelling, despite knowing that Ravana's life resided in his navel, Ram shot only at the head of Ravana as he was too proud a warrior to shoot below the neck. So Hanuman sucked air into his lungs and caused the wind to shift direction making Ram's arrow turn and strike Ravana's navel.

Hanuman's association with Shiva, and with celibacy, was reinforced by Hanuman's association with the various ascetic schools of Hinduism, including the Nath-yogis who followed the path of Matsyendra-nath from around 1,000 years ago, to the Vedantic mathas who followed Madhwa-acharya from around 700 years ago, and Sant Ramdas who inspired many Maratha warriors 400 years ago. The latter sages, especially during the Bhakti period, introduced the idea of connecting celibacy with service; you give up your worldly pleasures and work for the worldly aspirations of society. Just as the hermit Shiva became the householder Shankara for the benefit of Humanity, these sages spoke of how the ascetic Hanuman became Ram's servant for the benefit of society.

At one time, women were not allowed to worship Hanuman. By his mere radiance, it is said in many stories, he can make them pregnant. In the stories of Nath-yogis, one learns of queens who become pregnant by simply listening to the song of Hanuman, or fish becoming pregnant by consuming the sweat of Hanuman, for his radiance permeates into his voice and his sweat. As the centuries passed the overtly masculine nature of Hanuman was toned down. Just as Shiva was domesticated by Shakti, Hanuman's gentle side is evoked by Sita. Since there can be no Shiva without Shakti, many say that Shakti took the form of Hanuman's tail and always accompanied him. Hence, today women also worship Hanuman to solve their problems.

Chaupai 7: Clever and Concerned

विद्यावान गुनी
अति चातुर ।
राम काज
करिबे को आतुर ॥

**Vidyavaan guni
ati chatur.
Ram kaj
karibe ko aatur.**

*Educated, virtuous
and clever.
Ram's tasks
you always do eagerly.*

In the very first chaupai of the Chalisa, Hanuman is described as the ocean (sagar) of knowledge (gyan) and virtue (gun). This verse also reinforces Hanuman as being knowledgeable and virtuous, and adds that he is also clever (chatur). This tendency to complement one quality with another is a typical Indian idiom. Just as one spice does not create a dish, and just as a good curry is a clever combination of various spices, even a good person is a combination of various qualities.

In nature, we often say that the strong dominate the weak. But nature does not discriminate against the weak. They are given smartness to compensate for their physical weakness. Strength and smartness are tools to find food and security, to survive and thrive. Hanuman is strong *and* smart and thus has the best of animal qualities. His knowledge and virtue are what make him human and divine.

This verse reminds us that the educated man is not smart and the smart man is not educated. And a smart educated man is dangerous unless he has virtue. What is virtue? The ability to look beyond our own hungers and fears and be concerned of other people's hungers and fears. The way Hanuman behaves when he first meets Ram and Sita indicates how his knowledge, his cleverness and his virtue work together.

When he sees Ram and Lakshman wandering in the forest, looking for something, he realizes there is value in introducing them to Sugriv, the monkey-king. He approaches Ram, taking the form of a brahmin, and speaks in chaste Sanskrit, the language of the gods, which is an indicator that he has knowledge of the Vedas. Thus he evokes trust in the wary Ram, who is agonizing over the abduction of Sita.

Later, when it is time to meet Sita in Lanka, he wonders if he should speak in Sanskrit again while introducing himself. But he has seen Ravana speak in Sanskrit, and fears Sita will assume he is an imposter: Ravana's agent, or Ravana himself, posing as Ram's messenger. So he speaks to her in the organic language spoken by common folk. This is Prakrit (informal, organic language) as against Sanskrit (formal, designed language).

In neither situation is Hanuman trying to show off or intimidate the other with his knowledge. He is driven by concern for the other. He is not anxious of the other; he can sense the anxiety of the other. He is smart enough to anticipate how people react in stress: how they get startled at the sight of a stranger, and think the worst. The ability to adapt to the situation, and win the trust and confidence of both Ram and Sita through speech, reveals his sensitivity to people and to context, his communication skill, and most importantly, his empathy.

Chaupai 8: Other People's Stories

पर्भु चरित्र
सुनिबे को रसिया ।
राम लखन
सीता मन बसिया ॥

**Prabhu charitra
sunibe ko rasiya.
Ram Lakhan
Sita man basiya.**

*Ram's stories
you enjoy listening.
Ram, Lakshman
Sita as well, always reside in your heart.*

For Hindus, one of the ways to expand our mind, and discover the divine within, is by listening (shravana) to stories of the divine.

Puranic stories are containers (patra) of Vedic wisdom (atma-gyan). Stories are of different types: memoirs (itihasa), chronicles (purana), epics (maha-kavya), narratives (akhyana), glories (mahatmya), biographies (charitra), songs (gita), prose-poetry (champu). Hanuman nourishes himself intellectually and emotionally by listening to stories of Ram, as we learn from this verse.

Traditionally, in gatherings where Ram's story is read out, one seat is always left vacant. Hanuman is described as rasika, one who enjoys the aesthetic juices (rasa) of Ram's tale. As per Hindu aesthetics, a good story is like good food. It needs to have multiple flavours that stir the senses and arouse emotions, for only then can it incept thoughts that can help expand the mind.

In folk tradition, Hanuman grows up listening to stories of Ram narrated by his mother. How is that possible? How can Hanuman hear stories of events that he himself participated in? In the Hindu worldview, the world goes through cycles of re-birth and re-death, just like any other living creature. In each of its lifetimes (kalpa), the world has four phases, like all living creatures: childhood, youth, maturity and old age. These are the four yugas, identified as Krita, Treta, Dvapara, and Kali. The Ramayana takes place in Treta Yuga. Since the world has gone through infinite lifetimes, and in each kalpa there has been a Ramayana, everyone in every age knows the story of Ram. Anjana narrates to Hanuman stories of Ram from an earlier kalpa.

Hanuman is so excited to hear the story of Ram that he desires to meet Ram. And so he goes to the city of Ayodhya where he learns that Ram, the prince, is craving for a pet. Hanuman lets himself be captured by the soldiers who gift him to the prince. That way Hanuman becomes Ram's pet and also spends his childhood as Ram's companion. Thus, in local oral traditions,

Hanuman is with Ram throughout his life, not just after Sita's abduction as narrated in various Sanskrit and regional texts.

In the Valmiki Ramayana, when Ram and Sugriv meet for the first time, they exchange stories. Ram tells him his tragedy, how Ravana abducted his wife. Sugriv tells him his tragedy, how Vali usurped his kingdom. Hanuman realizes that Ram's story has a solution for Sugriv's problem, and Sugriv's story has a solution for Ram's problem. If Ram helps Sugriv get his kingdom, Sugriv will help Ram find his wife. Listening to each other's stories reveals mutual benefit. Had stories not been shared, neither would the problem be understood nor would a solution have been found.

To see the other is to hear their stories. Brahma, the creator of all living organisms, and his children, such as Indra, are not worshipped because they do not care for other people's stories; they are consumed by their own. In exasperation, Shiva beheads

Brahma, which is why Shiva is called Kapalika. Shiva has learned the importance of storytelling from Shakti. Together they establish their relationship by telling each other stories, stories that are overheard by birds and fish and shared with the rest of the world.

Vishnu hears the stories of Brahma's children, and nudges them to hear the stories of those around them. But reciprocity is not easy. By listening to Sugriv's story, Ram not only understands his problem, he also understands Sugriv's personality. He realizes that Sugriv sees him as an ally but has doubts. So Ram shoots a single arrow through seven trees, earning Sugriv's admiration and trust. Ram also realizes that after getting his kingdom, Sugriv will forget his end of the bargain, not because he is a cheat, but simply because he is so consumed by what he wants from others, that he is unable to see what others want from him. Still, he gives Sugriv the benefit of the doubt and helps him overpower Vali.

When Sugriv hears Ram's story, he sees a prince in distress and a potential ally in his fight against Vali. He sees what value Ram brings to him; he does not see Ram for what Ram is. By contrast, just by hearing Ram's story, Hanuman realizes that Ram is no ordinary human: his story has no villains, or victims, or heroes, just hungry and frightened humans seeking meaning. Hanuman recognizes Ram as the embodiment of divine potential, of atma, of dharma, all that is referred to in the Vedas, all that was taught to him by Surya.

Hanuman does Ram's darshan each time he hears Ram's story. He wants to participate in it, even as a minor character, for he relishes the idea of being part of Ram's story. One day, he narrated the story of Ramayana to his mother: how the monkeys and he built the bridge to Lanka, fought the rakshasas, killed Ravana and reunited Sita with Ram. Anjana was not impressed, for she felt her son was not living up to his potential. 'You could have just swung your tail and defeated the demons and rescued Sita without this whole charade of building a bridge and fighting a war. Why didn't you?' she asked. Hanuman replied, 'Because Ram did not ask me to.' Hanuman knew the Ramayana was Ram's story, not his. He did not want to control or appropriate or overshadow Ram's story. It was about Ram, not him.

It is significant that the very first narrator of the Ramayana is Hanuman himself: he describes Ram to Sugriv, he tells the story of Ram's adventures to Sita when he meets her in Lanka and does the same when he meets Bharat in Ayodhya. Later, he writes the first biography of Ram known as Hanuman Nataka, but destroys it so that Valmiki gets the credit of writing the first epic on Ram.

In stories, Hanuman observes Ram's relationship with Lakshman and Sita, and realizes how Ram's brother and Ram's wife complete him, and how he completes them. When Hanuman places all three of them in his heart, he is essentially placing in his heart the idea of relationship: that the self is incomplete without the other; that the self exists in an ecosystem of others. That is why in Hindu temples, no deity is placed alone: the deity always has a spouse, or a child, or a companion, or an attendant. Even Hanuman, who has no relatives, is not placed alone; we know that in his heart is present his master, who in turn is accompanied by his brother and his wife.

This value placed on relationship between the self and the other is key to Hindu stories. Most mythologies, ideologies and philosophies around the world can be broadly classified into two categories: individualistic and collectivist. Individualistic mythologies value the one over the group. Collectivist mythologies value the group over the one. Greek and Taoist ways, for example, are individualistic; Abrahamic and Confucian ways are collectivist. One can even classify Shaivite mythologies as individualistic and Vaishnavite mythologies as collectivist. However, that is not quite accurate. Hindu mythologies are best understood in terms of relationship: Shiva's relationship with Shakti and Vishnu's relationship with Lakshmi. Instead of the binary of the individual and the group, Hinduism focuses on the relationship between two individuals (the dyad). Shiva tends to withdraw from the other; Vishnu engages with the other.

When we relish the stories of the gods as Hanuman does, we see the gods truly, and recognize their presence or absence in us, just like Hanuman.

Chaupai 9: Adapting to Context

सूक्ष्म रूप धरि
सियहिं दिखावा ।
बिकट रूप धरि
लंक जरावा ॥

Sukshma roop dhari
Siyahi dikhava.
Vikat roop dhari
Lank jarava.

You took a small vulnerable form
before Sita.
You took a giant fearsome form
to burn Lanka.

In the first quarter of the Hanuman Chalisa, a lot of emphasis is placed on the origin, form and attributes, the role as well as the preferences, of Hanuman. We refer to his mother, his earthly and celestial fathers, we refer to his appearance and his symbols, his qualities and capabilities, his love for Ram's stories, and his desire to serve Ram.

With this verse we are describing his many feats: his ability to contract and expand himself physically as the situation demands. To the frightened Sita, he appeared as a small non-threatening monkey. To the arrogant Ravana, he appeared as a giant fearsome creature. Hanuman is thus no ordinary creature—he is a shape-shifter who knows what shape other people respond to.

In Hinduism, God is constantly playing games (leela) nudging the devotee-child to realize his divine potential. Thus God can expand or contract, encompass infinity (virat-rupa), and change shape and size for the benefit of all living creatures. Vishnu, for example, manifests as a fish, a boar, a priest, a king, or a cowherd. This ability to adapt for the benefit of the other is a hallmark of divinity, one that Hanuman also possesses.

The transformations of Hanuman described in this verse, of contracting and expanding in size, come from a chapter known as Sundar-kand in the Ramayana. The chapter is named beautiful (sundar) as it evokes hope: the possibility of Sita and Ram reuniting, thanks to the intervention of Hanuman. It is also thus named because it is the only place where he experiences the tenderness of Ram's love for Sita and Sita's love for Ram. Hanuman conveys Ram's words and describes Ram's sorrow to Sita, and Sita conveys her feelings to Ram through Hanuman, even sharing intimate secrets, such as how Ram used to rest his head on her lap when he was exhausted in the forest.

Hanuman's puny form makes Sita wonder how he could possibly have leapt across the sea. So Hanuman reveals his giant form and reassures her. Later, Hanuman lets himself be caught by Ravana's soldiers so that he gains an audience with the rakshasa-king. Hanuman is astute enough to realize that sensible words will not work with one such as Ravana who is consumed by his own self-importance, and is so frightened that he constantly feels the need to dominate those around him. Unable to break free from his animal nature, Ravana only understands the language of force. So when Ravana refuses to treat Hanuman as a messenger and give him due respect by offering a seat to him, Hanuman creates his own seat, extending and coiling his tail; only Hanuman's seat is at higher level than Ravana's throne, forcing Ravana to look up rather than down, a humiliation that Ravana cannot bear. Furious, unnerved, the king of Lanka orders his soldiers to set Hanuman's tail on fire. Hanuman responds by twirling his tail in every direction, setting fire to Ravana's beautiful palace and the city of Lanka around it, before leaping off the island-kingdom.

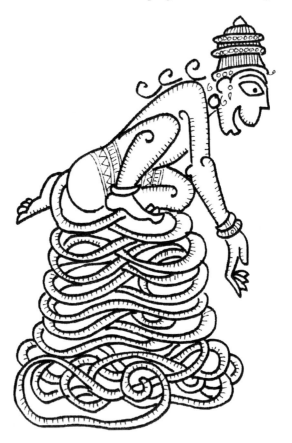

In India, there are broadly two types of monkeys—the red-faced monkey with golden fur and the black-faced monkey with silver fur. In folklore, it is believed that the soot of Lanka burning turned the red-faced monkey into the black-faced monkey.

In art, Hanuman images can be classified into two types depending on the location of the tail: if it is lowered, it indicates the gentle (saumya) form with which Hanuman approached Sita and Ram; if Hanuman's tail is raised, it indicates the fierce (rudra) form with which Hanuman stood up to Ravana. This reaffirms Hanuman's relationship with Shiva who is known for both his gentle (Shankara) and fierce (Bhairava) forms.

Hanuman is also depicted, especially in the south, with his arm extended as if he is going to slap someone. This is called 'tamacha' Hanuman: the form he took to humiliate Ravana. By contrast, when his image is placed next to Ram, his arms are in a position of veneration: this form is called Ram-dasa, the servant of Ram.

Chaupai 10: Demon-Killer

भीम रूप धरि
असुर सँहारे ।
रामचंद्र के
काज सँवारे ॥

**Bhima roop dhari
asur sanghare.
Ramachandra ke
kaj sanvare.**

*You took fearsome forms
to kill demons.
Ramchandra's
tasks were thus accomplished.*

A typical image of Hanuman enshrined in temples, shows him crushing a demon underfoot. Sometimes two demons—mostly a man, but sometimes a woman. These could be one of many demons that Hanuman overpowers in the Valmiki Ramayana and in the many regional and folk Ramayanas.

On his way to Lanka, Hanuman encounters three female demons—Simhika, Surasa and Lankini—who protect Lanka from intruders. Simhika has the power to capture her prey by its shadow; so she grabs hold of Hanuman's shadow and forces him into her mouth. Hanuman does not resist, he reduces himself in size so that rather than bite him, she is forced to swallow him. Inside her stomach, he expands in size and escapes by ripping out of her entrails, causing her to die.

Surasa blocks Hanuman's path in the middle of the sea and tells him that he cannot pass until he enters her mouth; that is a boon she has been given by the gods. Hanuman has no choice but to enter her mouth. He increases his size forcing Surasa to widen her jaws. Then in a moment, he reduces himself to the size of a bee, and zips in and out of Surasa's mouth. Surasa has no choice but to let Hanuman pass for he has outwitted her with his agility.

While he first contracts and then expands to escape Simhika, Hanuman expands and later contracts to escape Surasa, the mother of serpents. While he uses brute force to kill Simhika, he uses cunning to escape Surasa.

In Lanka, Hanuman simply shoves the guardian-goddess of Lanka, Lankini, to the ground, making her realize he is no ordinary monkey, but the monkey destined to defeat Ravana. The defeat of Simhika, Surasa and Lankini marks the beginning of the end of Ravana's rule.

The female demon depicted under Hanuman's foot is sometimes interpreted as Lankini, Surasa or Simhika. Some identify her as Panvati, or a malevolent astrological force that causes misfortune. Others see her as Surpanakha (Ravana's sister), embodying the lustful woman who is the opposite of the celibate sage embodied by Hanuman.

Some see this fierce relationship of Hanuman with female demons as a rejection of Tantra where female deities preside and the focus is the acquisition of occult powers. In folklore, the celibate male ascetics (jogi) are often in conflict with sexually alluring female sorceresses (joginis). This is seen as reflecting the conflict between the austere, refined Vedanta tradition where the focus was wisdom and liberation, and the crude Tantra tradition where the focus was power and control.

Not everyone appreciates the idea of violence against women, even if the woman is a demon. In most images, the demon under Hanuman's foot is male and identified as Kalanemi sent by Ravana to prevent Hanuman from finding the Sanjivani herb, or Mahiravana who Hanuman outwits to save Ram from Pa-tala. The demon embodies obstacles that come in the way of success. Crushing him marks the crushing of obstacles. That is why Hanuman is called the remover of obstacles (sankat-mochan).

The mighty Hanuman is imagined sometimes with ten heads (dasa-mukhi) or with five heads (pancha-mukhi). In the latter form, the extra heads are those of other animals: a horse, lion, eagle and wild boar. These indicate Hanuman's association with wisdom (horse), valour (lion), vision (eagle) and tenacity (boar). It also visibly reveals Hanuman to be more than a monkey. This form of Hanuman is called Maha-bali, and is seen as standing independent of Ram.

Hanuman displays his cosmic form (virat-swarup) in various situations, in various contexts: to impress Ram when they meet for the first time, to inspire the monkey army as he leaps across the sea, to overpower Simhika, escape Surasa, defeat Lankini, to instil hope in Sita isolated in Lanka, to intimidate Ravana in his court, and finally, in the Mahabharata, to teach Bhima humility. But at all times, this mighty form of Hanuman contains his humility, the desire to serve Ram always.

Chaupai 11: Saving Lakshman

लाय सजीवन
लखन जियाये ।
श्रीरघुवीर
हरषि उर लाये ॥

Laye Sanjivan
Lakhan jiyaye.
Shri Raghuvir
harashi ur laye.

By fetching the Sanjivani herb
you saved Lakshman.
Scion of the Raghu clan
hugged you in delight.

In the Ramayana, the rakshasa-king Ravana abducts Sita and takes her away to the south across the sea to the islandkingdom of Lanka. To save Sita, her husband Ram and Ram's brother

Lakshman take the help of the vanaras to build a bridge to Lanka and declare war against Ravana.

In the war that follows, Ravana's son Meghnad, also known as Indrajit, strikes Lakshman with a deadly arrow containing the venom of serpents. Lakshman loses consciousness and risks losing his life as the poison begins to spread through his limbs. Only a herb called Sanjivani can save Ram's brother, if applied to the wound before sunrise the next day. But the herb grows on a mountain far away in the north. Who can fetch it from so far, so soon? Ram wonders as the sun begins to set.

The vanaras shout, Hanuman, of course! Did he not leap across the ocean and reach Lanka as if jumping from one branch of a tree to another? Surely he can fly north and bring back the herb in one night. Ram looks at Hanuman with anxious eyes, his heart filled with deep despair at the thought of his dying brother. In response, Hanuman turns north and jumps.

As Hanuman rises to the sky, Ravana catches sight of him, and figuring out his mission, summons the magician Kalanemi and orders him to create obstacles so that Hanuman does not find the herb, and even if he does, he does not return before sunrise.

Kalanemi uses his magic to reach the Dronagiri mountain where the Sanjivani grows before Hanuman and waits there disguised as a hermit. On Hanuman's arrival, he welcomes him with words of praise and offers him food. Hanuman finds it inappropriate to say no to an offer of hospitality so he accepts the invitation, but insists on taking a bath before the meal. So Kalanemi directs him to a pool full of crocodiles. Hanuman not only takes a bath, he also kills the crocodiles when they attack him. The crocodiles turn out to be apsaras, celestial damsels cursed by Indra to live on earth as reptiles until liberated by a monkey. They thank Hanuman and reveal Kalanemi's true identity. A furious Hanuman attacks and strikes Kalanemi dead.

Much time has been lost, it is now the middle of the night and Hanuman has no time to find the herb on the mountain. It's too dark. So he picks up the entire mountain and flies back south to Lanka. Just as he is nearing Lanka he observes that the sun, goaded by Ravana, is being made to rise before his time. So with his free hand he grabs the sun, traps him in his armpit and makes his way to Ram, mountain in hand.

The herb is found, Lakshman is saved and the sun god released to rise, much to Ram's relief and delight. This very popular event from the Ramayana is described in this chaupai.

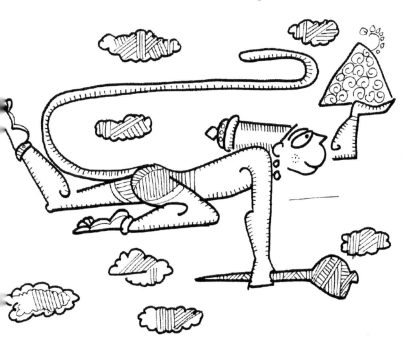

Hanuman with Kalanemi underfoot and Sanjivani in his hand is the form in which he is worshipped in most temples. Kalanemi represents the obstacles in our life. Sanjivani is the solution to our problems. The image captures the idea behind the worship of Hanuman—he removes obstacles and solves problems, which is why he is adored by all. Hanuman embodies the pragmatic aspect of Hinduism, quite different from the philosophical side.

There are many other stories of Hanuman carrying mountains, not linked to Sanjivani. The vanaras, we are told, carried many mountains from the Himalayas to build the bridge to Lanka. When the construction of the bridge was complete, all the vanaras were told to drop the mountains they were carrying wherever they were. All the mountains we see in the southern part of India, it is said, have their origin in the Himalayas and were brought south by the vanaras. The mountain being carried by Hanuman was called Govardhan. He felt bad that he would not see Ram. So Hanuman promised Govardhan that in a future birth, Ram would surely see him. So Ram took birth as Krishna in the Dvapara Yuga, and grew up on the slopes of Govardhan and even lifted him up with his little finger.

Chaupai 12: A Brother Like Bharat

रघुपति कीन्ही
बहुत बड़ाई ।
तुम मम प्रिय
भरतहि सम भाई ॥

**Raghupati kinhi
bahut badai.
Tum mam priye
Bharat-hi-sam bhai.**

*Ram sings
praises of you.
'You are as dear to me
as my brother Bharat.'*

Ram is so thankful for Hanuman's many interventions that enable him to succeed in his mission and so touched that Hanuman asks for nothing in return, except the pleasure of serving him, that he cannot stop himself from praising Hanuman and declaring that he is as dear to him as his brother, Bharat.

This comparison is significant. Bharat is the son of Kaikeyi, the second wife of Ram's father Dashrath whose machinations led to Ram being forced into exile in the forest for fourteen years. Bharat refused the crown. He did not appreciate his mother's ambitions and deceit. He begged Ram to return to the palace, but Ram refused as he had given his word to his father that he would stay in the forest for fourteen years. So Bharat returned to Ayodhya, placed Ram's footwear on the throne, and ruled the kingdom as Ram's regent until his return.

By comparing Hanuman to Bharat Ram elevates the status of Hanuman from servant to family. This indicates a significant elevation of Hanuman's status and his inclusion in Ram's heart. One cannot help but wonder if this narrative elevation of Hanuman is not political, an attempt by wise men of society to bridge the inequality, without threatening the old system: a calculated counter-force of wisdom that keeps the default social force of hierarchy in check.

In Eknath's Marathi Ramayana, when a childless Dashrath conducts a yagna for a son, he receives a magic potion from the heavens that he gives to his three wives who bear him four sons. A hawk grabs some of the potion and carries it to the jungle and puts it in Anjani's mouth. The son she gives birth to may be a vanara, but he is very much a brother of Ram, Lakshman, Bharat and Shatrughan.

In a folk variant of the Ramayana, when Hanuman is flying with the mountain southwards towards Lanka he passes Ayodhya. Fearing he is a rakshasa who intends to drop the mountain over the city, Bharat strikes Hanuman with an arrow causing Hanuman to descend. A duel is averted when Bharat identifies himself as Ram's regent and Hanuman reveals that he is Ram's servant. Hanuman then proceeds to tell Bharat the tragedy that has befallen Ram and how Ram is fighting Ravana to rescue his wife, Sita. The narration takes a long time. Hanuman suddenly realizes that the sun will soon rise and he is far away from Lanka. He fears he will not reach on time. So Bharat tells Hanuman to sit on his arrow, mountain in hand. He then fires the arrow, thinking of Ram, and the arrow takes Hanuman to Lanka in a fraction of a second, just in time to save Lakshman's life. Thus Bharat and Hanuman collaborate to save Lakshman and make Ram happy. Hanuman is thus included in the royal family of Ayodhya.

Chaupai 13: Vishnu's Avatar

सहस बदन
तम्हरो जस गावैं ।
अस कहि
श्रीपति कंठ लगावैं ॥

Sahas badan
tumharo jasa gaave.
Asa-kahi
Shripati kanth lagaave.

May thousands
sing your praises.
So saying
Shri's husband (Ram) hugs you.

With this verse begins the praise of Hanuman. Until now, we have focussed on the origin, the form and the feats of Hanuman. Now, we list all those who admire Hanuman's glory.

Ram tells Hanuman that thousands of beings will praise him. Here, Ram is identified as Shri-pati, lord of the goddess of fortune, meaning Vishnu. In which case, the thousands who praise Hanuman could refer to Adi-Ananta-Sesha, the cosmic serpent with thousands of hoods on whose coils reclines Vishnu, on the ocean of milk.

The linking of Ram to Vishnu means that Ramayana is being acknowledged as a subset of the Vishnu Purana, which in turn is a narrative expression of the Vedas.

In the Vedas, Vishnu is a minor deity, a younger brother of Indra, his companion, but he has nothing to do with preserving the world. He becomes a major deity—the preserver and protector of the earth—later in Puranic literature. In the Vedas, the king is identified with the conquering Indra and the moral Varuna, but in the Puranas, the king is identified with Vishnu, especially in the form of Ram, and Varuna is the god of the sea, father of Lakshmi, the goddess of fortune. Lakshmi chooses Vishnu as her guardian and consort. She manifests next to him as the embodiment of tangible assets (Bhu) and intangible value (Shri).

Sita of the Ramayana, is Lakshmi of the Puranas, who is Shri of the Vedas. The word 'Shri' is found in the Rig Veda, the oldest collection of Hindu hymns (mantra), over 4,000 years old, where it refers to affluence and abundance. In the Shri-Sukta, the goddess of fortune is invoked for grain, gold, cows, horses, children, wealth and health. The word 'Shri' also happens to be the first word in the Hanuman Chalisa, found in the very first doha, even before the word 'guru'. Some people believe that the guru being referred to in the doha is Sita herself, who is seen as Hanuman's guru in some Shakta traditions. Thus, while Vaishnavas see Hanuman as Vishnu's servant, and Shaivas see him as a form of Shiva, the Shaktas or Goddess worshippers saw Hanuman as a student of the Goddess, and Ram as the consort and guardian of the Goddess.

The Vishnu Purana informs us that Lakshmi was churned from the ocean of milk, a metaphor for domesticating and cultivating the forest. The division between the forests (aranya) and in the settlement (grama) is first found in the Sama Veda. In the Shiva Purana, the forest is Kali, mother of humanity, and the village is Gauri, daughter of humanity. Brahma is the creator, who turns forest into field, turns nature (prakriti) into culture (sanskriti)— where human rules apply.

However, the world created by Brahma is full of conflict and sorrow. His children, the devas and the asuras constantly fight each other. And so Brahma is not worshipped. Instead, prayers are offered to Shiva, the hermit, who rejects wealth and power, and withdraws from society, and returns to the jungle for peace. Shiva, the opponent of Brahma, is therefore described as the destroyer. Brahma's world brings prosperity but no peace. Shiva's world brings peace but no prosperity.

Vishnu, the preserver, stands in between Brahma and Shiva. He gets Brahma's quarrelling children to collaborate and churn Lakshmi out of the ocean of milk. Thus, like Brahma, he engages with society and generates and enjoys wealth, but unlike Brahma or his children, he does not see himself as the controller of Lakshmi. Instead, like Shiva, he has inner peace not to crave control over the wealth he generates. He is freely and fairly distributing it with detachment. This makes him Lakshmi's ideal husband. He protects her, enjoys her, but does not seek to control her. That is why Vishnu is called Lakshmi-vallabha, the beloved of Lakshmi, and Shri-pati, lord of wealth.

Vishnu descends on earth and takes various mortal forms, such as Ram, to show humans how to live life, generate, enjoy and distribute wealth without getting addicted to it. He speaks of dharma, the human ability by which the self (sva-jiva) can make room for the other (para-jiva), thereby creating a society where there is both prosperity and peace. This combination of abundance and happiness constitutes the idea of Shri. Because he makes this happen, Vishnu (hence Ram) is identified as Shri-pati.

Chaupai 14: Brahma and his Mind-born Sons

सनकादिक
ब्रह्मादि मुनीसा ।
नारद सारद
सहित अहीसा ॥

Sankadhik
Brahmaadi muneesa.
Narada-Sarad
sahita Aheesa.

Sanak,
Brahma, and other sages.
Narada, Saraswati,
alongwith the lord of serpents.

In the previous verse, Ram who is Vishnu praises Hanuman. In this verse, praise is being showered by Brahma and the sages.

Brahma is the creator-god of Hinduism, but never worshipped. The Creator in Hinduism is not a creator of material things, but the creator of self-identity (aham) and seeker of divine identity (atma). This creation happens on the canvas that is nature.

In nature, there are non-living things (a-jiva) and living organisms (sa-jiva). The living have awareness of death, and hence yearning for life, hunger for food and fear of becoming food. In humans, this hunger and fear is amplified. We imagine a world where there is ample food and no threats. Failure to get this world creates sorrow. We feel like victims, and are filled with self-pity. The creator of these emotions is not worshipped in Hinduism.

The destroyer of these emotions is worshipped in Hinduism. The creator of aham brings sorrow (dukkha). The destoyer of aham, the embodiment of atma, brings joy (ananda).

Happiness comes from knowledge, embodied as the goddess known as Saraswati, here referred to as Sharada. The sages (muni), including Sanaka and Narada, mark the struggle to acquire this knowledge. They worship Hanuman, as they recognize that Hanuman has this knowledge. Hanuman has this knowledge because he has genuinely seen Ram, recognized him as Vishnu, the embodiment of dharma, who has outgrown his own hunger and fear, and empathizes with other people's hunger and fear, and so is always in a state of ananda, despite huge calamities.

The first of Brahma's sons were the Sanat-kumars. They have various names such as Sana, Sanaka, Sanata, Sananda. Typically, they are visualized as four prepubescent boys. In the Puranas, sexual activity must not be taken literally: the male form represents the mind and the female form represents matter. The attraction of a sage for a nymph is a metaphor for the response of the mind to sensory stimuli. Prepubescent boys do not have the wherewithal to engage with the world, or even desire it. They wander everywhere seeking the wisdom that will bring happiness. As long as they don't grow up, and engage with the world, the knowledge will elude them. But they don't know that and so wander through space and time, never growing up or old.

Narada, born after the Sanat-kumars, is an adult, capable of engaging and desiring the world. However, he chooses not to be part of the material world, and goes around telling all living creatures that living in the material world is full of hunger and fear and suffering, and has no meaning, until he is cursed by Brahma that he will never escape the material world unless he gets everyone to engage with it. For unless one engages with the world, experiences hunger and fear, one will never outgrow hunger or fear, never gain empathy or find meaning. In other words, without the material, there can be nothing spiritual.

Saraswati is called Sharada because Sharada was the name of a popular script in India about a thousand years ago, used to write the Vedas, before the Devanagari script became popular. Brahma wants to possess her, and when he does that, she runs away from him, and Shiva beheads Brahma. Knowledge has to be internalized, transformed into wisdom, not memorized. Brahma is beheaded because he chooses the path of the brahmin (crumpled mind that seeks to dominate others using his knowledge and position) rather than the path of the brahmana (expanded mind that internalizes the Vedas and so feels no urge to dominate).

319

The Aheesha mentioned in this verse refers to the lord of serpents (naga), just as Kapish mentioned in the first chaupai refers to the lord of monkeys. It can refer to Vasuki, king of serpents, who rules the nether regions. It could refer to Adi-Ananta-Sesha, on whose hoods rests the earth. Or it could refer to the serpent Kundalini, coiled at the base of our spine, embodying our primal survival instincts, which can rise up and stir the flowering of wisdom in our mind, turn knowledge into wisdom. In wisdom, we see the world for what it is, rather than trying to control the world like Brahma and his children and being trapped in hunger and fear and meaninglessness, we become like Ram and Hanuman.

When Hanuman was a child, he did not know his strengths. He picked up boulders and mountains, trees and elephants, as if they were toys and hurled them around. So the sages declared that Hanuman would lose all memory of his great strength. It would reveal itself as needed. Every time Hanuman faced a crisis, or needed to solve a problem, he became aware of his hidden strengths and talents. In other words, the serpent of wisdom slowly rose up his spine, making him increasingly aware of the world, and the context, so that he could decide wisely how to make use of his incredible natural strength. Eventually, his great strength enabled him to leap across the oceans and carry mountains across land. But thanks to his teacher Surya, and thanks to his experience of Ram, he was able to transform knowledge into wisdom, use Saraswati not to cling to wealth (which is a mark of hunger) or dominate others (which is a mark of fear), but to outgrow his hunger and fear. This is why everyone adores him—Brahma, and his sons, the sages, even the goddess of knowledge and the serpent of wisdom.

Chaupai 15: Admirers in Every Direction

जम कुबेर
दिगपाल जहाँ ते ।
कबि कोबिद
कहि सके कहाँ ते ॥

Jam Kubera
Digpaal jahan te.
Kavi kovid
kahi sake kahan te.

Yama, Kubera
other guardians of the directions
Poets as well as scholars
cannot praise you enough

While the Hanuman Chalisa enables immersion into the idea of Hanuman, it also expands our understanding of the Hindu worldview. In this verse we are being introduced to the idea of Digpaal, or Digga-pala, the guardians of the sky who are located in eight spots: the four cardinal and the four ordinal directions. Here Hanuman's popularity is being reaffirmed. Even the guardians of space are singing praises of Hanuman, as are the poets (kavi) and scholars (kovid).

As the Puranas came to be composed, the Hindu universe came to have a unique architecture. The world was seen as a lotus flower, with continents spreading out like petals from a central mountain called Meru. The continent on which India is located is called Jambudvipa, stretching from the Himalayas to the oceans, and watered by seven rivers; it is the land of the blackbuck. Spreading over it like a canopy is the sky, pegged at eight different locations: north, south, east, west, northeast, northwest, southeast and southwest. At each peg is located a guardian (Digga-pala) and a pair of elephants (Digga-gaja).

The north is marked by the Pole Star, and is the land of permanence. This makes the south the land of impermanence, ruled by Yama, the lord of death. In the south rules Ravana, the king of rakshasas, who drove his elder brother Kubera, king of yakshas, to the north. If Ravana lives in Lanka, Kubera lives in Alanka, or Alaka. If Ravana grabs the fortune of others, Kubera, as the lord of treasures, gives fortunes to others. Metaphorically, the two directions counter each other. Yama fills life with fear while Kubera fills it with hope. Life is a combination of fear and hope. Both these deities complement each other, and both praise Hanuman.

Other Digga-palas include Indra on the east and Varuna on the west, who also complement each other: Indra embodies fresh water of rain while Varuna embodies saltwater of the sea. The ordinal directions are marked by the sun complemented by moon, and wind complemented by fire. These gods of space praise Hanuman. He is being adored in all directions.

Many Hanuman temples declare themselves to be Dakshina-mukhi, with Hanuman facing the south, the direction of death and decay. In this, Hanuman mimics Dakshina-murti, the south-facing form of Shiva found in South Indian temples. This form of Shiva is called the teacher of teachers as he gives discourse on the Vedas, Tantras, Nigamas and Agamas for the benefit of sages. But Dakshina-mukhi Hanuman is more ferocious than intellectual; he protects devotees from rakshasas, demons who reside in the south. This is not the literal south, but the metaphorical south.

One can say it refers to the negative impulses in our body, located in the lower part of the brain. One can say it refers to our base instincts or the base instincts of others, such as jealousy and rage that wreak havoc in relationships.

Hanuman has a special relationship with poets and scholars. Poets respond to the world with their heart, scholars with their head. Both adore this warrior monkey-god. Why? Because Hanuman is one of them: a poet and a scholar, and there are many stories testifying to that.

His love for knowledge is evident when he begs the sun god, Surya, to be his teacher, and reveal to him the secret of the Vedas. He does not mind suffering the glare of the sun while he is studying.

His love for storytelling is revealed when he narrates the story of Ram (Ram-katha) first to Sita in Lanka and later to Bharat in Ayodhya. In these narrations, he describes Ram using the most beautiful words and phrases. Hanuman's love for music is revealed when Narada, the musician-sage, watches him melt ice on the Himalayas with the sheer power of his singing the praise of Ram (Ram-bhajan).

Chaupai 16: Enabling Sugriv

तुम उपकार
सुग्रीवहिं कीन्हा ।
राम मिलाय
राज पद दीन्हा ॥

Tum upkar
Sugrivahin keenha.
Ram milaye
rajpad deenha.

Eternally grateful to you
is Sugriv.
You introduced him to Ram
who made him king.

This chaupai draws our attention to events in Kishkinda that led to Sugriv becoming king, thanks to Hanuman's intervention, with the help of Ram.

As stated earlier, the story of Ramayana draws attention to the state of affairs between three worlds: Ayodhya, where humans (manava) uphold dharma; Kishkinda, where monkeys (vanara) reside and struggle with dharma; and Lanka, where barbarians (rakshasa) reside and ignore dharma completely. Vanaras are thus located between the world of dharma and adharma.

In dharma, you give in order to get, and accept whatever you receive. In adharma, you grab whatever you want, as there is no concept of, or regard for, personal property. In between these two worlds is the world where you give and *take*: you are bound by obligations to fulfil. This is the world where you demand fair exchange, where fairness is not spontaneous, but enforced, through law or force. This is demonstrated in the politics of Kishkinda.

The king of Kishkinda, Riksha, once fell into a pond and turned into a woman. Two gods fell in love with his female form: the rain god Indra and the sun god Surya. From his union with the two gods, Riksha had two sons: Indra gave him the mighty Vali, and Surya gave him the meek Sugriv. Riksha, who had been both father and mother to the two brothers, asked them to share the kingdom equally after his death.

All was well until there was a misunderstanding. A rakshasa attacked Kishkinda and in the attack that followed, Sugriv assumed that Vali had been killed. But Vali had been victorious, and saw his brother's hasty conclusion as indicative of his guile and ambition. Rather than sort out the mistrust, and re-establish faith, Vali drove Sugriv out of Kishkinda by force and claimed the kingdom for himself. He made Sugriv's wife, Ruma, part of his harem. In other words, Vali behaved like a typical alpha male monkey who corners all the foraging lands and females of the troop for himself.

Had Hanuman not intervened, Vali would have killed Sugriv.

Hanuman was a student of the sun god and had been asked by the sun god to take care of his son Sugriv; and Hanuman had promised to protect him. Hanuman observed that Vali wanted to kill Sugriv and Sugriv survived by hiding atop Rishyamukh mountain—the one place that Vali feared to go. A sage had once cursed Vali that if he ever stepped on this mountain, he would die. So Vali, determined to hurt Sugriv, would fly over the mountain and kick Sugriv on the head. When Hanuman saw this happening day after day, he decided to stop Vali. He caught Vali's leg and threatened to drag him to the mountain top to perish. Vali begged for mercy and Hanuman let him go after threatening him with a slap (resulting in the icon known as 'tamacha' Hanuman) and extracting a promise: Vali would quit his petty behaviour and let his brother be. If Hanuman wanted, he could have hurt, even killed Vali. But he did not, as he had no quarrel with Indra's son. In other words, he did not interfere in the Sugriv-Vali conflict and focussed on taking care of Sugriv, as instructed by his guru.

It was Hanuman who spotted the jewels that Sita cast down to mark a trail as she was being taken to Lanka by Ravana on his flying chariot, the Pushpak-viman. This led Hanuman to Ram and Lakshman who were moving south in search of Sita. He introduced Ram to Sugriv. He felt the two could help each other: Ram could help Sugriv become king of Kishkinda and Sugriv could help Ram find Sita.

While Hanuman had sensed Ram's nobility and valour, Sugriv had no faith and wanted proof of Ram's talent as an archer. Ram had to shoot an arrow through seven trees, convincing Sugriv that he was indeed a worthy ally. Sugriv then challenged Vali to a duel and while the two were fighting, Ram who was hiding behind the bushes shot Vali dead with his arrow.

Vali condemned this act as cheating and Ram argued, 'One who does not know how to share, or forgive, one who lives by the jungle way, and uses his might to establish his authority, should not condemn the use of cunning in a duel, for that too is the jungle way, available for the survival of the meek. Besides, if I challenged you to a duel, by the ways of the jungle, Kishkinda would be my kingdom, not Sugriv's.'

Thus, with Ram's help, Sugriv became king. But when it was time to fulfil his end of the bargain, Sugriv said, 'Let's wait until the rainy season ends, travelling in the rain is dangerous.' While Ram waited patiently, Sugriv indulged in the pleasures of his harem, for even Vali's wife Tara was now his. He forgot all about his promise to help Ram even after the rains ended. Finally, an angry Lakshman decided to force Sugriv to help. 'I shall kill the cheat if he refuses to help,' declared Ram's brother. It was Hanuman who sensed trouble and restored peace. While he got Tara to calm the angry Lakshman down, he went to

Sugriv and told him to mend his ways, and keep his promise. Sugriv finally saw sense, apologized to Ram and organized his troops to find Sita.

Thus it was Hanuman who not only protected Sugriv from Vali's wrath but also enabled Sugriv to become king with Ram's help and protected him from Lakshman's outrage. Hanuman got Sugriv to follow the ways of dharma—not just take, but also give. Ideally, Sugriv should have helped Ram without any reminding or nudging. Hanuman had to remind Sugriv of his obligations.

While Lakshman expected Sugriv to keep his end of the bargain, Ram had no such expectation. For Ram was a yogi, who knows a man has rights only to action, not to the results of action. Only Hanuman noticed this and wanted to be the servant of the man who had no desire to be anyone's master.

Chaupai 17: Empowering Vibhishan

तम्हरो मंत्र
बिभीषन माना ।
लंकेस्वर भए
सब जग जाना ॥

Tumharo mantra
Vibhishan maana.
Lankeshwar bhaye
sub jag jana.

Chaupai 17: Empowering Vibhishan

Your counsel that
Vibhishan accepted.
Made him Lord of Lanka
as the world knows.

This verse reveals the difference between the Valmiki Ramayana, composed 2,000 years ago, and Tulsidas's Ram-charit-manas, composed 500 years ago, and draws attention to the many variations found in regional and folk retellings of Ram's tale. While everyone acknowledges Valmiki as the first poet to compose the Ramayana, the epic itself has been reimagined, and retold, in many ways in various Sanskrit plays, Prakrit compositions, and—from about tenth century onwards—in various regional languages.

The difference between the oldest work and the later compositions is of two kinds. First, is the theme: while the focus of the Sanskrit epic was dharma and the obligations of a royal prince, the focus of the regional epics came to be bhakti and the veneration of a deity by his devotees. The second is the change in plot.

In the Ram-charit-manas we find an episode that is not found in the Valmiki Ramayana: the meeting of Hanuman and Vibhishan when Hanuman visits Lanka in search of Sita. Hanuman finds a man chanting Ram's name in Lanka. It turns out to be Ravana's younger brother. After introductions are exchanged, Hanuman informs Vibhishan that Ram is coming to Lanka to set things right. Vibhishan then directs Hanuman to the Ashoka garden where Sita has been confined.

Vibhishan does not agree with his brother's action of abducting another man's wife and imprisoning her in his garden. There are many reasons for this. There is the moral reason of respecting a woman's consent. There is the ethical reason of respecting another man's wife. Then, there is the practical reason: Ravana's actions damage Lanka's reputation and threaten Lanka's security. There is also the dharma reason: a king's misbehaviour affects the welfare of the entire kingdom. Vibhishan wants his brother to see sense and Hanuman urges Vibhishan to have a talk with his brother.

Unfortunately, Ravana does not like Vibhishan's arguments and protests and kicks his brother out of Lanka. Hanuman gives Vibhishan the courage to take a decision to override his deep love for his brother, and join forces with Ram.

Vibhishan reveals the various secrets and weaknesses of Ravana that enables Ram to defeat the rakshasa-king. And so in popular lore, Vibhishan is not respected. He is seen as a traitor, a disloyal brother. He is contrasted with Kumbhakarna, another of Ravana's brothers who shares Vibhishan's stance in the matter of Sita's abduction, but remains loyal to Ravana. He attacks Ram and is brutally killed by Ram's army of monkeys in the battlefield. The question emerges: is loyalty superior to dharma? For Ravana, the one who grab's another man's wife, is no follower of dharma.

Kubera, the king of yakshas and elder brother of Ravana, was the one who built the city of Lanka. Ravana drove Kubera out of Lanka and made himself king. Thus Ravana behaved as animals do, using force to establish his authority. This action is an even greater tragedy because Ravana is no barbarian; he is a Brahmin well versed in Vedic knowledge. But he misuses Vedic knowledge to dominate and exploit the world. In other words, he is not interested in the fundamental theme of the Vedas—atma-gyan, or self-awareness, which enables humans to outgrow animal instincts and empathize with the world.

Hanuman gives Vibhishan the strength to choose dharma over

loyalty. Loyalty indulges the self-image at the cost of the other. It values reputation of the self (sva-jiva) over the welfare of the other (para-jiva). Dharma is all about the other. It is what defines our humanity.

After the defeat of Ravana, Vibhishan marries Ravana's widow and becomes king of Lanka. He rules as a good king should—taking care of his people, rather than getting people to take care of him.

Chaupai 18: Sun as Fruit

जुग सहस्त्र
जोजन पर भानू ।
लील्यो ताहि
मधुर फल जानू ॥

**Jug sahastra
jojan par Bhanu.
Leelyo tahi
madhur phal janu.**

*The distant
faraway sun.
You mistook
for a tasty fruit.*

The Hanuman Chalisa is not linear. So the story of Hanuman's life does not appear sequentially. One moves back and forth. And so, after speaking of how Hanuman helped Ram, Sugriv and Vibhishan, this verse goes back in time to Hanuman's childhood when he mistook the rising sun for a fruit and jumped into the skies to grab it.

This fantastic tale reveals how Hanuman is able to contract space and time. He is able to travel a huge distance as if he is jumping across the branch of a tree. And he is able to consume the vast fiery ball that is the sun as if it is a fruit.

Some people have taken the phrase 'jug sahastra jojan' to refer to the distance between the earth and the sun, proof therefore that ancient India knew how to calculate distances in space using observation. They have taken jug or yuga to mean 1,200, sahastra to mean 1,000 and jojan or yojan to refer to 8 miles (approximately 13 km). So the line, they suggest, means roughly 150,000,000 km, in other words, the distance of earth from the sun. However, yuga refers to traditional time measurement (an era), and jojan refers to a traditional distance measurement. When you multiply the two you get speed, not distance. Such interpretations, however appealing, are misleading. It simply refers to Hanuman's ability to bend space and time, to not only reach the sun but also consume it by increasing his relative size. Hanuman does this as a child, without any training, without any knowledge of his own strength.

This is when the gods panic and Indra, god of the sky, hurls his thunderbolt at Hanuman, causing him to come crashing down to earth, disfiguring his jaw, giving him his name—Hanuman. But Vayu gets annoyed at the way Indra treats his son and hides in a cave with his son, until the gods beg Vayu's forgiveness and ask him to leave the cave and enable all creatures to breathe once again. In exchange, Indra and all the gods bless Hanuman with many powers.

In some stories, during his journey to the sun, Hanuman assumes all the other celestial bodies (grahas) and the constellations (nakshatras) to be toys and tosses them around. Hindus believe that the location of the grahas, relative to each other and relative to the nakshatras, provides the map of human destiny. The purpose of astrology (Jyotish) is to appreciate this cosmic pattern. Hanuman has the power to change the location of these celestial bodies, hence the power to change human destiny. The sun impacts our radiance, the moon impacts our emotions, Mars our aggression, Mercury our intelligence, Jupiter our rationality, Venus our creativity, Saturn our patience, Rahu our clarity and Ketu our calm.

People pray to Hanuman on Tuesday and Saturday so that he ensures the grahas exert positive, not negative, influence. The verse tells us how for Hanuman the flaming ball of the sun is equivalent to a juicy fruit. We also know how he held the sun in his armpit, and some say his mouth, while finding Sanjivani. Hanuman is therefore considered a force that can change our destiny, influence the power of the grahas, remove their malevolent influence and enable their benevolent influence.

The sun god is also Hanuman's guru. Hanuman wanted to learn everything that there was in the world. He was advised to go to Surya, who sees all things. But Surya refused to be Hanuman's teacher arguing that he was busy travelling all day and at night he had to rest and so had no time to teach. Hanuman then began flying in front of the sun's chariot, facing the sun, suffering his glaring heat, determined to learn whatever the sun god could share during his daily journey from the east to the west. Impressed by this display of determination, the sun—who is lord of all grahas—taught Hanuman many things, amongst them how to counter the ill effects of dangerous planets, plants and animals. Therefore, one prays to Hanuman in times of crisis.

In the Ramayana, Ravana is a great astrologer who wrote the Ravana-samhita, a treatise on astrology. But he did this to figure out a way to manipulate the stars and planets to grant him fortune. Hanuman does not seek fortune. And he uses his strength to limit the malevolent influence of celestial bodies, and to give humans the strength to cope with the malevolent influence of celestial bodies. For Ravana, the sun has to be controlled. For Hanuman, the sun is a toy who entertains, and a teacher who enlightens.

Chaupai 19: Monkeyness

प्रभु मुद्रिका
मेलि मुख माहीं ।
जलधि लाँघि
गये अचरज नाहीं ॥

**Prabhu mudrika
meli mukh mahee.
Jaladhi langhi
gaye achraj nahee.**

*With Ram's ring
in your mouth.
You leapt over the sea
how amazing is that.*

Being knowledgeable and wise does not stop Hanuman from popping Ram's ring in his mouth while leaping over the sea. Mundane rules of propriety make no sense to Hanuman, reminding us of his animal side. His monkeyness evokes his childlike nature. In this, he reminds us of Bholenath, the guileless, innocent form of Shiva. This form of Hanuman is often addressed as Balaji, or the child-like form of Hanuman.

Hanuman's paradoxical qualities mirror the paradoxical qualities of Shiva. Both are wise and mighty, yet both are totally unaware of worldly ways. Shiva may have the power to destroy the three worlds (which is why he is call Tripurantaka) and enlighten the sages on the wisdom of Vedas and Tantras (which is why he is called Dakshina-murti), but he does not know how to function as a husband, a father, or a son-in-law, and has to be taught the ways of a householder by his patient wife, Parvati. Likewise Hanuman, who can leap over the sea with a mountain in hand and the sun in his armpit, does not know the value, and status, of a king's ring and does not understand why humans find his act of keeping Ram's ring in his mouth inappropriate.

The concept of 'value' exists only amongst humans. For

animals, food has value. For humans, an object becomes valuable based on what meaning we attribute to it. Meanings are given randomly. They are cultural: of a set of people, by a set of people, for a set of people, making no sense to outsiders or non-humans.

For example, the idea of contamination by the touch, saliva or even shadow of a person from certain communities, to establish the draconian caste hierarchy of India, of making some communities the embodiments of pollution in order to make other communities embodiments of purity. In the Ramayana, Lakshman is horrified when Shabari offers him berries after tasting them to check if they are sweet; he considers the food contaminated, but Ram has no problem eating the berries for he rises above such cultural meanings and is able to recognize that they exist in context and are not universal. What makes sense in one culture may not make sense in another. This discomfort with contamination following contact with saliva is implied in the verse where Hanuman casually puts Ram's royal ring in his mouth.

The ring is nothing special; it is simply a tool by which Sita can identify a messenger sent by Ram. It is the clever Hanuman who asks Ram to give him something by which he can win Sita's trust, for he can foresee a captive Sita being too insecure to trust him only on the basis of his words of instruction. For the poet, Ram's ring has much greater sentimental value, which makes little sense to a monkey whose focus is more pragmatic: finding and rescuing Ram's beloved.

Once, Sita gave Hanuman a string of pearls. He kept biting the pearls as if they were nuts. The residents of Ayodhya laughed at this, exclaiming that a monkey could not know the worth of pearls. When asked to explain his behaviour, Hanuman said, 'I was biting to see if Ram resides in these pearls. He doesn't, so they are useless to me.' The people found this to be an absurd idea, for Ram sat on a throne and could not be seated inside pearls. But Hanuman was surprised at their assertion and confidence. He just tore open his chest and there within his heart was Ram with Sita by his side. Suddenly, the people of Ayodhya realized what Hanuman was innocently drawing their attention to. For him, a thing had value if it was either food, or if it evoked divinity. He saw no value in expensive, royal pearls—for they neither nourished his body, nor his mind, as Ram did. Possessing pearls could make people rich. But engaging with Hanuman could make people experience what it meant to be Ram.

Just as humans give value to things, we also give value to gestures. Animals recognize only two kinds of gestures—those that threaten their security, and those that assure them of security. Humans, however, have complex gestures to establish hierarchy that are beyond Hanuman's understanding, for he does not understand the need for hierarchy when one has experienced Ram.

Once Narada told Hanuman that he had to bow to all the sages who paid a visit to Ram, everyone except Vishwamitra, who did not like anyone bowing to him. Hanuman complied, not knowing that this was Narada's trick to create a rift between Hanuman and Ram. Vishwamitra saw this as an insult and demanded that the monkey be killed. So Ram raised his bow and shot arrows at Hanuman. Hanuman simply chanted Ram's name—and such was the power of Ram's name that it created a force field that even Ram's arrows could not penetrate. Everyone bowed to Hanuman who showed the world in his very innocent way, that the *idea* of Ram is greater than Ram the king.

Thus, as the verse reiterates, Hanuman amazes you with his many incredible qualities—his ability to leap over an ocean, rip his chest open, resist Ram's arrows by chanting Ram's name. Simultaneously, he amazes you with simian innocence— holding Ram's royal ring in his mouth, biting pearls, trusting the mischievous Narada. This reminds us that Hanuman has no desire to impress anyone. His knowledge and powers exist to help others, materially and spiritually; else he is happy being a monkey.

Chaupai 20: In Southeast Asia

दुर्गम काज
जगत के जेते ।
सुगम अनुग्रह
तुम्हरे तेते ॥

**Durgam kaj
jagath ke jete.
Sugam anugraha
tumhre tete.**

*All tough jobs
in this world.
Become easy
with your grace.*

A few years ago, Indian media went abuzz with the news that Barack Obama, former President of the United States of America, carried, amongst many things, an image of Hanuman in his pocket. On closer examination, it turned out to be not the image enshrined in Hindu temples of India, but the image of Hanuman popular in Thailand. Hindus who see this image will not feel the same emotion they feel on seeing a Hanuman image from India.

Be that as it may, Hanuman grants everyone the psychological strength to cope with crises, which makes solving problems easier. Even an exiled Ram was able to raise an army of monkeys, build a bridge across the sea, defeat Ravana and his army of demons, and rescue Sita, with Hanuman by his side.

This story of Hanuman's ability to solve problems travelled beyond Indian shores on merchant ships travelling to Southeast Asia, which Indians knew as the golden land, or Suvarnabhumi. It is said that on the long sea voyages, sailors created the art of shadow-puppetry projected on the ship's sail using leather dolls, to tell the story of the Ramayana. Hence, along the coast of India and in many islands of Southeast Asia one finds this art form even today. In Thailand, the old capital was called Ayutthaya, the local name for Ayodhya, and the kings were seen as descendents and embodiments of Ram. The Southeast Asian Ramayanas include the Hikayat Seri Rama of Malaysia, Yama Zatdaw of Burma, and Ramakien, the national epic of Thailand. In these epics, one encounters a local version of Hanuman.

There are three differences between the Hanuman of India, and the Hanuman of Southeast Asia. First, the Ramayana mingles and merges with the local Buddhist lore of the regions. Second, the Hanuman depicted in these regional epics is a more strong and clever and funny monkey; loyal to Ram, but not quite a wise devotee, suggesting that the stories reached there from Indian shores over a thousand years ago, before the widespread popularity of the Bhakti doctrine. Third, Hanuman is not necessarily depicted as a celibate brahmachari or yogi; he is a charming rake, and a powerful warrior who battles demons and is able to satisfy the demonic desires of rakhasa women including Ravana's sister, Surpanakha, and his wife, Mandodari.

In the Vedas, there is a ribald argument between Indra and his wife Indrani over a huge male monkey, Vrishakapi, who happens to be Indra's friend. The conversation deals with Indra's lack of virility, Vrishakapi's excess virility, and Indrani's frustrated desires. It ends with the journeys and sacrifice of the monkey who restores Indra's power and Indrani's fertility. Some people postulate that this Vedic Vrishakapi transforms into the Ramayana's Hanuman. Details of his potent sexuality were rejected in India where society preferred a Hanuman with control over his senses, emotions, and desires. However, this idea may have travelled to Southeast Asia where Hanuman is known for his humourous erotic adventures.

There are many stories of Hanuman that are unique to Southeast Asian retellings. In one story, he battles the mermaid queen Suvarna-maccha (golden fish) who tries to disrupt the building of the bridge across the sea to Lanka. In another story, Benyakai or Benjkaya, the daughter of Vibhishan, uses her magical form to appear like the dead body of Sita washed up on the shores; Hanuman senses mischief and decides to cremate the 'dead body', which suddenly comes alive as the flame rises and runs away. When Ravana tries to break the bridge to Lanka, he expands in size and stretches his tail so that Ram and the army of monkeys can cross to Lanka with ease. These tales remind us how Hanuman, even in other lands, makes the toughest jobs look easy, even fun.

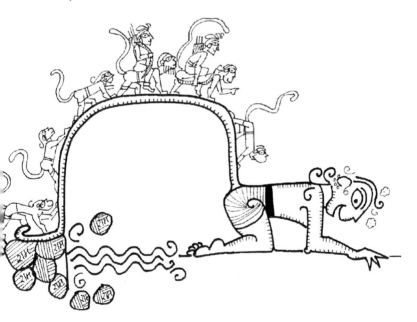

Chaupai 21: Doorkeeper

राम दुआरे
तुम रखवारे ।
होत न आज्ञा
बिनु पैसारे ॥

Ram dwaare
tum rakhvare.
Hoat na agya
bin paisare.

Ram's door
has you as guardian.
Without your permission
no one can cross it.

Doorkeepers of the gods are very important in Hindu mythology. The door marks the liminal in-between space between outside and inside, wild and domestic, nature and culture. Like security guards and secretaries, the doorkeeper maintains the integrity of the inner world. They decide who gets access to the deity within the temple, and who does not. In Puri, Odisha, at the Jagannath temple, for example, Hanuman stands outside, they say, preventing even the sound of the sea from entering the temple and disturbing the deity inside.

The doorkeepers' presence draws attention to the hierarchy of communities (jati) that characterize Indian society. For centuries, a resident of India was identified by the larger community his family belonged to. Usually, members of a community followed one profession. Each jati isolated itself, like most tribal communities around the world, by not permitting marriage with outsiders, thus protecting its knowledge system, which was its source of income. About 500 years ago, Europeans who visited India used the word 'caste' for jati, as it reminded them of the clan system in Europe where blood purity mattered greatly.

There are over 2,000 jatis in India today. For centuries, people have been trying to classify these into a fourfold hierarchy (chatur-varna), with Brahmin priests at the top, powerful landowners after them, followed by rich traders and the rest below. But what makes the jati system unique is not the economic and political hierarchy, but the concept of purity: some communities are seen as intrinsically pure (priests, for example), while others as intrinsically impure (janitors, butchers, undertakers, for example). The 'impure' were denied access to temples, kitchens, and even the community well. Thus, in a grand temple, only the pure could access the inner shrine where the deity was enshrined, while the impure ones had to stay outside, outside the door, at times even outside on the street.

Those who were not allowed to enter the temple, naturally, turned to Hanuman whose image was located outside the temple, at the entrance, or even on the street. He was far more accessible than the royal Ram, who sat deep within the complex, accessible only to the elite.

Hindu history reveals a long tension between the hierarchy of purity imposed by priests and the doctrine of atma revealed by the poet-saints. The latter doctrine led to the ritual of the gods going out on processions regularly, stepping out of the temple on palanquins and chariots, to meet those communities who were not allowed inside the temple. It also led to many doorkeepers being made to look very much like the deity enshrined within the temple. This was to assure those being excluded that while humans may exclude humans, God excludes no one.

The doorkeepers of Vaikuntha are called Jaya and Vijaya. The doorkeepers of the sacred groves of the Goddess are called Maya and Laya. Nandi the bull is Shiva's doorkeeper and vehicle (vahana). Hanuman is Ram's doorkeeper, messenger, secretary, and strongman.

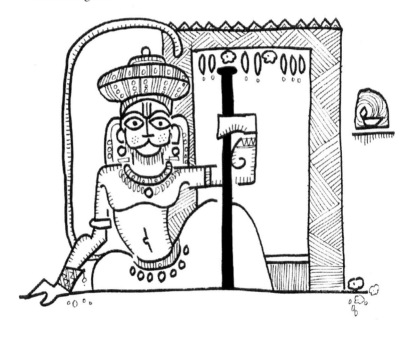

Once Ravana paid a visit to Shiva but was stopped by Nandi at the door as Shiva was with Shakti, and the couple wanted privacy. Ravana did not like being stopped, and without heeding Nandi, tried to get past him. When Nandi blocked Ravana, Ravana called Nandi a monkey. Nandi did not appreciate Ravana's rudeness, for he was only carrying out his duty. He cursed the arrogant Ravana that monkeys would be the cause of his downfall. To make this happen, it is believed, a portion of Shiva's divinity manifested on earth as Hanuman. Nandi, the doorkeeper of Shiva, was avenged through Hanuman, Ram's doorkeeper, who defeated Lankini, Ravana's doorkeeper.

With Hanuman guarding the gates of Ram's palace in Ayodhya, even the god of death, Yama, feared entering the city when it was time for Ram to leave his mortal body and return to Vaikuntha. Finally, Ram moved Hanuman from the gates so that Yama could do his duty. Ram dropped his ring in a crack in the palace floor and requested Hanuman to fetch it. Hanuman entered the crack in the palace floor in the form of a bee, only to discover it was a tunnel leading to the land of serpents (Naga-loka) where he found a mountain made of Ram's rings. He wondered what was the secret. To this Vasuki, king of the nagas, said, 'The world goes through cycles of birth and death just like all living creatures. Just as every life has a youth, so does the world have a Treta Yuga when Ram rules the world. In this yuga, each time, a ring falls from Bhu-loka to Naga-loka, a monkey follows it, and Ram up there dies. As many rings as there are Hanumans and Rams. Nothing lasts forever. But what goes, always comes back.'

In north India, temples of many mountain goddesses who are manifestations of the tiger-riding Sheravali are guarded by Bhairo-devata and Langur-devata, the former looks like a child-warrior who drinks bhang (a narcotic), the latter looks like a monkey who drinks milk. Both these deities embody domesticated masculinities, the principles of brahmacharya (celibacy, continence) and yoga (inward orientation). Nowadays, many identify the Langur-devata with Hanuman.

Chaupai 22: Guardian of Fortune

सब सुख
लहै तुम्हारी सरना ।
तुम रच्छक
काहू को डरना ॥

Sub sukh
lahae tumhari sarna.
Tum rakshak
kahu ko darna.

All joy
exists in your shelter.
With you as guardian
there is nothing to fear.

This verse seeking shelter and protection from Hanuman evokes humanity's most primal needs. Every village in India had a guardian-god (vira) who protected the village from danger: wild animals and raiders. He or she protected the settlement (kshetra-pala). Hanuman emerges from the kshetra-pala tradition. He protected Sugriv, and he protected Ram, and he protects Ayodhya.

The idea of submitting to a divine being and seeking his shelter is prevalent in most religions. However, the reasons are different.

A Buddhist surrenders (sharanam) to the Buddha, as he seeks freedom from a world of suffering. A Christian seeks shelter in the love of Christ, as he abandons his way of sin and returns to God's fold. A Muslim submits to Allah, promising to live by His commandments revealed by His final prophet, Muhammad. These ideas informed the idea of submission in the Bhakti period of Hinduism.

The Hindu devotee submits (sharanagati) to either Ram, or to Shiva or Shakti who are worshipped by Ram, or to Hanuman, who worships Ram. The object of adoration (aradhana) could be all of them simultaneously, or each one of them sequentially, depending on need and mood. This complication arises because Hinduism is not monotheistic and does not seek to be monotheistic unlike most religions and doctrines. It acknowledges the diverse needs of people, and so the need for different deities for different people, each form being seen as one of the myriad manifestations of the divine.

In Hinduism, unlike Buddhism or Christianity or Islam, submission does not mean following a particular doctrine or a set of rules. It is submitting to the will of the divine, which in earlier pre-Bhakti times meant submitting to what is determined by one's karma. If things happen as we desire, it is the grace of God (Hari-krupa). If things don't happen as we desire, it is the will of God (Hari-ichha). Hari is another name for Vishnu. It is also another word for monkey. And monkey is a metaphor for the restless human mind.

Western scholars using Western religious frameworks and the atheistic contempt for religions, often reduce Hindu devotion (bhakti) to some kind of feudalism with God presiding as master. They ignore the strong component of affection and love in the relationship, like a parent's for a child (vatsalya-bhav), like a lover for their beloved (madhurya-bhav), like a friend for a companion (sakha-bhav). Bhakti is essentially the construction of an emotional highway connecting the devotee to the divine. God is not always in a position of power: he can also be the playful child, the gullible hermit, the mischievous monkey; which enables the devotee to take on the role of a parent, or a friend. Hanuman can be at once awesome (adbhuta) and silly, displaying monkey qualities (kapitva). The latter part is missing in most non-Hindu religions.

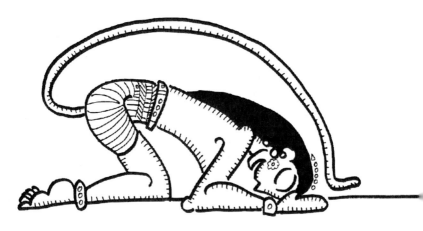

If one looks at the verse carefully, one realizes that the deity works for the devotee. The devotee submits and then the deity works to enable the happiness and security of the devotee. And so, in this verse, the protection is a kind of spiritual hug from God that comforts the frightened and lost devotee. The emotional aspect of the divine elevates the stature of the otherwise rustic guardian and fertility gods of the village. From material, he becomes spiritual, transcendent. He makes the devotee feel that he matters, for there is someone celestial watching out for him, even if fellow humans do not. Thus the devotee is granted meaning.

Chaupai 23: Three Worlds

आपन तेज
सम्हारो आपै ।
तीनों लोक
हाँक तें काँपै ॥

**Aapan tej
samharo aapai.
Teenhon lok
hank te kanpai.**

*Your glory
You alone can contain.
The three worlds
Tremble when you roar.*

This verse refers to the glory of Hanuman manifesting as his radiance and his roar. No one can contain his radiance and no one can withstand his roar. Yet, despite this great power, Hanuman does not seek to dominate the three worlds, which distinguishes him from other powerful people. His power is balanced by his immersion in the idea of Ram.

The quest for power (siddhi) from the divine is the central theme of Tantra, while the quest for immersion in the divine (samadhi) is the central theme of Vedanta. These two arms of Hinduism complement each other. In Tantra, the world is power (shakti); in Vedanta, the world is delusion (maya). Tantra seeks control over nature; Vedanta seeks transcendence. Tantra binds us to the earth and the world below, while Vedanta elevates from the earth to the world above. Hanuman's tales span the dark regions below the earth to the bright regions above the sky. In other words, he features across Tantrik as well as the Vedantic landscapes, adored by followers of Tantra and Vedanta, who would otherwise be rivals. Between these two antagonistic worlds is the world of Bhakti, the emotional highway between devotee and deity, the self and the other.

The concept of three worlds is found in the Vedas and the Puranas, but is very different in both. In the Vedas, the three worlds are the earth, the sky and the atmosphere in between. Indra separates the earth and sky and creates the three worlds. His younger brother, Vishnu, can traverse it in three steps and is hence known as Trivikrama, conqueror of the three worlds. The Vedic gods are classified as those who live on earth (fire, for example), those who live in the sky (the sun, for example) and those who live in between (wind, for example).

In the Puranas, on the other hand, the three worlds refer to earth, the celestial regions (Swarga), home to the devas, and the nether regions (Patala), home to nagas and asuras. Initially, there was not anything negative about the nether world. The two were just different. But gradually, perhaps under the influence of Christianity, or Islam, as society became increasingly linear in its worldview, the devas came to be seen as forces of good, while the asuras came to be seen as forces of evil. Devas started being associated with Vedanta, while asuras were linked with Tantra.

Patala was equated with hell (Naraka) and Swarga with heaven.

There are two Adbhut Ramayanas, both written roughly 500 years ago, one in Assamese and one in Sankrit, which reveal the different ways in which Patala was seen. In both, Hanuman plays an important role.

In the Assamese Adbhut Ramayana, Hanuman enters the kingdom of serpents, Naga-loka, located under the earth, to rescue Luv and Kush, abducted by Vasuki, king of serpents, on the instructions of Sita, who misses her children. The story comes from a local retelling of the final chapter of the Ramayana where gossip in the streets of Ayodhya about Sita's relationship with Ravana leads to Ram casting her away in the forest while she is pregnant, an episode that bothers most devotees of Ram. Sita raises her two children, the twins Luv and Kush, on her own and lets them go back to their father, but refuses to return to Ayodhya herself, choosing instead to descend into the earth, for she is the daughter of the earth. But then she misses her children and wants Vasuki to bring them from Bhu-loka to Naga-loka. In the war that follows, a compromise is reached. The children return to earth and Sita promises to visit them and their father in secret. Thus the royal family of Ayodhya is reconciled thanks to Hanuman.

The idea of Hanuman watching over Sita and her children when she was in the forest is a theme found in many folk retellings of the final chapter of the Ramayana. He takes the form of a monkey and plays with Luv and Kush, watching over them, providing them food and revealing to them the secrets of the forest. Only Sita knows what Hanuman is up to.

In the Sanskrit Adbhut Ramayana, also based on regional stories from the eastern part of India that is renowned for its

Tantra followers, Hanuman goes to Patala where he encounters not nagas, but asuras, demons and ghouls who worship Kali, perform human sacrifices and practice sorcery.

In this work, Ravana invokes his sorcerer brother, Mahiravana, who abducts Ram and Lakshman and takes them to Patala to offer them as sacrifices to Kali or Bhairavi. In the previous verses, we learnt of Hanuman as a doorkeeper and a guardian and provider of shelter. In the Adbhuta Ramayana, Hanuman uses his tail to create a fortress in which Ram and Lakshman can be safe. He lets no one in. Still, Mahiravana is able to outwit him and abduct the two brothers and take them to a place below the earth where there is no sun or wind.

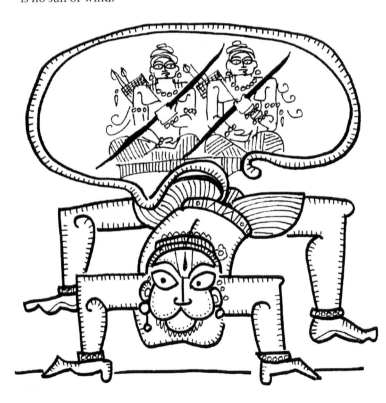

At the entrance of Patala, Hanuman meets a doorkeeper, who is part monkey and part fish, who refuses to let him in. In the duel that follows, Hanuman realizes he has met his match. 'Who are you?' he asks. The doorkeeper identifies himself as the son of Hanuman. How is that possible, wonders Hanuman, for he is a celibate ascetic. The warrior explains that he was born when a fish in the sea consumed a drop of Hanuman's sweat that fell as he was flying across to Lanka. When Hanuman reveals his identity, his son bows to him, and lets him pass, revealing to him the many secrets of the subterranean region.

Hanuman enters Patala, defeats the demons and ghouls there and outwits Mahiravana who he eventually beheads, thus pleasing Kali and asking her to never demand human sacrifice again. Kali places the condition that Hanuman should serve her, after Ram leaves the earth. Hanuman agrees.

In one of the many plots of this story, Hanuman has to simultaneously extinguish five lamps located in five different directions to kill Mahiravana's son, Ahiravana, which he is able to accomplish by sprouting four extra heads—that of an eagle, horse, lion and wild boar. This form of Hanuman with five heads transforms him from a god who is part of Ram's entourage, to an independent god in his own right. In other words, this story transforms Hanuman from being dependent on Ram to becoming dependable for Ram, from devata to bhagavan, from Ram-das to Maha-bali, from karya-karta to karta, for he takes initiative and decisions on his own, and not instructions from Ram.

The Hanuman who went to Patala, or Patali Hanuman, is a special form of Hanuman invoked for protection from sorcery. Patali Hanuman's temples are often located close to temples of the Goddess. Near Indore in Madhya Pradesh there is a temple to Ulte (upside down) Hanuman, for it is believed that everything in Patala is upside down.

Chaupai 24: Frightens Away Ghosts

भूत पिसाच
निकट नहिं आवै ।
महाबीर
जब नाम सुनावै ॥

**Bhoot pisaach
nikat nahin aavai.
Mahabir
jab naam sunavae.**

*Ghosts and ghouls
don't come near.
Hanuman's name
when they hear.*

This is undoubtedly the most popular verse of the Hanuman Chalisa, chanted when one is frightened and restless. It is said to drive away ghosts and spirits, or at least give one the strength to face what we believe to be ghosts and spirits.

Until the rise of modern psychology and medicine, around the world, mental disorders were seen as the work of ghosts and spirits. And so, this hymn has as much to do with the paranormal as it has to do psychiatry. Those who believe in ghosts believe that this hymn drives ghosts away. Those who see ghosts as merely external manifestations of internal fears believe this hymn helps strengthen the mind to overcome internal fears. It is not by accident that the word for ghost, 'bhoot', also means the past.

The idea of ghosts is different in different cultures. In Greek mythology, a ghost is believed to be the aspect of a living person that outlives death. Ghosts need to travel from the land of the living to the land of the dead, across the River Styx. Those who are unable to make the journey make life miserable for the living with their mourning, wailing and rage at their unfulfilled desires. In Christian mythology, the word soul is used instead of ghost. After death, souls wait in purgatory for Final Judgement. Then, depending on the deeds of their life, God takes them to Heaven or casts them in Hell. Some escape purgatory and haunt earth and have to be driven away using God's name.

In Hindu mythology, the River Vaitarni separates the land of the living from the land of the dead and souls move both ways continuously, as Hindus believe in multiple lives. The beings in the land of the dead are called pitrs, or ancestors. The dead who are trapped in the land of the living turn into pretas, or ghosts, colloquially known as bhoot. They torment the living. They hunger for a proper death ritual and rebirth. Some pretas refuse to become pitr as they have unfulfilled wishes that they need the living to assure them will be fulfilled. Other pretas refuse to become pitr as they are consumed by a sense of injustice, having died in a violent death, for instance, and so they yearn for justice. Many pretas are simply those who died while travelling and whose relatives do not know of their death and so have not conducted suitable rites for their passage across the Vaitarni.

Pisachas, or vetals, are different from bhoot and pret. They are one of the many sets of children fathered by Kashyapa, son of Brahma, such as the deva, asura, rakshasa, yaksha, naga, garuda, gandharva, apsara, and kinnar. They prefer night to day. They hang from solitary trees and prefer crematoriums. They speak a secret language called Paisachi. They enchant travellers in the forest and eat them alive, enjoying their flesh and their fear. They can have sex with a living creature that is asleep and such a person wakes up mad; this is why sex with a sleeping person is described as Paisachi maithuna.

Images of Shiva and Hanuman are kept in Hindu crematoriums to protect the living from pretas and pisachas. In folklore, Hanuman's father, either Kesari or Vayu, had another wife who was a cat and she gave birth to Preta-raja, lord of ghosts, who some identify with Yama. As a half-brother of Preta-raja, Hanuman is invoked to get rid of negative and malevolent forces that can afflict people tormented by ghosts and ghouls. One temple where this idea of exorcism is the central theme is the Mehendipur temple of Balaji Hanuman in Rajasthan.

There are also folktales that describe wandering preta or pisacha being captured by a sorcerer and made to do his bidding. So even the pretas and pisachas who encountered Hanuman's power during his adventures in Patala, worship Patali Hanuman to protect them from such sorcerers. Hanuman, thus, protects the living from the dead and the dead from such sorcerers.

In Tantrik lore, Chamunda is seen in crematoriums riding pretas with an entourage of pisachas. She is worshipped in this form at Betal-Deul in Bhubaneswar, Odisha. This ghastly site can drive people insane unless they seek the protection of Shiva and Hanuman.

This verse refers to chanting the name of Hanuman as protection from these external, malevolent forces. Chanting the name of the divine (naam-jap) became a very popular means to invoke the divine in the Bhakti period. In Vedic times, in order to invoke the gods Brahmins had to know Sanskrit hymns, their complex pronunciations and meaning, and chant them at appropriate times, with appropriate gestures and rituals. But with time, and the rise of Bhakti, people rejected the complex ways of priests and came to believe that faith alone could invoke the divine. Faith was expressed by simply concentrating on the deity. And this was facilitated by chanting their name, or a set of names, or a sound (bija mantra) that represented the deity.

Many people believe in the concept of aura or energy fields that surrounds all things. Everyone has an inherent aura but it depletes over time. It can be replenished from outside as well as inside. Humans especially can invoke it from within—through prayer and faith. Many are unable to regenerate their own auras and so need the help of external instruments, such as talismans, crystals, gemstones, beads and coloured cloth. Then there are humans who feed on other people's auras like predators feed on prey. To create a force field around oneself from such predators, to combat the drain of energy created by social trauma, psychological afflictions and paranormal phenomena, and to restore health and harmony, one can invoke positive energies simply by chanting Hanuman's name.

Chaupai 25: Takes Away Ailments

नासै रोग
हरै सब पीरा ।
जपत निरंतर
हनुमत बीरा ॥

Nase rog
harae sab peera.
Japat nirantar
Hanumat Beera.

All diseases
and pain vanish.
When one continuously
chants your name.

If the previous chaupai focussed on mental health and paranormal phenomena, this chaupai focuses on physical health. Hanuman, the mighty warrior and patron god of bodybuilders and wrestlers, is seen as an agent of good health, one who gets rid of diseases and pain.

Hanuman is closely associated with Ayurveda, the traditional Indian system of health and healing, according to which health is the outcome of harmony between water (kapha), fire (pitta) and wind (vata) in the body. Disharmony results in disease. Hanuman, son of the wind, helps in maintaining harmony.

Hanuman is closely associated with yoga, which the yoga sutra defines as de-crumpling the mind crumpled by hunger, insecurity and imagination. Doctors have always known that many physical ailments such as insomnia, skin rashes, allergies, asthma, hypertension and indigestion are actually psychosomatic—having their origins in the mind—and so calming the restless and frightened mind, by a rhythmic, repetitive activity, like chanting God's name, arrests unnecessary thoughts and resolves many health issues too.

This de-crumpling of the mind can be achieved by various modulations of breath and body postures. Hanuman is associated with pranayama, breathing exercises that ensure proper oxygenation of the blood and also relieve mental stress. He is also associated with asanas, physical postures invented by Hanuman as he jumped from tree to tree and mimicked various forest creatures. Asanas strengthen the joints, the muscles and the ligaments of the body, and when done in alignment with breath, these postures affect the oxygenation of blood and can calm the restless mind.

Hanuman also designed the Surya-namaskar (sun salutation) to venerate his guru, the sun god. He designed the physical discipline of Malkhamb, popular in Maharashtra, wherein boys and girls go up and down a pole, like a monkey on a tree, to improve their flexibility and agility. The act of chanting plays an important role in calming the restless and tumultuous mind preventing the release of body-harming hormones and chemicals.

Hanuman's association with Sanjivani has linked him to all herbs that cure the most lethal of ailments. The Dronagiri mountain that he brought from the Himalayas to Lanka to save

Lakshman from near death is said to be the source of various medicinal herbs. Offerings to Hanuman include preparations of urad dal, til and butter that are rich in protein and fat, necessary for fighting disease, firing up the metabolism and lubricating the joints. The poisonous Arka leaves and flowers he is offered at temples are a reminder of how he is the embodiment of all antidotes, and can withstand the fiercest of toxins.

Chaupai 26: Aligning with the Divine

संकट तें
हनुमान छुड़ावै ।
मन क्रम बचन
ध्यान जो लावै ॥

**Sankat te
Hanuman chudavae.
Man, kram, vachan
dhyan jo lavai.**

*Problems
Hanuman takes away.
When the heart, action and word
are fixed on him.*

In this verse, we discover how we can get the grace of Hanuman: he will remove our problems provided we concentrate on him, aligning mind (man), action (karam) and speech (vachan).

The key word here is dhyan. It means focus or concentration

and is a kind of mental exercise that is part of the yogic tradition. This word became cha'an in China, and zen in Japan, as Buddhism spread to the Orient.

Concentration may have been a part of Vedic rituals, however it was the Buddha who, nearly 2,500 years ago, transformed it into a technique to awaken the mind so that one could witness the truth about the world, that it is impermanent and our desire for it is the cause of our suffering. By the Bhakti era, 500 years ago, concentration had become a tool to invoke Hanuman to solve one's problems—whether psychological (stress, fear, ghosts), physical (ailments, pain), or social (danger, misfortune)—and take away our suffering (sankat). Sankat Mochan, or the remover of problems, is a popular form of Hanuman; it is the name by which he is revered in the city of Varanasi.

While monastic orders are all about withdrawing inwards into the mind by shutting the senses, Hinduism functions from the premise that not all humans can go through life simply by withdrawing inwards; they need external support. This consideration for diversity, and avoidance of homogeneity, is a hallmark of Hinduism.

The average human being needs a god out there who listens and cares. We realize this need clearly when we trace the history of Buddhism. As Buddhism spread, the concept of the Bodhisattva—who was very different from the Buddha—emerged. While the Buddha shut his eyes and trained his mind to concentrate on the truth, training others to do the same, the Bodhisattva kept his eyes and ears open to hear the suffering of the people, and stretched out his hand to help them. The suffering concentrated on the saviour Bodhisattva, rather than the teacher Buddha. The Theravada (original school) Buddhists, who preferred focussing on the Buddha's way, broke away from Maha-yana (elevated school) Buddhists, who encouraged worship of the Bodhisattva.

In Hinduism, there was no such breakup between the intellectual and the popular. The Gurus of Vedanta who wrote in Sanskrit and discussed complex theories of truth—such as Shankara, Ramanuja, Ramananda, Madhwa, Vallaha—all saw the value of devotion as complementing the intellectual and meditative approach. At one level they spoke of abstract Vedic ideas; this was Nigama parampara. Simultaneously, they spoke of the worship of various Hindu deities, Hanuman included; this was Agama parampara.

Hanuman becomes a form through which a devotee in stress can regain hope and strength. The act of praying to him, concentrating on him, gives strength—strength to be patient until fortune arrives, and strength to face misfortune when it arrives. Hinduism turned the act of prayer into simultaneously an external theistic practice (invoking God) and yogic practice (de-crumpling the mind crumpled by stress).

The word dhayan in this verse reveals an implicit understanding of yoga, the de-crumpling of the crumpled mind through restraint (yama), discipline (niyama), breathing (pranayama), postures (asana), withdrawal (pratyahara), concentration (dhayan), awareness (dharana) and immersion (samadhi).

Yoga also means alignment. By asking the devotee to align his concentration on Hanuman in mind, action and word, there is an implicit reference to Sankhya (Hindu metaphysics) that forms the canvas on which yoga is based. In Sankhya the world is divided into soul (dehi, or purusha) and body (deha, or prakriti). The body in turn is constituted by elements (mahabhutas), sense organs (gyan-indriyas), action organs (karma-indriyas), the heart (chitta), intelligence (buddhi), imagination (manas), memory (smara) and ego (aham). Problems arise when there is misalignment between what we think, what we do, and what we say—when we are forced to repress our feelings and pretend. Hanuman grants us the strength to cope with these everyday issues.

Yoga is also the process by which we discover the divine within us; bhoga is the indulgence of desire that seeks to ignore the truth of our body, our mind and our world. Yoga helps us place bhoga in perspective, recognize that pleasure is temporary, addictive and delusion-inducing, and not let desire sweep away all good sense. Hanuman is a yogi but not a bhogi. He has full perspective on the nature of desire, and desires nothing. We are bhogis, but not yogis. We seek his help in giving us the mental faculties we lack, and taking away the mental afflictions we suffer from.

Chaupai 27: Serving the Hermit-King

सब पर राम
तपस्वी राजा ।
तिन के काज
सकल तुम साजा ॥

**Sab par Ram
tapasvee raja.
Tin ke kaj
sakal tum saja.**

*Ram who rules over all
Is the hermit-king.
All those tough tasks
You accomplish them easily.*

The Chalisa gently makes its way from the external to the internal, from conversations on material success to psychological and physical well-being, to the idea of yoga, and the connection between a living creature and the divine. In the verse, all of us are described as the subjects of the hermit-king Ram, whose tasks are executed by Hanuman.

At one level, this verse establishes the relationship of Ram and Hanuman. Ram is the karta, the responsible leader, and Hanuman is the karya-karta, the obedient and effective follower. At another level, we are made to feel that it is Hanuman who enables Ram's rule, and so prayers to him are worthwhile, for one who makes the life of the king so easy can surely make the life of his subjects easy too.

This division between the grand but passive divine and the accessible and active divine is a common theme in many theistic schools around the world. In Christianity, even Zoroastrianism, there are archangels who carry out the will of God. In medieval India, the common folk rarely saw the king. They saw bureaucrats and soldiers fulfil the king's will. This is why worshippers of Shiva invoked Nandi, devotees of Vishnu invoked Garuda, and devotees of Ram invoked Hanuman.

Ram is the hermit-king because he desires neither kingship nor the fruits of kingship, these are his duties as the eldest son of the royal family. For him kingship is a role; he is not nourished by or dependent on the power that comes with the crown, which is why it is very easy for him to give it up. When he is asked to let his half-brother Bharat be king, he gives up his claim to the crown without regret or remorse. He is as happy in the forest as he is in the palace.

Both Ram and Hanuman are as happy in the forest as they are in Ayodhya, but Ram is obliged to be in Ayodhya because of his duty, while Hanuman gives up the forest out of love for Ram. Does that make Hanuman superior to Ram? One wonders. Thus one is cleverly drawn into the Vaishnava-Shaiva conflict that was prevalent in Varanasi at the time the Hanuman Chalisa was written. Ram, who is a Vishnu avatar, is burdened by kingship, and Hanuman, who is a Shiva avatar, helps Vishnu bear the burden with ease.

Hanuman's love for Ram is different from the romantic love of Sita for Ram, or Ram for Sita. Hanuman's love for Ram is the love of a devotee for a deity, of a seeker for a guru, of a student for a teacher, for the latter enables the former to transform himself, rise above his limitations. In other words, his mind expands: he moves from being dependent on the world to being independent of the world, and yet dependable *for* the world.

In medieval India, kings started identifying themselves as Ram, or descendants of Ram. They expected their followers to be like Hanuman, Sugriv and the obedient monkey army (vanar-sena). And so we find a large number of temples dedicated to Hanuman built by kings of the Vijayanagar and Maratha empires. They were inspired by acharyas such as Madhwa and Ramdas, who made Hanuman serving Ram and Bhima serving Yudhishitra, who in turn served Krishna, their models.

Love in political spaces is often described as standing by the beloved loyally no matter what and doing things for them without expecting anything in return. This logic is self-serving and does not see the larger narrative. For by this logic, Kumbhakarna's love for Ravana is no different from Hanuman's love for Ram.

Many loyal followers insist they are Hanuman, doing what their leaders tell them to do, thus implying that their leaders are Ram when, in fact, they are simply Kumbhakarnas who are following Ravana. The difference between Ram and Ravana is that Ram is a hermit-king. Ram desires nothing, least of all dominating people and establishing territory. He is content with himself. He does not even seek, or need, Hanuman's love. Ram is king by social obligation, not ambition, unlike Ravana. Ayodhya needs Ram; Ram does not need Ayodhya. By contrast, Ravana needs Lanka and the unconditional control over the rakshasas to feel powerful. For him, disobedience and disloyalty are indicators of a lack of love. Hence, he kicks Vibhishan out of the house and when Kumbhakarna dies, he blames Ram, refusing to see his own role in the unnecessary war.

Ravana is consumed by his ego, and so does not see the hurt he causes. All he sees is the hurt caused to him by others who do not obey him or who are not loyal to him. He sees Ram as the enemy, even though it is he who has captured Sita and kept her in Lanka against her consent. His craving for power and control reveals how hungry and frightened he is. He is no Ram. Ravana 'consumes' those who love him. Ram 'nourishes' those who love him. In serving Ram dutifully, Hanuman nourishes himself. He moves from being va-nara, less than human, to being Nara-ayana, refuge for humans.

Chaupai 28: Chariot of Desire

और मनोरथ
जो कोई लावै ।
सोई अमित
जीवन फल पावै ॥

Aur manorath
jo koi lavai.
Sohi amit
jeevan phal pavai.

Any wish
one comes with.
Endless
fulfilment he receives.

In this verse, wishes are described as 'mano-rath', the chariots of the mind, that propel our actions, and hence our life.

While Buddha said desire is suffering, and established monasteries, Hinduism advocated dharma, doing one's social role. The former disrupted social structure, the latter maintained social structure. Buddhist shrines (chaityas) were centres of silence and discipline, and introspective art. By contrast, Hindu temples (mandir) were centres of song and dance and food and celebratory art; the walls had images of beautiful women adorning themselves as men went about doing their duties.

When Buddhism waned, many Buddhist ideas expressed themselves in Hindu form: Hindu monasticism became a dominant force, challenging Hindu worldliness. The hermit sought liberation (moksha) from the world, while the householder spoke of social obligations (dharma) that sustained the world. Shiva, the hermit god was patron of the mathas (monasteries) where ash-smeared ascetics focussed on burning their desires just as Shiva had set aflame Kama, the god of desire. Vishnu, the householder god, was enshrined in grand temples that had separate sections such for food (bhoga-mandapa) and theatrical performances (natya-mandapa). How does one balance between moksha and dharma? This was done through the Goddess.

Every human being was seen as existing within an ecosystem of others. The relationships between humans were governed by desire and action. From desire came all the mental modifications: yearning, attachment, greed, pride, jealousy, frustration, rage; the source of all problems. Action, however, sustained the social fabric. The Goddess demanded focus on action and detachment from desire. In other words, plant the seed, do not desire the fruit. When put in a social context, this means working to satisfy other people's hunger and taking away other people's fear; striving hard to outgrow, rather than indulge, one's own hunger and fear.

And so the Goddess turns Shiva the hermit into Shankara the householder and gets him to descend from his mountaintop abode of Kailasa to the city of Kashi in the plains. Likewise, the Goddess becomes Lakshmi and Saraswati, and asks Vishnu to serve as her guardian. Brahma and his sons, be it the devas or asuras, nagas or yakshas, embody the other or those who are so focussed on their own hunger and fear that they are uninterested in the hunger and fear of the others. Hanuman, a student of the Goddess, on the other hand, focuses on satisfying the desires of others and seeking nothing for himself.

Hindu rituals are designed around this principle. Whether it was a Vedic yagna, or a later day puja at a temple, the yajaman makes offerings to a god and hopes to get something in return. Thus his desire is regulated: he does not just ask, or grab, he is made to first give something to the deity. He can give a gift (flowers, food, incense), or even words of praise (bhajan), or simply the gift of attention (darshan, dhayan). Then we pray the deity reciprocates. We have control over what we offer, how we offer it, when and where and to whom we offer it, but no control on what we receive, or don't receive. What we get is a function of whether the deity is pleased or not, and whether the deity is willing or not, or if the deity feels obliged or not. We have to accept what we get with grace and be at peace with what we don't get. So it is with the deity, so it is in life.

The chariot of desire is not the only force that governs the world. There is also karma, the cycle of actions and reactions. We may or may not get what we desire, but we certainly get what we deserve, based on the reactions of the past, and the actions of the present. Hanuman ensures we get what we should, and he ensures we have the strength to cope with what we don't get. That strength to enjoy what we get and be at peace with what we don't get is the eternal (amit, or amrit) fruit (phal) promised in this verse.

Chaupai 29: Four Eras

चारों जुग
परताप तुम्हारा ।
है परसिद्ध
जगत उजियारा ।

**Chaaron jug
partap tumhara.
Hai persidh
jagat ujiyara.**

*Across four eras
Spans your glory.
Your fame
radiates through the world.*

As mentioned earlier, Hindus believe that the world goes through cycles of birth and death, just as all living creatures go through cycles of birth of death. The 'world' here refers more to human culture, an organization or a system, rather than nature.

The lifespan of a world is called kalpa. It has four quarters (yuga, or jug, referred to in this verse): childhood, youth, maturity and old age known as Krita, Treta, Dvapara, and Kali, respectively. Ram lives in the Treta, hence he is called Treta ke Thakur. Krishna lives in the Dvapara, hence the name Dvapara ke Thakur. Hanuman lives across the four ages, hence he is also called Chiranjivi, the immortal one.

As Ram dies and returns to Vaikuntha at the end of the Treta yuga and Hanuman outlives him, greater emphasis is placed on the worship of Hanuman. People believe he still wanders the earth, and seek him out. There are legends that describe him living in the Himalayan region in a valley where there is a banana (kadali) grove (vana). During ritual readings of the Ramayana, a seat is placed specially for Hanuman, so that when he comes he has a place to sit and enjoy what he enjoys most—the story of his beloved Ram. Stories, and even photos, of his sightings are not uncommon. Some say he is the legendary Yeti or Big Foot of the mountains. For the believer, this is true; for the sceptic, it is simply the power of faith.

Since he is immortal, Hanuman plays an important role in both the Ramayana and the Mahabharata. In the Ramayana, he serves one avatar of Vishnu (Ram), and in the Mahabharata he helps another avatar of Vishnu (Krishna) enlighten the Pandava princes. He teaches the arrogant Bhima humility by taking the form of an old monkey and asking the mighty prince to lift his tail. A similar encounter takes place between Hanuman and Arjuna.

When Arjuna wonders why Ram did not build a bridge of arrows across the sea to Lanka, Hanuman, again in the form of an old monkey, replies saying such a bridge would not have been able to bear the weight of the monkey army. Arjuna tries to disprove this by building a bridge across a river using his own arrows, but the bridge breaks as soon as Hanuman steps on it. Then Krishna advises Arjuna to chant Ram's name while shooting his arrows. This time the bridge does not break. Arjuna realizes that it is not just the material strength of arrows, or stones, that creates the bridge; it is also the grace of Ram's name.

A humbled Arjuna asks Hanuman to sit atop his chariot during the war against the Kauravas. Arjuna declares his flag to be kapi-dhvaja, as it displays the image of a monkey, a symbol of the restless mind which can transform into Hanuman when it has faith in Ram.

Chaupai 30: In China

साधु संत
के तुम रखवारे ।
असुर निकंदन
राम दुलारे ॥

**Sadhu sant
ke tum rakhware.
Asur nikandan
Ram dulhare.**

*Sages and saints
are protected by you.
You who destroy demons
are much loved by Ram.*

Over 1,500 years ago, many pilgrims from China came to India seeking original Buddhist manuscripts. During their travels here they came upon stories of Hanuman which they carried back with them. These stories mingled with ancient Taoist stories of an incredible white monkey who had miraculous strength and powers. And so, in Chinese literature we find a Chinese version of Hanuman, one who travels with a Chinese monk, Hsuan Tsang, in his perilous journey through the west (India). His name is Sun Wukong. And he does precisely what this verse states: protects sages and destroys demons. Coincidentally, the famous Chinese novel describing this monkey-king's feats was written in China around the same time the Hanuman Chalisa was written in India.

Born from a rock that was touched by the wind, Sun Wukong is incredibly strong and fast and had powers to change his form, just like Hanuman. Unlike Hanuman, he makes himself king of all the monkeys by displaying his incredible powers and strength.

In Sun Wukong's hand he has a special magical staff, much like Hanuman's mace, but while the monkey-king's staff is an important aspect of his personality and plays a key role in his adventures, Hanuman's mace has only symbolic value in Hindu iconography. It is entirely possible that originally Hanuman was shown holding the trunk or branch of a tree as a weapon which eventually metamorphosed into the mace (malla, or gada, in Sanskrit) used by bodybuilders and wrestlers.

Like Hanuman, the monkey-king did not know his strength; his unruly wild side needed to be contained. So in the Ramayana Hanuman was cursed to forget his powers until the time was right, while in the Chinese novel, after the Jade Emperor of Heaven was unable to stop him from consuming the Peaches of

Immortality, the heavenly Adi Buddha intervened, to humble him. The Buddha asked the arrogant monkey to find the edge of the world. Sun Wukong found it and boasted that he had made a mark on one of the five pillars that stand at the edge of the world. 'Is this the mark?' asked the Buddha, showing him one of his fingers. On seeing it, Sun Wukong realized that what he thought was the whole world was just the palm of the Buddha's hand.

The humbled monkey was given the task of helping Hsuan Tsang retrieve sacred Buddhist texts from the west in exchange for freedom. But to control this mischievous rake, the Bodhisattva Guanyin got Hsuan Tsang to trick the monkey-king into wearing a headband. The monk could constrict the headband, and the resulting headache would rein in the monkey-king whenever he got too unruly. This taming of the monkey theme is not found in the Ramayana. Hanuman voluntarily submits to Ram, and venerates his divinity. Ram neither seeks Hanuman's submission nor does he display his own divinity.

After many adventures, one of which involved defeating a demon who had abducted a princess and reuniting her with her beloved, the pilgrim returned to China, his mission successful, thanks to the help of the monkey-king. The monkey-king Sun Wukong was rewarded with Buddhahood and revered by all as the 'Victorious Fighting Buddha,' an important character in Chinese Buddhism.

Chaupai 31: Goddess and Tantra

अष्टसिद्धि
नौ निधि के दाता ।
अस बर दीन
जानकी माता ॥

**Ashta-sidhi
nav-nidhi ke data.
As bar deen
Janki mata.**

Eight powers
Nine treasures you bestow.
As per the wishes of
Janaka's daughter (Sita)

This verse explicitly elevates Sita to the level of Goddess and establishes her connection to Hanuman, revealing the influence of the Shakta school of Hinduism. Initially, Hanuman was linked to Vedic gods, then to Vishnu, then to Shiva, and finally to the Goddess. Here, Sita is presented not just as the wife of Ram, but also as the daughter of Janaka, himself a hermit-king. She is being addressed as mother, which is a title of respect as well as a term for the female divine. Sita blesses Hanuman that he can grant the seeker both siddhis and nidhis. Siddhis refer to powers that enable one to manipulate one's body and one's ecosystem and nidhis refer to secret treasures. Embodied, 'Siddhi' and 'Nidhi' can be seen as Tantrik forms of Saraswati and Lakshmi.

Hinduism has two branches—Vedanta, which is spiritual and mystical, focussing on the mind and soul, and Tantra, which is material and occult, focussing on the body and the world. The object of worship in Vedanta is the male form of the divine—Ram—while the object of worship in Tantra is the female form of the divine, so Sita.

Around 500 years ago, many Shakta Ramayanas were written that linked Sita to the Goddess. Here she is described as the wild Kali who voluntarily becomes the demure Gauri, embodiment of forest and field, enabling Ram's greatness. While Ram could kill the ten-headed Ravana, Sita secretly killed a thousand-headed brother of Ravana, a secret that Ram revealed to Lakshman. In these Tantrik tales, the Goddess enables God; without Shakti,

Shiva is a mere corpse (shava), and Ram would not be able to establish Ram-rajya. It is she who gives Hanuman the power to defeat demons and rescue her.

The various siddhis are the ability to reduce one's size (anima), expand one's size (mahima), make oneself heavy (garima), make oneself weightless (laghima), acquire anything from any space (prapti), satisfy any desire (prakamya), duplicate oneself (ishtva), and dominate all (vastva). Hanuman's many adventures reveal that he has access to this knowledge which is why he can change his size and shape, and fly. In one story, he asks the rakshasas to move his leg and they are unable to, for such is his strength.

The secret treasures have many names such as Mahapadma, Padma, Sankha, Makara, Kacchapa, Mukunda, Kunda, Nila and Kharva. Though Hanuman has access to so much power and wealth, he wants nothing because he is a yogi who has everything but wants nothing. This is why all the gods adore him. This is what makes him the chosen deity of many followers of Tantra.

Both Kali and Hanuman are part of the pantheon adored by the Nath-jogis, or Nath-yogis, who see Shiva as the Adi-guru, or teacher of teachers. These ascetics believe in celibacy and own no property, but are believed to have immense power (the siddhis) and access to many treasures (the nidhis). Their first teacher, Matsyendra-nath, was a fish who overheard a conversation between Shiva and Shakti and so became a human and a jogi. His student, Gorakh-nath, was created from cowdung ash.

In Nath folklore, if a yogi acquires power by resisting sex, then the yogini acquires power by seducing the yogi. This makes them antagonists. The yoginis live in an enchanted banana grove that turns all men into women. Only a yogi can resist the spell of these women and enter this enchanted grove. Matsyendra-nath was ensnared by the queen of these yoginis and had to be rescued by Gorakh-nath who entered this kingdom of women by disguising himself as one. When the women of this kingdom wanted children, they begged the Goddess to help. She sent Hanuman. Hanuman, however, being a brahmachari wondered how he could satisfy the wishes of these women and keep the word of the Goddess. Seeking a solution, he began to sing a song in praise of Ram. So powerful was the song, its words and its tune, and the voice of Hanuman, that all the women who heard this song became pregnant.

Historically, this branch of Hinduism originated about a thousand years ago, around the time when Hinduism became increasingly monastic and many monks chose to be wandering warriors, offering their services to local warlords and kings, but refusing to marry and settle down. They saw themselves as embodying the principle of the immortal Hanuman, who promised to help the world even after Ram returned to Vaikuntha.

Chaupai 32: Serving God

राम रसायन
तुम्हरे पासा ।
सदा रहो
रघुपित के दासा ॥

**Ram rasayan
tumhare pasa.
Sada raho
Raghupati ke dasa.**

*Ram's chemistry
Is known to you.
May you forever be
Servant of the lord of the Raghu clan (Ram).*

If there is one thing that Hanuman wants, it is to serve Ram.

One day, Hanuman asked Sita why she marked her forehead with a red dot. She told him that it was a sign of her love for Ram. Hanuman concluded that the colour red indicates the chemistry (rasayan) between devotee and deity. Hanuman wondered how much red colour he would need to indicate his love for Ram, since he was a mere monkey, and a servant, far lower in stature to Sita, the consort of Ram. He finally decided to colour his entire body with red powder, which is why Hanuman images are coloured red in temples dedicated to him, it is believed. Deities associated with the Goddess, such as Ganesha (her son) and Hanuman (her guard), are typically coloured red, a colour usually associated with the Goddess.

Hanuman used to serve Ram diligently, so much so that no one else had the pleasure of taking care of Ram's needs. Exasperated, one day Ram's brothers and Sita and other members of the Raghu clan decided to make a list of all of Ram's needs and divide the chores amongst them. Hanuman was left with nothing to do. Hanuman did not mind, after all, he realized that everyone needs the pleasure of taking care of Ram. But he was keen to do something for Ram. He noticed that the list did not have one task: snapping fingers when one yawns. The people of Ayodhya believed that if you did not snap your fingers while yawning, disease-causing spirits entered the body. Surely, the act of snapping fingers while Ram yawned could be outsourced to him, thought Hanuman. Better a monkey do this menial task than Ram himself, or anyone else in the family, for that matter. So Hanuman kept following Ram everywhere, to everyone's annoyance, carefully waiting for the moment Ram would yawn so that he could click his fingers. But at night, he could not enter

Ram's private chambers. He waited at the door, wondering how he would know when Ram yawned inside. Rather than wait for Ram to yawn, Hanuman thought of snapping his fingers continuously—that way, whenever Ram happened to yawn at night, he wouldn't miss it. Unfortunately, his plan had a disastrous impact—every time he snapped his fingers Ram would start yawning inside, so that his devotee's chores did not go waste. All night, Hanuman kept snapping his fingers, and Ram, instead of sleeping, kept yawning. When the reason for this was discovered, everyone laughed. They realized they could take Hanuman away from Ram, but not Ram away from Hanuman.

Stories such as these, popular in the oral tradition, seek to convey the deep bond of the relationship between Hanuman and Ram.

The idea of selflessly serving Ram who seeks the welfare of the world is often used by politicial leaders who want their followers to be like Hanuman, and serve their constituency. But such a parallel is dangerous. For it assumes that leaders are Ram and followers are Hanuman, by default.

Both leaders and followers work hard to project that they are indeed hermits, seeking no personal gain from their political powers. So they shun family, property, luxury and pleasure, and are seen in public wearing white or saffron clothing. They understand that the masses equate the superficial with the psychological.

We can see matter, not mind. We can see saffron costumes, not the yogic mind. We assume that those dressed in simple clothes, who shun wine, and sex, and non-vegetarian food, must be hermits. But these are assumptions, matters of faith.

Just as we can see clothes and not the mind, we can see wealth not power. A leader or follower may not care for wealth, but they often seek power. This hunger for power manifests in the desire to control people, dominate people, direct people and in territorial behaviour. This is seen in political parties as they fight for votes, and the power to control people through law enforcement. This is seen in spiritual organizations where the only decision-maker is the guru. This is seen in institutions that split after the charismatic 'hermit' founder-leader dies. This is seen in the constant yearning for social status and respect and media attention that many 'gurus' crave for, even as they give elaborate, hair-splitting arguments about how desire is different from ambition, and how their business and political activities are actually manifestations of dharma.

Power is Durga, who rides a lion. Durga is as seductive as

Lakshmi but far more insidious. Even those who seek Saraswati, scholars, experts and artists, and who insist they don't care for Lakshmi, eventually use their knowledge and skill and art to dominate, argue, direct, control and assert authority. These are all signs that the aham is thriving and the atma is eclipsed.

When the atma shines, we don't crave wealth, power or knowledge, as we are wealthy, powerful and knowledgeable, like Ram and Hanuman, we are happy in the palace as well as in the forest. When the atma shines, the other matters more than the self. And it is the other who decides who is a leader. Ram does not want to be the leader. Hanuman, however, wants to follow Ram. To realize this is to realize Ram's chemistry (rasayan).

Chaupai 33: Karma and Rebirth

तुम्हरे भजन
राम को पावै ।
जनम जनम के दुख
बिसरावै ॥

**Tumhare bhajan
Ram ko pavai.
Janam-janam ke dukh
bisraavai.**

*Singing your praises
leads to Ram.
Sorrows accumulated over lifetimes
are hence forgotten.*

In this verse, we learn that the benefit of adoring Hanuman is not to just get fruits in this life, but also to forget the sorrows of multiple lives, by finding Ram.

The idea of living multiple lives distinguishes the Indic faiths from Abrahamic faiths. In Hinduism, Buddhism and Jainism, we live multiple lives, whereas in Judaism, Christianity and Islam it is believed that we live only one life. In one-life cultures, we have one life to lead a perfect life; in multiple-life cultures, every life is an outcome of the ones that came before. In one-life cultures, the quest is to align oneself to the rules of God revealed through His messenger; in multiple-life cultures, the quest is to either stop the cycle of rebirths, or overpower the suffering that comes as a carry-over from each life. In one-life cultures, God is outside, watching us, loving us, judging us, as we live our one and only life; in multiple-life cultures, God is within, awaiting discovery patiently over multiple lives.

Karma means action. Karma also means the reaction to that action. Reactions to past actions create the circumstances that we encounter in our present life. Thus, when we face an opportunity, it is because of something we did in our past. And if we face a threat, it is also because of something we did in our past. How we react to an opportunity or a threat determines our present and our future. This is karma. This is very different from the popular understanding of karma as some kind of cosmic justice: as you sow, so you reap. And certainly not fatalism: your life is determined by past deeds. All the things that are not in our control are born of past actions. What is in our control is our current action. If the circumstances in our life are full of sorrow and misfortune, it indicates the terrible burden of past actions. Can we change the circumstances? No. What, then, can we do? This verse suggests we sing the song of Hanuman and find Ram.

The Ramayana reveals how bad things happen to the best of people for no fault of theirs, for reasons beyond their control. Ram is exiled to the forest, because of circumstances, because his father made a promise to his stepmother and because his stepmother was ambitious and because he, as a prince, was obliged to uphold a royal promise. It was not because he was a bad person or because anyone in his household hated him or wanted to hurt him. Likewise, Sita was doing a good deed: she was feeding a hungry man. But the results were bad: the hungry man turned out to be a demon who abducted her. Neither Ram nor Sita are ever angry or upset with the people around them, nor do they blame them for their misfortune. They suffer, without judging others, and find the inner strength to cope with the suffering. That inner strength comes from atma. Aham makes us blame.

In Hindu mythology, even God is not outside the realm of karma. In the Naradeya Purana, one hears the story of how once Narada asked Vishnu to give him Hari's face. Hari is a proper noun, the name of Vishnu, as well as a common noun, referring to a monkey. Narada wanted Vishnu's face to impress a princess but Vishnu gave him a monkey's face. When the princess saw Narada's new face she burst out laughing. When Narada discovered Vishnu's prank he cursed Vishnu that when he would descend on earth as Ram his success would depend on a monkey. So it came to pass that Ram needed Hanuman's help to find Sita and overpower Ravana. Curse is a mythological tool to explain karma. Even Vishnu, who is God, cannot escape the reaction to his actions.

Chaupai 34: Heavens

अंत काल
रघुबर पुर जाई ।
जहाँ जन्म
हरिभक्त कहाई ॥

**Ant-kaal
Raghubar pur jayee.
Jahan janma
Hari-bhakt kahayee.**

Eventually,
one goes to Ram's heaven.
Where for eternity,
one is known as Ram's devotee.

If the previous chaupai spoke of rebirth, this chaupai refers to immortal life in Ram's heaven. In the previous verse, singing the praises of Hanuman enables us to cope with this life's suffering born of actions in previous lifetimes. In this verse, the same activity grants us immortality and peace in the hereafter. Thus, these two verses deal with Hindu eschatology: death, rebirth and liberation. With this verse, we are now in the fourth quarter of the Hanuman Chalisa. Just as the verses in the first quarter deal with birth (of the deity) the verses in the final quarter deal with death (of the devotee).

In Hindu funeral rites, the dead body is cremated and the bones cast in a river. Thus fire and water claim the dead. Fire embodies the promise of immortality, while water embodies the promise of rebirth. Immortality and rebirth are the two options after death.

The Vedic Samhitas, over 3,000 years old, speak of an entity (prana, atma, jiva) outliving death. But the idea of rebirth fully develops only in the Upanishads, 2,500 years ago. The idea of Swarga, a temporary paradise of pleasures for those who have earned good merits in their life, and Vaikuntha, for those who want to break free from the cycle of rebirths, first appears in the Mahabharata roughly 2,000 years ago.

In the Puranas, one can be reborn in Swarga, where the fruits of good deeds are enjoyed or in Naraka, where one must suffer the consequences of bad deeds. The former is ruled by Indra, the king of devas and the latter is ruled by Yama, the king of pitr and preta. But stay in either location is temporary, as we learn in the Mahabharata. We can tumble down from Swarga when we use up our karmic equity, or rise up from Naraka when we exhaust our karmic debts.

In the Garuda Purana this is further elaborated with detailed descriptions of multiple hells to punish people who have committed different misdeeds. Chitragupta, assistant to Yama, maintains the book of accounts, determining if we are to go to heaven or hell, and if heaven, then which heaven and for how long, and if hell, then which hell and for how long. We keep going up and down over lifetimes depending on karmic baggage.

Freedom is breaking free from the karmic cycle, a balance sheet with no debts to repay. Then we go to the heaven of our choice and are there forever, experiencing neither death nor sorrow, gazing upon the deity of our choice. In the Vishnu Purana and Shiva Purana, there are heavens for Vishnu (Vaikuntha) and Shiva (Kailasa). Later, we find references to the heaven of Krishna (Go-loka), and the heaven of Ram (Saket, or Raghuvir pur). Still later, there are heavens for other gods which rise in popularity, like those of Ganesha (the sugarcane forest, ikshu-van) or that of Hanuman (the banana grove, kadali-van).

These structures gave form to abstract ideas like moksha to the common man. He realized that after death, there was the possibility of living in a world without any suffering, gazing upon the face of Ram, embodiment of atma, with the help of Hanuman. It was a world where there was no hunger or fear, no dearth of food, and no threat to our existence. It is the kingdom governed by Ram, with Sita and Lakshman by his side, and Hanuman at his feet.

Chaupai 35: One is Many

और देवता
चित्त न धरई ।
हनुमत सेई
सर्ब सुख करई ॥

**Aur devta
chitta na dharehi.
Hanumat se hi
sarba sukh karahi.**

My Hanuman Chalisa

All other deities
Do not connect.
Hanuman alone
Gives full delight.

This chaupai raises the question: is Hinduism polytheistic or monotheistic? For in this verse Hanuman is seen as the source of all happiness, so why bother with other deities. The other deities are not derided; they are just seen as not needed.

This question of monotheism and polytheism did not matter until the rise of European Orientalist studies in the 19th century. After having established their authority in the subcontinent, the Muslim rulers did not bother so much with this question, which is why Muslim communities and Hindu communities lived in relative harmony. But all this harmony was disrupted when European rulers kept wondering: what is true religion? In their view, polytheism was definely primitive, pagan, false, hence myth. Monotheism was true, especially one that saw Jesus as the son of God, not one that saw Muhammad as the last and final Prophet of God.

With the rise of postmodern studies in the late twentieth century, the politics underlying the word 'myth' was revealed and its association with falsehood and fiction discarded. Today, both polytheism and monotheism, like ideology and theology, are classified as different kinds of mythology, conceptual cultural truths, and distinguished from measurable and verifiable scientific truths. Of course, fundamentalists, and even many historians, academics and scientists, still cling to the old, outdated colonial meanings, and the binary of truth and falsehood.

Greek mythology is polytheistic while Abrahamic mythology is monotheistic. When the Roman Empire became Christian, polytheism was rejected as false religion. Hindu mythology has always been simultaneously polytheistic and monotheistic: the same God (spelt with capitalization) manifests as multiple gods (spelt without capitalization). In other words, the whole manifests as parts, and every part is an expression of the whole. The whole is limitless, and the part limited; the limitless whole is accessed through the limited part. This approach is unique to Hinduism, and remains unfathomable to most non-Hindus.

A word commonly used for Hinduism is kathenotheism, where one god is worshipped at a time, without disrespecting other gods, and that god is seen as representative of the limitless formless divine, or God. Hence the concept of ishta-devata, the One Being invoked, through whom the devotee accesses the cosmic soul (param-atma). Each deity is like a portal to the same divine entity, and each deity, despite its finite form, is the perfect embodiment of infinity.

In Hindu temples, Hanuman can be seen as an independent deity, or as a deity who is part of Ram's entourage, just as Ganesha or Murugan can be seen as independent deities, or a deity who is part of Shiva's family. A deity exists in an ecosystem of many deities and at the same time contains all deities within them.

Hanuman is one. But simultaneously, he is many. Through him, one accesses the hermit Shiva, the householder Vishnu, and the Goddess who embodies nature. He is a Vedic scholar as well as a potent Tantrik warrior. He is the embodiment of Bhakti. He is linked to literature and poetry, with song and music, with physical prowess as well as marital arts. He brings with him Durga (power), Saraswati (knowledge) and Lakshmi (prosperity).

For those uncomfortable with the idea of worshipping a celibate man, there are temples in India where Hanuman has a wife (in Hyderabad, for example), and also one where he wears a nose-ring to appear like the Goddess (in Ratanpur district, Chhattisgarh). So, says this verse, the most efficient way to worship infinity is through this one single deity.

Chaupai 36: Problem-Solver

संकट कटै
मिटै सब पीरा ।
जो सुमिरै
हनुमत बलबीरा ॥

Sankat kate
mite sab peera.
Jo sumirai
Hanumat Balbeera.

Problems cease
pain goes away.
When one remembers
Hanuman, the mighty hero.

This chaupai reiterates what Hanuman can do for us: remove problems and take away pain.

In the Ramayana, Hanuman solves Ram's problems. He finds Ram's missing wife, Sita, by leaping across the sea to the kingdom of Lanka. He saves Ram's injured brother, Lakshman, by carrying a mountain of herbs across the sky. He even saves Ram from being sacrificed by Mahiravana to Patala Bhairavi. If he can help God, surely he can help humanity. Perhaps this explains Hanuman's mass appeal.

Across India, at the start of roads that wind up hills and mountains, one frequently finds temples of Hanuman. People driving past in cars, buses and trucks, throw money at these temples, offerings to the great hero, to give them the strength to overcome the obstacle before them, and to keep out all obstacles from their path. A temple is also located at the end of the journey, on the other side of the mountain, where the travellers can thank Hanuman for protecting them from all potential danger.

At the frontier of most villages, and in most Hindu crematoriums, we find red-orange images of Hanuman, glistening with til oil, bedecked with Arka leaves and flowers, protecting the village from the wild, from diseases and demons, ghouls and ghosts. He embodies the positive side of masculinity (strength) but not the negative side (domination).

When Hanuman was flying over the ocean to Lanka, he defeated many monsters. But he did not stop to rest. Mount Mainaka rose from under the sea and requested Ram's messenger to sit on his slopes for a bit. Hanuman politely refused, for he had a task to complete. Thus Hanuman embodies selflessness, commitment, and integrity, the one who completes the most arduous task without resting. We yearn to have someone like Hanuman on our side. And to have him on our side, we need to invoke Ram in our hearts.

In folk retellings of the Ramayana, Ravana had locked up Shani, lord of Saturn; Mangal, the god of Mars; and Preta-raja, or Mahakala, or Yama, lord of disease and death, under his throne. Hanuman released them and so Shani, Mangal, and Mahakala are in Hanuman's debt. If one prays to Hanuman on Saturday, the day associated with Saturn, then Shani, who delays things, does not assert his malevolent force. If one prays to Hanuman on Tuesday, the day associated with Mars, then Mangal, who causes strife, does not assert his malevolent influence. And if one worships Hanuman at night, when Preta-raja rules, then disease and death, caused by negative energies and black magic, fail to act.

The Nawabs of Lucknow started the Bada Mangal festival, when Hanuman is worshipped with great fanfare every Tuesday in the summer month of Jyestha (May-June). This practice began after an image of Hanuman was found at a construction site. The story goes that the elephant carrying the deity to its new location stopped at one point and refused to budge. So the temple was built at the spot the elephant stopped. In this festival, local Hindus and Muslims participate, the latter providing water to the long queues of devotees who stand all through Tuesday night to see Bada Hanuman.

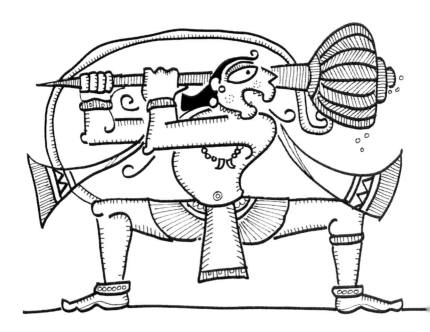

My Hanuman Chalisa

This verse reveals the most elemental form of Hanuman and resonates with humanity's most primitive past, when the things one wanted from divine forces were as basic as protection from dangers and cures from diseases. In the verses that follow, the higher needs of humanity are addressed, revealing Hanuman's versatility spanning from the most elemental to the most refined.

Chaupai 37: Guru and Gosain

जै जै जै
हनुमान गोसांई ।
कृपा करहु
गुरुदेव की नांई ॥

Jai Jai Jai
Hanuman Gosain.
Kripa karahu
gurudev ki nyahin.

Hail, Hail, Hail
Hanuman, lord of senses.
Be as kind
As the master.

In this chaupai, Hanuman is identified as gosain and is being asked to be as kind as his guru. So Hanuman, who in previous verses is being asked to solve material problems and relieve material pain, has here been sought to grant spiritual wisdom that will liberate us from material bondage.

The word gosain, or go-swami, is a Vedic metaphor. Ancient Hindus were aware that our understanding of the world begins with sensory awareness of the world around us. The five sensory organs (gyan-indriya) carry information to our mind (manas) and provoke emotions (chitta) and finally get our intellect (buddhi) to take decisions that are manifested through the five action organs (karma-indriya). Our intelligence is controlled by our ego (aham) and only a guru's guidance can help us break free from ego, and discover our soul (atma), our true self, that fears no death, is neither hungry nor insecure, and so can empathize with the other (para-jiva). The indriyas that continuously engaged with the world of sensory stimulations were metaphorically described as cows (go) grazing (chara) in a pasture. The one who had complete control over them was the go-swami, or gosain, master of the sense-cows. Gosain, thus, is a word for yogi commonly used by Vaishnavas and followers of Krishna. It was a title bestowed on students by their gurus.

If Hanuman is the gosain, who is Hanuman's teacher? Is it Surya, the sun god? Is it Ram, lord of the solar dynasty? Or is it Sita, the shakti of Ram? Maybe all three. This difference between guru and gosain reflects the difference between Jehovah and Jesus in Christianity, Allah and Prophet Muhammad in Islam, and the Buddha and Bodhisattva in Buddhism. In religious traditions around the world, there is invariably a medium between the spiritual and the material, between the deity and the devotee, between the transcendental and the phenomenal. That is the role being attributed to Hanuman, the gosain of the guru.

The Hanuman Chalisa was composed in times when the Mughals established their authority over the Gangetic plains.

The locals were very familiar with Islamic ideas of God and prophet, that had entered India five centuries prior to Tulsidas, that is, almost a thousand years ago from today. For local Hindus, the guru became the Hindu equivalent of the Islamic prophet, one who shows you the path to God. If Muslims had a paigambar for Allah, then Hindus had a Ram-doot for Ram. The similarity was convenient but deceptive. Convenient because it helped establish a connection between the two faiths and facilate dialogue, in the spirit of plurality. And deceptive because Hindu ideas of God and teacher are very different from the Islamic idea of God and messenger.

God in Islam is formless and firmly located outside space and time, while his prophet has form and is located in history and geography. God in Hinduism is simultaneously formless and has form (Shiva, Vishnu), is simultaneously outside space and time (Vishnu) and inside history and geography (Ram and Krishna). The guru can be a real person located outside (Shankara-acharya, Ramanuja-acharya, Madhwa-acharya, Ramananda, Tulsidas), or a deity (Hanuman), or a voice inside our heart and head. In the Bhagavat Purana, the primal teacher (adi guru) Dattatreya describes nature as his guru. In Tantra, Shiva is Shakti's guru, Shakti is Shiva's guru. Thus in Hinduism, guru is gosain and gosain is guru, and guru is God and God is guru. The message and the messenger mingle and merge. Time, space and people are simultaneously outside and inside, literal and metaphorical, immanent and transcendent, objective and subjective, physical and psychological. This fluid aspect of Hinduism is most confounding to the outsider, as confounding as the Indian headshake.

Chaupai 38: Liberation

जो सत बार
पाठ कर कोई ।
छूटहि बंदि
महा सुख होई ॥

Jo sat bar
path kar koi.
Chhutehi bandhi
maha sukh hoyi.

Whoever a hundred times
recites this song.
Will be liberated
and very happy.

This chaupai states that chanting the Hanuman Chalisa a hundred times will grant us liberation. Hanuman will make this happen; it is the kindness he is asked to bestow upon us in the previous chaupai.

Happiness in Hinduism is of two types: material and spiritual. In material happiness, our desires are met. In spiritual happiness, we outgrow desire itself. The technique for the latter is known only to gurus, who reveal it to deserving students, the gosains, who master the techniques of yoga. But according to this verse, simply chanting the Hanuman Chalisa will invoke Hanuman who will grant us spiritual happiness. This outgrowing of desire is liberation.

Many people confuse the Hindu idea of liberation (mukti) with the Christian idea of salvation. In Christian mythology, humans are born in sin and can be saved from eternal damnation if they accept the love of Jesus Christ, the son of God, who takes upon himself the sins of the world. This is salvation. In Hindu mythology, humans are born in debt and incur more debt by indulging desires. Liberation happens when we repay this debt, and incur no more debts.

In Vedic times, the purpose of a yagna was simply to invoke deities for the sake of material happiness. But then the Buddha came along and declared this desire for material happiness as the root of all misery. He encouraged people to become monks. As more and more chose the monastic life over marriage, social structure was threatened. So the Dharma-shastras came to be written, and the idea of debt was elaborated upon. It was argued that liberation could not happen unless debts were repaid to the ancestors (pitr): they gave us life and were now in the land of the dead patiently waiting for their descendents to facilitate their return to the land of the living. Stories were told of forest hermits tormented by visions of suffering ancestors demanding they marry and produce children. Liberation could only follow the fulfilment of worldly obligations. In other words, after retirement!

Later, in the Bhagavad Gita, we find the idea that one does not have to renounce the world, or wait for retirement, to be liberated. We can be liberated while living the life of a householder, if we do our duties, without any expectations. This idea of one who is liberated while being a productive member of society is embodied in the idea of Ram. He is engaged with society, yet free. Chanting the Hanuman Chalisa, we are told, will give us the strength to fulfil our duties and so repay our debts, and at the same time, overcome our desires and prevent incurring new debts.

If we spend our life indulging our hungers and fears then we generate a debt which we are obliged to repay in future lives. Thus we are trapped in the cycle of birth and death. The only way to break this cycle is to stop generating debt. This demands outgrowing hunger and fear. This can only happen when we empathize with the hunger and fear of those around us. When we empathize with the other, and work for them, like Ram, and like Hanuman who serves Ram, we become one with Ram, who has no debts, or desires, and so is eternally tranquil. This union of the self (jiva-atma) with the divine (param-atma) is called moksha. And the easiest way to achieve this is to chant the Hanuman Chalisa a hundred times.

Chaupai 39: Title of the Poem

जो यह पढ़ै
हनुमान चालीसा ।
होय सिद्धि
साखी गौरीसा ॥

**Jo yeh padhe
Hanuman Chalisa.
Hoye siddhi
sakhi Gaureesa.**

*Whoever reads
these forty verses of Hanuman
Will achieve whatever he desires
a claim to which Gauri's lord (Shiva) is witness*

This verse contains both the title of the poem, as well as the promise of the poem. Here, for the first time, we learn that this work is called Hanuman Chalisa. And we are being told the benefit of reading it. This is phala-stuti, chanting of benefits. If a Hindu ritual begins with sankalpa, sowing the seed of desire, it always ends with phala-stuti, enumerating the fruits that are promised by the enterprise. And the fruit being guaranteed is the achievement of any desire.

We may want a material desire to be fulfilled, such as the removal of problems, freedom from physical pain, success in an enterprise; or we may want occult help, like powers to control the world; or psychological help, such as contentment and freedom from fear; or we want spiritual success in the form of liberation from the cycle of rebirth. Whatever we desire, this verse guarantees that we will get it when we read the Hanuman Chalisa repeatedly.

What is curious is the word witness (sakshi). It is almost as if the poet is using the traditionally Abrahamic phrase, 'As God is my witness!' The idea of a witness turns the promise into an objective fact, not merely a subjective promise. The witness is

Shiva, the husband of Gauri, who is a guileless hermit, who has no reason to bear false testimony. The chaupai thus amplifies the validity of this composition's promise.

But there is another way to consider this witness. Who is the ultimate witness of the universe? In the Vedas, we come upon the line, 'The bird who watches another bird eating the fruit!' We are the bird eating the fruit, seeking fulfilment of our desires, and the bird watching us eat the fruit is Gauri's lord, Shiva.

Shiva, the hermit form of God, is never hungry, while Vishnu, the householder form of God who manifests as Ram, enables the hungry bird—with the aid of Hanuman—to eat fruit. So while Hanuman enables us to achieve what we desire, the whole act is being watched by the atma within, Shiva, who desires nothing. Perhaps one day, having achieved all that we desire, we will realize how desire never ends, and will see the futility of achievement, and so become witnesses ourselves of the world, and the hunger that motivates people to act and react, die and be reborn.

Chaupai 40: About the Poet

तुलसीदास
सदा हरि चेरा ।
कीजै नाथ
हृदय मँह डेरा ॥

Tulsidas
sada Hari chera.
Keejai Nath
hriday mein dera.

Tulsidas,
God's eternal servant
Yearns that the lord
reside forever in his heart

In this chaupai, we learn that the name behind this composition is Tulsidas. In oral traditions, it was common practice for the poet to insert their name in the composition itself. It was akin to an author signing their name in a written text.

When we study the life of Tulsidas we understand what made him compose the rather simplistic and popular Hanuman Chalisa, after having completed the magnificent and literary Ram-charit-manas.

Tulsidas was born nearly 500 years ago, in the Gangetic plains, and abandoned by his parents at birth because his astrology chart revealed he would herald misfortune. He was named Rambola as the first words he spoke were, 'Ram, Ram!' The nurse who raised him died when he was still a child. When he went looking for his biological parents, he discovered they were already dead. Left to fend for himself, he survived for a long time begging from door to door until, noticing his brilliant command over language, Naraharidas, a disciple of the Ramananda order, took young Rambola under his wing and named him Tulsidas. Tulsidas was educated in Sanskrit and Vedic scriptures as well as the regional language, Awadhi, in Ayodhya and in Varanasi. He heard the story of Ram for the first time from his guru.

In some accounts, Tulsidas did get married. He had a child who died at birth. He was very fond of his wife, and one day, when she decided to stay in her mother's house on the other side of the river, Tulsidas swam across a turbulent river in the middle of the night to meet her. His passion embarrassed her and she yelled, 'If you loved God as much as you loved me, you would have attained moksha!' Thus chastised, Tulsidas left her house. On the way back, he realized that the vine he had held on to, to enter her bedroom, was actually a snake and the log of wood he floated on to get to the other side of the river was actually a corpse. Lust had blinded him. Disgusted, he decided to become a hermit and devoted his life to writing songs about God.

One day, while offering water to a tree, a ghost (preta) appeared before him and offered him a boon for having quenched his thirst. Tulsidas said that he wished to see Ram. So the preta pointed him to Hanuman who was disguised as a leper and had came to Varanasi to hear the narration of the Ramayana. Tulsidas thus saw Hanuman and begged him to show him Ram and Lakshman, and by Hanuman's grace, he saw the brothers riding horses near Chitrakuta, and the next day, Ram appeared before Tulsidas as a boy while Tulsidas was performing his morning ritual of preparing sandal paste. Spellbound by these visions, Tulsidas decided to compose the Ramayana. He first thought of composing it in Sanskrit but Shiva and Shakti appeared in a dream and ordered him to write it in the local language, such that it could be used in a play, and create harmony between the bickering Shaivas and Vaishnavas.

Tulsidas wrote the Ram-charit-manas and it was a huge success. People concluded that Tulsidas was a great saint, for only a saint could write a vernacular work that had the melody of the Sama Veda. Local priests were dismissive of a work not composed in Sanskrit, so to test it they placed it at the bottom of a pile of Sanskrit manuscripts and locked it in the Vishwanath temple of Shiva in Kashi. At dawn, when the bundle of manuscripts was opened, Tulsidas's work was on top with the words 'Satyam, Shivam and Sundaram' on the first page, written by Shiva himself, who had declared the work to be the embodiment of truth, auspiciousness and beauty.

As Tulsidas's work became popular his fame spread far and wide. People said he could even bring the dead back to life by the sound of magnificent poetry. When the Mughal emperor Akbar heard this, he ordered Tulsidas be brought to his court in Agra. Tulsidas was reluctant to travel because he was old, with joint pains and several health problems, including boils on his body. Poverty had taken its toll. However, he was forced to go.

The emperor demanded that the saint show him some miracles. Tulsidas said he was no sorcerer, just a poet and Ram's devotee. Mistaking his honesty for impertinence, Akbar had Tulsidas thrown in jail.

While in jail, Tulsidas composed the Hanuman Chalisa, recollecting how Hanuman had helped Ram, and Sugriv, and Lakshman, and Vibhishan, how he could sort out astrological misalignments, restore physical and mental health, solve the most mundane of problems as well as bestow everything from occult powers to spiritual wisdom to the seeker, while seeking nothing for himself. Suddenly, for apparently no reason, a monkey troop wreaked havoc in the city of Agra and made life miserable in the bazaars, and in the palace. This continued for days, until Akbar let Tulsidas go back to Varanasi, where the poet-saint spent the rest of his life immersed in Ram, and his devoted servant, Hanuman.

Doha 3: Becoming Hanuman

पवनतनय संकट हरन मंगल मूरति रूप ।
राम लखन सीता सहित हृदय बसहु सुर भूप ॥

Pavan tanay sankat harana mangala murati roop
Ram Lakhana Sita sahita hriday basahu soor bhoop

Son of the wind, remover of problems, embodiment of
auspiciousness
Along with Ram, Lakshman, Sita dwell in my heart forever

With this doha, ends the Hanuman Chalisa. This is the exit from the mind-temple, where we have invoked, observed, adored, venerated, and petitioned Hanuman, who we describe here in three ways: based on his origin (son of the wind god), based on his function (remover of obstacles) and based on his form (embodiment of auspiciousness). We now invite him to dwell forever in our heart along with Ram, Lakshman and Sita. What do we mean by that? A story explains this well:

Once Hanuman wrote the biography of Ram on a banana leaf. When Valmiki read it, he began to cry, because Hanuman's Ramayana was outstandingly beautiful, of perfect melody and metre, so beautiful that it would overshadow his own work, the Valmiki Ramayana. Feeling sorry for Valmiki, Hanuman tore the banana leaf with his Ramayana on it, and swallowed it whole, thus destroying his Ramayana forever. When Valmiki asked Hanuman why Hanuman had done this, Hanuman replied, 'Valmiki needs Valmiki's Ramayana more than Hanuman needs Hanuman's Ramayana. Valmiki wrote the Ramayana so that the world remembers him; I wrote the Ramayana because I wanted to rediscover Ram. I have achieved my objective. Valmiki needs to achieve his.' Thus, for Hanuman, his work was not about fame and glory, it was yoga: a tool to realize divinity within his heart.

Valmiki bowed to Hanuman for revealing to him the great secret of the Ramayana. It is said that Valmiki therefore took birth again and again, in different times of history, in different geographies, to recompose the Ramayana in different languages, so that he too could re-discover Ram as Hanuman did. Many people see Tulsidas as Valmiki reborn.

The gods are already in our heart and around us. It is upto us to discover them, both without and within. Hanuman Chalisa begins with acknowledging the Hanuman outside. It ends with acknowledging the Hanuman within. What does this mean in practical terms?

To understand this we have to remind ourselves that all living creatures are consumed by hunger and fear. In humans, this hunger and fear is amplified infinitely by imagination. To cope, we use imagination to invent technology and gather resources. But all the resources in the world do not explain the purpose of our life. We remain restless. We either cling to wealth, or use power to dominate others.

In the Puranas, Brahma is blamed for misunderstanding the Vedas and creating a culture that values wealth and power. That is why he is not worshipped. Instead worship is offered to Shiva, the ascetic, who shuns wealth and power, and does not participate in culture.

Shiva beheads the fifth head of Brahma and holds it in his hand for the entire world to see. This fifth head embodies ego (aham), the crumpled mind, which is the offspring of imagined hunger and fear that makes us cling to wealth and seek control over others. Hindus worship Shiva, the destroyer, as he reveals this Vedic wisdom, which the Upanishads call atma-gyan.

Vishnu takes a different approach: he acknowledges and accommodates, even appreciates, the crumpled mind of those around him, and continuously makes available wealth, power and knowledge for them, hoping patiently that they will use their life to outgrow their addiction, and de-crumple their mind. He does not always succeed. But he does not give up. For the world is infinite, and every creature has infinite lifetimes to live, and he has infinite faith in the human potential and infinite patience. Hence, he is the preserver.

In the Ramayana, Brahma is embodied in the ambitious Kaikeyi, in the stubborn Ravana, and in the gossipy public who live in Ayodhya. All three are so self-absorbed that they are

oblivious to the consequences of their action on others. Their
actions cause the separation of Ram and Sita.

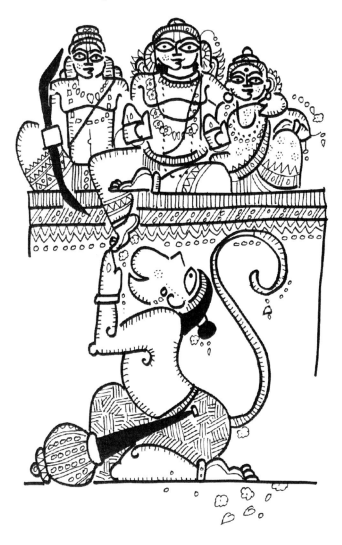

Hanuman is Shiva. The colloquial meaning of his name is the destroyer of the ego. He does not seek wealth, power or knowledge. He is content. He has no reason to participate in the Ramayana, yet he does. He helps reunite Ram and Sita. And watches with amazement how this divine couple conducts their life.

Hanuman witnesses how Ram, unlike Lakshman, is not angry with Kaikeyi, or with Ravana, or even with the people of Ayodhya who benefit from his rule and yet gossip about the character of Sita and her suitability to be their queen. He never judges them for being so mean and petty. He asks Lakshman not to judge them, but does not try to control Lakshman's behaviour, letting Lakshman figure out his own path.

Hanuman also witnesses how Sita is not angry with Kaikeyi, or Ravana, or the people of Ayodhya, or even with Ram who abandons her following public gossip. Like Ram, she sees the underlying fear, and the crumpling of the mind, hence the ego that makes Kaikeyi insecure about her future, and Ravana insecure about his station in society. She watches how Ram's subjects, despite being showered with wealth and security by the grace of Ram, seek out 'pollution' to cast out of their city to make it 'pure'. This yearning for purity, this lack of compassion for the 'polluted', is also fear at work. We are so frightened that to make ourselves valid we render others invalid, to make ourselves feel superior we do not mind gossiping about the inferiority of the king's chaste wife.

How can you be angry at the frightened? How does it help? Instead, Ram and Sita focus on yoga, on uncrumpling the mind, unravelling aham so that atma shines forth.

As embodiments of atma, Sita and Ram have no hunger or fear, hence they do not crave wealth or power, or the approval of those around them. They do not seek to control others. They are not dependent like Brahma; they are not independent like Shiva; they choose to be dependable, no matter what the situation.

By repeating the story of Ram again and again, Hanuman understands Ram, and discovers the Ram within him, the ability to be dependable for those who are dependent, even those who are unworthy, like the stream of hungry and frightened devotees who venerate him in his temples.

Likewise, by chanting the Hanuman Chalisa again and again, we hope to understand Hanuman and discover the Hanuman within us.

Further Reading

- Aryan, KC & Aryan, Subhashini. *Hanuman: Art, Mythology and Folklore.* Delhi: Rekha Prakashan, 1994.

- Lutgendorf, Philip. *Hanuman's Tale: The Messages of a Divine Monkey.* New York: Oxford University Press, 2007.

- Nagar, Shantilal. *Hanuman in Art, Culture, Thought and Literature.* Delhi: International Publishing House, 1997.

Acknowledgements

Prof. Purushottam Agarwal, former member of Union Public Service Commission, and former chairman of Centre of Indian Languages, School of Language, Literature and Culture Studies, Jawaharlal Nehru University. The team at ABP News for producing the show on Hanuman Chalisa, which inspired me to go deeper into the poem.

28/01/23
300-100
200

500-100
200
181

owa + hing
+ honey

nilgiri tel

apple + dadim.